THE TRUTH ABOUT PATRIOTISM

STEVEN JOHNSTON

The Truth about Patriotism

DUKE UNIVERSITY PRESS

DURHAM AND LONDON

2007

For Dad

Contents

Acknowledgments

For reading early versions of various chapters, commenting on confer-
ence papers, offering invaluable advice, and providing resource materials
I thank Jane Bennett, Bill Chaloupka, Bill Connolly, Brian Danoff, Tom
Dumm, Tom Eagles, Stephen Engelmann, Leonard Feldman, Kathy Fer-
guson, Kennan Ferguson, Kirsten Fischer, Jason Frank, Michael Gibbons,
Cheryl Hall, Stacy Jacobson, Jennifer Culbert and the noontime semi-
nar series of the political science department at Johns Hopkins, Brenda
Johnston, Timothy Kaufman-Osborne, Brad MacDonald, Tom Mertes,
Laurie Naranch, Mort Schoolman, Verity Smith, Simon Stow, Roy Tsao,
Stephen White, and Nick Xenos.

Earlier versions of chapters 1, 4, and 5 appeared respectively in *Polity* 34,
no. 3 (spring 2002); *Theory and Event* 5, no. 2 (August 2001); and *Strategies*
15, no. 2 (November 2002). Chapter 4 was reprinted in *The Politics of Moralizing*, ed. Jane Bennett and Michael J. Shapiro (New York: Routledge,
2002).

Thanks to the anonymous readers for Duke University Press who provided extensive and provocative comments and suggestions for revisions.
The considerable time and effort that they devoted to the project is a
tribute to their scholarly commitment. The advice, often contradictory,
made me think even harder about the manuscript. Thanks also to Court-
ney Berger, whose timely counsel proved indispensable to submitting and

completing the manuscript. Finally, I greatly appreciate Fred Kameny's superior copy-editing skills, which provided the necessary finishing touches to the book.

Bruce Springsteen has generously agreed to let me quote from many of his songs in the manuscript. Thank you. And thanks to Mona Okada for guiding me through the permission process.

To Kirsten Fischer I owe a founding debt. Early on, we talked for countless hours about the book-to-be. Her intellectual curiosity and passion forced me to focus and refine vague notions into a viable project.

Mike Gibbons is a great friend and an indispensable colleague. Not only did he read several drafts of most of the chapters; he would allow, even welcome, me into his office several times a day as I experienced my latest enthusiasm, discovery, or (alleged) insight about patriotism. Mike makes writing books not only a considerable challenge but also enormous fun.

Judy Gallant teaches me every day about love, compassion, patience, and kindness. I can't imagine my life without her and us, and it's my great good fortune that I don't have to.

A lot can happen in the years it takes to write a book.

The book is dedicated to my father, Ted Johnston. My father died on June 30, 2004. The last couple of years of life were painful for him. I saw him on Father's Day, a couple of weeks before he died. He knew that he didn't have long to live. He told me he wasn't afraid to die. He wasn't; rather he was busy making suggestions about possible book covers, and he was doing so because I asked. I was desperately trying to keep him connected to us and to the world for as long as possible. I had hoped to surprise him with the dedication. I never got the chance.

Though my father served in the Korean War and was proud to be an American, that's not why I am dedicating the book to him. He was a man of integrity, truthfulness, decency, and generosity. My father also possessed a deep skepticism and though we argued passionately over many of the ideas in the book, his influence can be found throughout it. I dedicate the book to him because of the love, friendship, and indestructible bond that we shared for a short forty-four years. There are few things as wondrous as having a Dad you adore.

Hence the cautious, stumbling manner of this text . . . it is not a way of saying that everyone else is wrong . . . rather than trying to reduce others to silence, by claiming that what they say is worthless, I have tried to define this blank space from which I speak, and which is slowly taking shape in a discourse that I still feel to be so precarious and so unsure.—MICHEL FOUCAULT, *The Archaeology of Knowledge*

Love turns, with a little indulgence, to indifference or disgust: hatred alone is immortal . . . The pleasure of hating . . . makes patriotism an excuse for carrying fire, pestilence, and famine into other lands: it leaves to virtue nothing but the spirit of censoriousness, and a narrow, jealous, inquisitorial watchfulness over the actions and motives of others.—WILLIAM HAZLITT, "On the Pleasure of Hating"

Patriotism no one thinks discreditable; nor does any one deny that war is the romance of history. But inordinate ambitions are the soul of any patriotism, and the possibility of violent death the soul of all romance.—WILLIAM JAMES, "The Moral Equivalent of War"

How does it happen that the state will do a host of things that the individual would never countenance? . . . Through the interposition of the virtues of obedience, of duty, patriotism, and loyalty.
—FRIEDRICH NIETZSCHE, *The Will to Power*

"Without External Picturesqueness,"
Or, Why I Am Not a Patriot

These are patriotic times. United States troops make war in Afghanistan and Iraq. Possibilities of apocalyptic violence from named but invisible enemies haunt the home front. Lifetimes of fear and insecurity await coming generations. Add structural economic fragility, planet-wide pandemics, a rise of "natural" disasters, and global environmental meltdown to the mix and America faces impressive challenges. This is the very stuff of patriotism: epic problems call for virtuoso performances.

Nevertheless, I would like to make the case against patriotism.[1]

In 1973 John Schaar, writing in the face of Vietnam and Watergate, deemed patriotism the sine qua non of democratic politics.[2] Much could be said on the fate of Schaar's plea for patriotism. Regardless, thirty-four years later I would like to revisit Schaar's claim on behalf of democratic politics. Like Schaar I have little hope of success. Like Schaar I sense thoughtlessness afoot. Like Schaar I think that citizens won't need the argument and that noncitizens will be prone to reject it. Like Schaar I will carry on nonetheless, for patriotism's dangers are endless and the case for democratic politics is one that always needs to be made. Though events of 2001 confirmed these truths, they did not invent them.

To exemplify the themes that preoccupy the book, I offer two distinct versions of politics. The first, patriotic, has two constitutive elements—a willful enmity and a logic of sacrifice—that compromise or even destroy what they claim to privilege; the second, democratic, aspires to a magnanimous, chastened agonism that serves as a spur to others and requires a direct, participatory version of civic engagement disinclined to cheer itself.

PATRIOTISM OF HATE

For a politics of enmity, consider first the conduct of presidential politics in 2004. Democratic opposition to George Bush's bid for election centered on his conquest of Iraq. John Kerry charged Bush with gross incompetence, dishonesty, and malfeasance. Having failed to prepare for occupation, America found itself fighting Bush's war a second time—and losing. Moreover, the Iraq invasion turned out to be gratuitous. Saddam Hussein's dictatorship posed no threat to the United States; moreover, it had no involvement with the attacks of late summer 2001—despite what the administration, against the evidence, repeated ad nauseam. Bush's Iraq obsession diverted attention from critical military operations in Afghanistan, which enabled Osama bin Laden to escape and al-Qaeda to reconstitute itself in more dangerous form.

Bush responded to criticism of his Iraq war in predictable fashion. He changed the subject and rendered suspect the very idea of criticism. Bush insisted time and again that the commander in chief had to be resolute, stay the course. No other posture would be thinkable for the president. To challenge the war's rationale, to question its execution, would send the wrong message to American troops fighting and dying on behalf of the country. Such slander would reach not only American soldiers but, more importantly, the "terrorists." To treat with disrespect, dishearten, and thereby undermine the military would embolden and empower the evil-doers. As if summoning the American spirit of calumny (read: sedition), Bush effectively equated criticism with aiding and abetting the enemy, fratricide. Bush, moreover, identified himself with American troops to the point of convergence. Trying to account for failure while refusing to admit its possibility, Bush quipped: "We thought we'd whip more of them going in." The implications of Bush's mantras were unmistakable: to challenge the president amounts to unpatriotic, arguably treasonous, behavior. If Bush's silencing strategy succeeded, it would place him beyond reproach. Patriotism can be the first as well as the last refuge of the scoundrel.

While George Bush maintained his presidential composure, David Brooks expressed and perfected patriotism's counterpart. Just days before the election, Brooks delivered an indignant broadside on behalf of the Bush campaign. John Kerry, he insinuated, had not established his patriotic credentials. What led Brooks to this assessment? Kerry's lack of what Brooks deemed the proper visceral response to September 11 and Osama bin Laden. Like Bush, Brooks did not hesitate to speak on behalf of the American people. Responding to bin Laden's pre-election video-tape, Brooks wrote, "What we saw last night was revolting. I suspect that more than anything else, he reminded everyone of the moral indignation we all felt on and after Sept. 11." Brooks then took the occasion to convert bin Laden's narcissism into a new presidential criterion. The sermon continued with a declaration: "One of the crucial issues of this election is, Which candidate fundamentally gets the evil represented by this man? Which of these two guys understands it deep in his gut—not just in his brain or in his policy statements, but who feels it so deep in his soul that it consumes him?" Here Brooks enunciated an affective loyalty test. You are what you feel. You must feel what we all feel. You must show it. And you must show it in a way that we can recognize and affirm. Bush passed his test; he responded to bin Laden by insisting that America would not be intimidated. Kerry failed; he dared criticize ("attack") Bush for losing an opportunity to capture bin Laden. Drawing on the authority of the American people, Brooks made an astonishing claim: "Many are not sure that [Kerry] gets the fundamental moral confrontation. Many people are not sure he feels it, or feels anything." Brooks concluded by professing one of patriotism's tenets, "We are revealed by what we hate."[3]

Let us take Brooks at his word. After November's election Kerry's status notably altered. Once Bush had been "returned" to the presidency, Brooks, in a follow-up piece, identified Bush's new enemy: the CIA. With Democrats reduced, for the time being, to mere opponents, the CIA drew Brooks's wrath because it first questioned and then resisted Bush's Iraq war policies; worse, it did so during a campaign season. It sabotaged Bush through anonymous leaks and stealth publications. It even voiced disdain for him at meetings. Since Brooks couldn't countenance the idea that the CIA had an obligation to the truth and an obligation to challenge Bush's repeated falsehoods, distortions, and misstatements about Iraq as he tried to fix responsibility for war failures on the agency, he believed that it must be called to account for having "violated all standards of honorable public service." Brooks also couldn't abide the idea that the CIA's principal allegiance was to the American republic. Just the opposite: "This is about more than intelligence. It's about Bush's second term." CIA employees, accordingly, do not work for America; they serve instead "on the president's payroll." What should be done with the "mutineers"? Brooks fantasizes mass slaughter and individual execution. He won't call directly for death, but projects lethal possibilities onto a distant past that knew how to deal with disloyalty. In Brooks's nostalgic daydream, Langley would be laid waste, with heads displayed on "spikes." Absence of punishment, after all, amounts to appeasement; then "everything is permitted."[4] From presidents to pundits, patriotism speaks its truths to the enemies it creates and permits itself wide latitude rhetorically, politically, and militarily when it comes to the country's defense. Not only does hate reveal identity; its performance constitutes identity.

I now turn to a topic closely allied with the politics of hate: patriotism's logic of sacrifice. In *The Genealogy of Morals* Nietzsche theorizes the relationship between a political order and its creators. Once upon a time, peoples believed that their well-being depended on the accomplishments, the sacrifices, of ancestors, which amounted to a gift that kept reiterating itself, generation after generation. Founders thus lived on in highly productive fashion. As a result, peoples felt a profound sense of indebtedness to forebears, and what was owed demanded payment: hence the advent of public rituals, tributes, ceremonies, and monuments to express not just gratitude but also love for the order bequeathed.[5]

Frederick Douglass confirms Nietzsche's analysis of a founding's patriotic productivity, the very Frederick Douglass who, speaking before the American Anti-slavery Society in New York in 1847, declared: "I have no love for America, as such; I have no patriotism. I have no country."[6] Douglass cannot be taken at his word, however. Consider his account of the Fourth of July, then America's sacrosanct patriotic holiday. Speaking to the Rochester Ladies' Anti-slavery Society in 1852, Douglass retells the inspirational tale of American freedom. It is an inspiring story partly because no one thought it would ever be told. Independence seemed doomed from the start, a romantic notion at best, a suicidal undertaking at worst. And yet seven decades later, here are Douglass and the members of the society celebrating the country's day of days. America's fathers were patriots, heroes, warriors; they privileged the common good over self-interest. They were animated by principle, not profit.[7] Freedom is their legacy—to some. Yet restrictions cannot derail the celebration.[8]

While Douglass addresses the society's members as fellow citizens, he refuses to claim joint political ownership of America with them. This is not his country, nor is it his holiday. These are yours, he tells them.[9] Yet Douglass's oration places him within patriotism's ambit as he understands it. More than mere celebration, patriotism involves, nay requires, serious criticism. No country is served by the bland recapitulation of congratulatory self-images. Hard truths need to be told. Accordingly, Douglass recovers July 4 by narrating it for the slave to his fellow citizens. The very fact of July 4 celebrations exacerbates the evils of slavery and makes the day, as well as its ideals, an unparalleled obscenity for blacks. No occasion brings America's crimes into perspective like the Fourth. It is a day of pretense, hypocrisy, ridicule, vanity, impiety, self-satisfaction, bombast, fraud, and deceit.[10] "There is not a nation on the earth guilty of practices more shocking and bloody than are the people of the United States, at this very hour."[11] The cries from chains grinding human beings bloody, he informs his audience, overwhelm the tumult of joyous celebration. It's not just that slaves can hear the "jubilee shouts." It's that America cannot "hear the mournful wail of millions!" Douglass deploys every linguistic resource at his disposal to focus the public mind: "I will, in the name of humanity which is outraged, in the name of liberty which is fettered, in the name of the constitution and the Bible, which are disregarded and trampled upon, dare to call in question and denounce, with all the emphasis I can command, everything that serves to perpetuate slavery—the great sin and shame of America!"[12]

Douglass's masterly performance places his audience in an uncomfortable position. Having reminded people of what they already know, they now have to justify what was once unassailable, namely their patriotism, their love of country. Slavery's history is America's history. The country's constitution presupposed and affirmed slavery. There is no America without slavery. As such, love of country seems impossible in front of Douglass. How can they love the country now that they see it, at this moment, as he sees it? He won't draw the conclusion they must draw for themselves. It's as if he is forcing them to do it by refusing to do so himself.[13]

Still, Douglass takes comfort and finds hope in America's youth. Among nations it is but an infant. Despite a wayward life of seventy-six years, time remains for America to correct its ways. Thus while the patriot's gaze is sickened, the patriot's heart is gladdened.[14] Douglass is to America in the mid-nineteenth century what the revolutionaries were to the colonies in the late eighteenth century. He will rouse the country from a life of prosperity and ease. One problem—the country epitomizes self-regard: "the American side of any question may be safely left in American hands."[15] Surely, Douglass believes, if America can work itself into a frenzy of historic proportions over a minuscule tea tax, it can summon the outrage needed to fell slavery, an ill that fouls every aspect of American life.

Douglass ultimately takes refuge in the Constitution. It can vindicate the founders—not the reverse. As if by magic, it can undo, in retrospect, undeniable founding crimes. America, from birth, has possessed the political means to right its perpetual defects.[16] Douglass embraces this argument once he has been mysteriously freed from a politics rooted in an understanding of "the pro-slavery character of the Constitution."[17]

Douglass's critical engagement with America embodies Schaar's account of "patriotic radicalism."[18] According to Schaar, to wage successfully a serious oppositional politics, you must persuade fellow citizens that you share "a country with them" and that you care for the "common things," though you may also violently disagree in certain respects.

Schaar's account of a self-styled patriotic politics suggests that Douglass loves America despite his protestations to the contrary.[19] He cares with such passion that he cannot let go of his critical engagement with America. Douglass's military service—recruitment—during the Civil War ups the ante of his commitment. Deeds match rhetoric. Douglass almost seems to be making an installment on Founding debt even though he, by rights, should be a recipient of payment. Regardless, Douglass's wartime efforts ultimately reveal a fatal flaw in his critical patriotism. Previously without country, Douglass now senses one within reach. The Civil War represents a political opportunity not to be missed, and Douglass's contribution places him within America's wartime patriotic tradition. He wants "colored men" to be included one day in the great patriotic narrative that will frame the war. The struggle between North and South names an epic battle of right versus wrong.[20] Patriots rush to defend Liberty against its southern traitors and join the ranks of America's heroes. Neutrality disrespects morality. You are either with the government or against it.[21] Patriotism's call must be answered, and this chapter in American history must not be absent colored contribution.[22] Douglass does not fear Jefferson Davis's criminal war policies as much as he desires patriotism's approving retrospective judgment. To fall within patriotism's embrace means dying for your country, history notwithstanding, even if it's not your country.[23] This in turn presupposes an America defined by its potential rather than by what Douglass calls its dead past.

Douglass sustained his enlistment drive despite the unequal treatment that black soldiers received. Union forces refused to pay, equip, or adequately train them. Moreover, upon capture Confederate forces would execute blacks, wounded or not, on the spot—while the Union maintained official silence. Douglass, in the end, scoffs at such hardships, for the "colored soldier" becomes the true patriot aiding a country that can't admit he belongs to it. He alone fights for republican principle, on behalf of an idea, devoid of "brutal malice."[24] Those who fight for America, Douglass insists, thereby make America theirs. Blood's investment makes the claim undeniable, impossible not to respect.[25] Recognized or not, they will be patriots.

Yet surely Douglass must suspect that if the price of citizenship means having to prove that you are ready to die for country, die in an internecine war not of your making, then your attempt to be accepted has little hope of success. Has not the ability to die in the project of nation building defined your lot in life since inception? The irony is that those who enslave—who admit that they cannot do for themselves what they impose on others—thereby declare themselves unworthy of democratic citizenship. Douglass's efforts to prove the patriotism of colored people—and thus make them worthy of citizenship—have already been implicitly considered and rejected by the very country to which he appeals. For blacks have already sacrificed generations to found and build America and to win its wars, starting with the revolutionary struggle. Douglass's calls for sacrifice thus follow countless sacrifices previously made to prove what's already been proven. Douglass's position seems no-win. If citizenship were granted, what would it say about America that it took three-quarters of a century and additional horrors for it to accede? While Douglass's politics seem calculated to generate moral pressure on the North, his rendering of patriotism here involves a commitment and sacrifice that exceed patriotism's standard operating terms. Douglass's enlistment logic dictates that you willingly sacrifice yourself and your children now so you can enjoy the right to have your future country impose on you the duty to be sacrificed later.

Thanks to Douglass, patriotism thus makes demands to which it is not entitled in a republican context, yet which appear imperatival or even persuasive. This is patriotism without limits. One gets the sense that Douglass's demands upon America, once granted, would change the country and make it worthy of the love offered. But death as the catalyst would seem to discredit rather than commend America. Perhaps it's only once you possess the object of your love—no longer distracted by the struggle to win it—that you can see it for what it is by virtue of what it took from you, what it cost.

Either way, Frederick Douglass proves himself a patriot, which partly explains why I am not one. If the country were worthy of the love that patriotism insists upon, it would not be able to accept it from Mr. Douglass, what with the sacrifices involved. The very idea of such taking would be unthinkable, especially insofar as the Union starts to mimic the very Confederacy with which it is at war. Patriotism would have to say no to itself and thus cease to be.

In short, if John Schaar is correct that patriotism, love of country, derives its sense and significance from belonging to a family of words, words including roots, covenant, legacy, gift, debt, reverence, and loyalty, then that family must be enlarged to include, and emphasize, crisis, threat, enemy, hate, death, dying, sacrifice, killing. Patriotism cannot be without the self-regarding, self-destructive logics informing them. Or, better, through the exemplary affirmations of patriots like Schaar, explored in chapter 2, the case for patriotism flounders not because it cannot keep the promises it makes to democracy; rather, democracy's undoing flows from patriotism's uncanny success in realizing the full potential of its union of sacred words.[26]

WITHOUT EXTERNAL PICTURESQUENESS

For the second version of politics promised, I turn from Bush, Brooks, and Douglass to another Massachusetts veteran, Robert Gould Shaw. Thanks to the good fortune of northern triumph and southern defeat, Shaw lives on in America's collective imagination. His fame derives from his having led the Massachusetts 54th, a regiment of black soldiers. Shaw was white. He led a doomed charge against Fort Wagner in the summer of 1863 and was killed in the attack. Thus official memory holds that America's division by race dissolved before the cause of Union. With the country imperiled, the 54th answered the call to arms and overcame difference to save the nation. It thereby prefigured a new order of things. The Robert Shaw I wish to recover, however, evades such traditional patriotic deployment. Hence the Shaw conjured and bequeathed by William James in 1897.

A monument to Shaw adorns the edge of Boston Commons across the street from the Massachusetts State House. Though striking, like many memorials it has become part of the fabric of the city in which it stands—more or less invisible. For my purposes, the monument's reputation can be revived by its commemoration ceremony, notable for the presence of James, who gave a dedication speech. It may be his finest piece of writing.[27] Certainly it does not lack ambition—for James would subvert the very ritual he ostensibly serves.

The beginning of the speech seems innocent enough, as James pays homage to the nature of the occasion. Citizens are indebted to those who bravely serve their country in time of crisis. Memory in the face of inevitable forgetting is thus a civic duty. At the same time, James calls the civic event into question. How is it that "only a young colonel, this regiment of black men and its maiden battle—a battle, moreover, which was lost—should be picked out for such unusual commemoration?"[28] Permanent public tributes tend to favor famous generals or the nameless, faceless warriors who secured a great victory fighting for them. Not so here. James reminds his audience that when it comes to history's actions or events, significance matters. Thus Bunker Hill, a military defeat, thrives in American memory, since America proved its would-be military mettle. Insofar as the Civil War was fought over the nature of the union itself, victory is best "symbolized and embodied" by Shaw and the 54th. James honors them for their composition, not their military achievements, if any.

James quickly turns back on his own discourse, however. He emphasizes the relative ordinariness of Shaw and his men. This is partly what makes them worthy of acknowledgment and representation. Yes, with their country in crisis these men were willing to sacrifice everything for the cause of Union. Yet thousands of other young men were willing to do likewise. On what basis should Shaw and the 54th be singled out for honors? Can selection be left to the contingencies of war itself, as the vagaries of battle provide fortune for some and send others to oblivion?

James refuses to worship at the altar of military valor. The idea of war as a school of manly virtue defines commonplace; and the value of military prowess suffers from civic exaggeration. Alas, there is never a shortage of those ready and able to throw themselves at death—provided that thousands of others are ready to accompany them (itself never a problem). Battlefield heroics have become instinctive, bred into each human being's nature. Not even centuries of peace could cure the species of its brutal leanings, reinforced by collective applause. War needs no further assistance from the poet or the orator.

James accordingly relocates the honors accorded to Shaw. With the assault on Fort Wagner at best secondary, he singles out in Shaw a rare civic courage. The irony is that precisely what makes Shaw deserving of memorial salute does not lend itself to oral testimony. Before taking command of the 54th, Shaw was an up-and-comer in the famous Massachusetts 2nd. When asked to take command of the 54th he ultimately accepted—though as a career choice this was dubious, all the more so for an ambitious young officer. His thinking was not colorblind. "Shaw recognized the vital opportunity: he saw that the time had come when the colored people must put the country in their debt."[29] James calls this a lonely courage and advises that the monuments of nations be erected to it. Not designed to call attention to itself, this courage was outside public view. And once it became known, it would likely be no more popular than, initially, the war itself. Shaw's courage was made possible by living a certain kind of life. Shaw's decision thus precedes the celebratory, that is, patriotic appropriation of his career and service.[30] James pays tribute to the Shaw whose action was complete unto itself. Contra traditional patriotic understandings, it did not require death to bring it to life. It was the life lived that gave meaning to the death.[31]

James situates Shaw within his version of American exceptionalism. Echoing Lincoln's Gettysburg Address, James adds a dose of candor. Given the impossible combination of freedom and slavery, America was an anomaly from its inception. Despite boasting of liberty America's empire of property in human beings demanded unconditional rule. This tension gave the lie to the country's vaunted self-conception. Ultimately the irrepressible voice of the abolitionists drove the "fanatics of slavery" to madness, and the South brought destruction upon its cherished institutions and way of life.[32] The founding generation, august reputation notwithstanding, especially in Boston, dared not touch the founding contradiction. It was left to the likes of Robert Gould Shaw and his comrades to redress it. They exemplified the "American religion" at its best.[33] They lived and thereby enacted freedom's creed; in the process they defeated its enemies once and for all. It is of Shaw's fidelity to the common political faith that James writes: "we wish his beautiful image to stand here for all time, an inciter to similarly unselfish public deeds."[34]

What kind of public deeds does James envision? He privileges the everyday, the routine, the banal: conduct that does not necessarily stand out when it is performed. Democratic conversation and engagement, whether through speaking, writing, or, less frequently, voting thoughtfully, exemplify indispensable "common habits" for a democratic agonism. Once acquired, these habits enable citizens to execute the responsibilities of citizenship. These in turn require stern discipline and sound temperaments. Democracies entail opposition and conflict, governing and being governed in turn, the affirmation of which entails relationships of critical engagement, contestation, doubt, and dissent on the one hand and modesty, respect, and generosity on the other. After all, politics and defeat are synonymous. Nothing can prevent reversals of fortune. In light of these political facts of life, a resentment-driven turn to war can become an irresistible temptation in the absence of equanimity when you find yourself on the losing end. The destruction of public peace, however, receives zero toleration. Remember: "the Slave States nearly wrecked our nation."[35]

James insists that the fate of the American democracy remains uncertain. The sacrifice of Shaw, as well as hundreds of thousands of others, cannot secure the country's future. Yet what made Shaw Shaw is unclear. James speaks of the civic genius of the American people, but he does not delineate or explain it: "neither laws nor monuments, neither battleships nor public libraries, nor great newspapers nor booming stocks, neither mechanical invention nor political adroitness, nor churches nor universities nor civil service examinations can save us from degeneration if the inner mystery be lost."[36] The common habits that James lauds as the inner mystery are anything but common. He describes them as homely, by which he appears to mean simple, reflexive, and unpremeditated. Honoring Shaw, James recommends emulation. Decisions such as Shaw's—quotidian, innumerable—form the nation's character. If James's counsel were to prove successful, the irony is that Shaw would be effectively erased. *Eventually the mark of a democratic people is precisely that no one can be singled out and distinguished from the rest. Decency would prevail and we would be one, as it were, in our homeliness. Patriotism would dissolve in the face of ordinary citizenship.* The likes of George Bush and David Brooks would be exposed as what James calls "rabid partisans and empty quacks."[37]

Shaw may nevertheless appear to be a patriot. While I find Shaw's life admirable, his protean ethical sensibilities, though placed in service to the nation, cannot be reduced to patriotism. Some of Shaw's qualities may be critical to patriotism but they are also separate and distinct from it. Thus I would argue that Shaw is no patriot. I believe the same can be said of James, the James who posits a future polity where Robert Shaw is anything but idiosyncratic.

The juxtaposition of Shaw and James with Brooks and Bush highlights something fundamental about patriotism: despite the promise that it seems to possess, it tends to disappoint and destroy. Is there not something inherently suspicious about an ethos that dwells upon distinguishing its true, genuine, or healthy instantiations from its allegedly false, counterfeit, perverted forms? Patriotism, I argue, cannot reliably deliver as advertised the political goods that it claims to produce, especially under pressure. What might be the reason? It is, in short, that patriotism at its best begets patriotism at its worst. Among other things, patriotism, as a first move, insists on the articulation of criteria through which it establishes itself and simultaneously forges its enemies, namely those whose failure to meet the criteria by definition poses an existential threat to the political order. Patriotism's Manichean logic forges a central divide in the structure of the body politic, thus posing a permanent, continual threat poised to erupt. Patriotism, to be, posits a complex relationship of self-destruction: it legitimizes actions taken in the name of basic political principles that traduce those same principles; it accords itself a special, perhaps higher, authority to monopolize politics and to silence, marginalize, and ultimately disable opposition, particularly when opposition matters most; it induces affective states that lead to plans and policies otherwise objectionable or even unthinkable; it conceals the damage that it does through professions of love and declamations of terrible necessity that adherents would recognize; it emerges as a primal, preemptive force precisely because polities cannot face the cruelties, injustices, and exclusions that characterize them. Thus perhaps patriotism cannot but be insistent, imperatival, and univocal. In sum, patriotism proves itself to be anything but indispensable to democracy; rather democracy's future depends on its emergence from patriotism's self-obsessive grip.

THE IRREDEEMABILITY OF PATRIOTISM

Perhaps it is time to listen to a "new" claim: patriotism as impossibility. Let us consider the notion that you cannot "love" your country, for no country can be worthy of the moral crown that is love. If anything, patriotism is already dead; it has killed itself—though its aura may linger for generations. Patriotism itself makes such thoughts possible, perhaps necessary.[38] Despite historical variations, patriotism evidences a handful of transcendent features: wars celebrated, death glorified, martyrs incarnated, sacrifice worshiped, enemies vilified, hate encouraged, killing sanctified. Yet these familiar, all-too-familiar patriotic phenomena can be recovered and experienced anew. James again offers assistance. In "The Moral Equivalent of War," he endeavors to wage war against the very ideal of war. His self-assignment runs counter to millennia of history. The war spirit has been bred into the species, James insists, forming part of our genetic makeup. After national civil conflict, however, war's popularity has suffered. James observes a difference between affirming, in retrospect, a war fought and won and a willingness to refight it now—despite its just character. The former sentiment flourishes; the latter one wanes. The shift provides James with an opening.[39]

James takes patriotism as a given. To oppose it strikes him as futile, in particular if the opposition consists of sheer moralizing. Regarding service to country, disclosing war's horrors, for example, cannot hope to succeed, since horror provides war with one of its many attractions. Life lived at the edge, with death a serious prospect, offers meaning and purpose. A world without war and its attendant dangers would be dull, banal, and stultifying. Thus from ancient Greece to contemporary America, love of war persists. Patriotism counts on and cultivates it.[40] What is to be done?

James argues that to move an (intellectual) opponent from a stronghold, you must first enter deeply into his position.[41] The problem with those who condemn and denounce war is not only that they fail to understand its pleasures; lacking such an understanding, they offer no substitute for it, no moral equivalent. James would fill the void he identifies by declaring war on Nature.[42] In effect, James recovers Rousseau's notion of corvées and proposes the formation of youthful civic work gangs to build and rebuild the nation's basic institutions. Social service would name a new kind of conscription. Everyone would be drafted into an army trained to fight and conquer Nature, an enemy that defies permanent defeat. James seeks a new and improved martial ethos, a better patriotism, a project for the ages.[43]

Pace James, I believe that entering more deeply into the position of an opponent might yield different results. James may be right that horror can be thrilling—when contextualized in terms of heroic response and civic glory as nations go to war. What if, however, horror can be restored to itself? What if cruelty, violence, death, and war can be reinvented, can be unleashed and set loose upon themselves? Insofar as they form the core of patriotism, what if they were stripped of their patinas of romanticizing, mythification, and deification? If James is right that patriotism does not appreciate the price it exacts for its exercise, perhaps it can be induced to reevaluate itself if seen from a new angle of vision. What if patriotism can be shown to bring about stands and affirmations that violate the principles constituting its very reason for being? What if patriotism can be shown to depend on and produce a cult of endless enmity? What if patriotism can be shown to feed on death to the point of addiction? What if patriotism can be shown to care principally for its own credentials, its own bona fides, in short, itself? The chapters that follow are placed strategically to put pressure on patriotism, so that it might conduct a candid self-appraisal of its enabling-cum-disabling logic.

Chapter 2 explores calls by contemporary democratic theorists and public intellectuals for patriotic renewal aided by the articulation of great national stories. Speak well of America and its distinctive past, Richard Rorty, Walter Berns, and others argue, if you wish to inspire generations working for a better, more progressive future. For Rorty, alas, this project presupposes finessing the less attractive episodes in America's history, as well as a tendency to vilify potential allies who would confront the country's past. When it comes to the subject of Vietnam, for example, Rorty begins by acknowledging America's war crimes, perpetrated for no good reason other than macho stupidity. Yet Rorty soon folds Vietnam into a larger cold war context, the evident nobility of which excuses any mistakes that might have been made on behalf of a global crusade against evil. Rorty thus rewrites and erases Vietnam from America's troubled history as he ostensibly addresses it. (Berns does the same with America's founding and slavery.) Thus good patriotic tales are told. The price is a cruelty that Rorty abhors; the reward is license to act on the world's political stage as history's designated agent. Here patriotism is its own worst theoretical enemy.

Following Rorty's patriotic example, chapters 3 and 4 trace patriotism's love of epic drama, highlighting citizen-heroes fighting against great odds with life on the line—whether it's Socrates lecturing an Athenian jury while on trial, Will Kane in *High Noon* addressing the good citizens of Hadleyville at Sunday services, or Captain John Miller scouring the war-ravaged French countryside in search of Private Ryan. Yet what appear at first to be doomed opposition to state-sanctioned injustice; solitary, perhaps futile resistance to unmitigated evil; and an ethical mission-impossible that must succeed no matter the cost appear otherwise with a second look. Socrates provokes Athens at the end of his life, with death a pleasant, even essential prospect; Will Kane usurps the badge after forced retirement to what he considers a worthless way of life; America gambles the lives of exhausted men after the bloody success of D-Day on a task whose moral point—not to be confused with its stated objective—revolves around the deliberate humiliation of a superfluous solider. With each drama unfolding late in the day, so to speak, at patriotism's behest, they may turn out to be self-indulgent exercises (bordering on narcissistic display) that subvert the larger principles supposedly being enacted. In the absence of patriotic moralizing, not only might death have been sidestepped. My claim is that life, democratic life, could have pursued new avenues of adventure.

Chapters 5 and 6 consider patriotic monuments and memorials that seek to eternalize love in public space. What, if anything, renders self-applause problematic? It's not just that countries alternate between pride and shame, as Rorty observes. It's not just that countries are unable to acknowledge their mistakes, especially crimes, as again Rorty observes (with others). It's not just that instances of patriotic pride result in by-products that can't be countenanced. It's that the acts typifying patriotism, love of country at its best, lead to violence and cruelty destructive of privileged national self-conceptions. As a result, the will to self-congratulation tends to preclude innovative architectural design that might capture history's complexities and enact democratic values. While the World War II Memorial, its triumphal arches and self-satisfied inscriptions, might seem the premier instance of collective preening on the Mall, I believe that the Japanese-American Memorial to Patriotism during World War II best captures patriotism's relentless self-regard. Denied a memorial dedicated to the arbitrary incarceration by Franklin Roosevelt in 1942 of American citizens of Japanese descent, the Japanese American Memorial transformed itself into a salute to America, the country that can and did publicly acknowledge its error. Our beneficence is worth monumental marking—rather than fixation on an ancient crime that everybody agrees to agree was an unfortunate wartime mistake. America's racial transgression, already forgiven, becomes an isolated incident with the country trusted never to repeat it—despite the repetition characteristic of American history. Thus does patriotism's version of the past presage the country's future. America now locates its gulags abroad.

Chapter 7 investigates patriotism's affective fuels, death and dying. In need of constant replenishment, war's carnage can't do the job by itself.

Renewable resources must be developed. Such permanent shortages help to illuminate the veritable cult surrounding John Kennedy's gravesite at Arlington National Cemetery. Owing to the shortness of Kennedy's presidential tenure and his concomitant lack of accomplishment, the stone inscriptions that surround the eternal flame speak to what perhaps might have been rather than to any real achievement. Thus the gravesite's location in Arlington and its enduring popularity name political and cultural oddities. Enter Oliver Stone's *JFK* and Don DeLillo's *Libra*, the latter a disturbing investigation of America's body politic. Thanks to DeLillo's presentation, Kennedy's murder suggests that killing on behalf of country names the definitive patriotic act. More than a willingness to sacrifice yourself, the willingness to sacrifice others, much more one of your own, proves telling. Kennedy's murder, transformed by a cold war context in which the country finds itself in great peril, becomes a heroic sacrifice made on behalf of the country, perhaps especially if performed unknown to the president himself. All the president's men knew what he would have wanted done in his name. They are entrusted to read his mind. Though DeLillo has no apparent interest in shedding light on patriotism, his novel reveals the various forms that love of country can take. This is not patriotism perverted, in other words, but patriotism honed and perfected. In short, it may take a novel to complete a memorial.

Chapter 8 discloses patriotism's great irony: love of country in search of consummate expression reveals its own impossibility. Thanks to Bruce Springsteen's career-long meditation on the American Dream, a country self-consciously loved proves itself indifferent, unmoved—in a word, unlovable. This insight can be gained only by working through the very love that is taken for granted and judged susceptible of definitive representation. In the course of professing love, whether by describing the sacrifices offered to country or the successes it was thought to have made possible, America turns out to be something other than initially believed. Given what countries routinely, matter-of-factly expect, demand, and extract, once the truth of these takings is experienced in its raw immediacy there is a moment of recognition when love of country becomes impossible. When your prospects in life are fixed by the lowly circumstances attending birth, when your way of life moves overseas as a result of the hard work that defined your career, when the country to which you gave your life to defend inflicts harms that even its enemies cannot match, when your children are killed fighting gratuitous and losing wars against foes that vanish with their victory, you sense that love, when it comes to country, is at best a misplaced sentiment, at worst ethically indefensible. Constant investment and projection cannot be reciprocated but result only in further offerings: patriotism as the mirage that never fails to entice. Yet, Springsteen's songs prove, life's events can be retold as tragic tales that in turn generate pressures, demands, forces, and potentials seeking an expression, an outlet. Tragedy provokes action.

DEMOCRACY RESTORED

Having worked through patriotism, what might follow, theoretically and politically, from a world without it? Insofar as patriotism's operationalism relies on a sophisticated blend of the real and the imaginary, the concrete and the figurative, it simultaneously points to the lived presence of actualities (conflicts, failures, sufferings, cruelties, losses) that can inspire a tragic appreciation of democracy. What might this mean?

George Steiner contends that tragedy essentially names an ontological condition: homelessness.[44] The human condition, characterized by alienation and estrangement, follows a cataclysmic fall from grace. Steiner thereby makes tragedy something achieved, something for which humankind is responsible—through a foundational sin, for example. Steiner insists that tragedy properly understood belies hope, but the very notion of a fall driving even his version of tragedy presupposes the possibility of some kind of redemption—if not now, later; if not here, elsewhere; if not by human hands, other hands.[45] Either way, homelessness engenders homesickness, a yearning to be one with the world to which you belong. This longing, anti-tragic to the core, encompasses patriotism and the professions of love defining it—which, if anything, bring the very object of love, namely country, into being in the first place.

While I concur with Steiner that tragedy speaks to an ontological event, it strikes me as coterminous with life. Unlike Steiner, I do not doubt the possibility of atheist tragedy; rather, I take it for granted.[46] The world, uncreated, unplanned, is indifferent to the human being and its projects, including politics; this leads to a perverse condition in which success and frustration, joy and futility invariably combine. Thus I take tragedy's ontological starting point to be thrownness.[47] We live in the breach, in the middle of things. Life, including politics, proceeds in complex situations of no one's making, consisting of forces not necessarily susceptible to understanding, let alone control. Life marks the effort to do the best possible with the resources available. With regard to democracy, this combination makes for complicated successes, strange victories, ambiguous achievements, skewed results, and uncertain outcomes. Ironically, however, tragedy can inspire at the level of both thought and action. Even if the world foils well-planned interventions, politics can be approached ingeniously, as if it were a solution in need of, well, a solution. Tragedy's challenge is that it makes you work in reverse. If you know, in advance, that things must go awry, the question becomes, before you start, what response might be apt this time around, for this set of circumstances to what you might do—a response itself in need of response. And so on. Hence tragedy's vexing and productive circle.

Following James, I would affirm that life is hard, defined by struggle, pain, antagonism, and injury. Thus life suggests the indispensability of democratic politics, which, as it addresses life's tragic necessities and mysteries, routinely, necessarily produces tragic outcomes of its own. The stuff of politics, composed of tragic projects and conflicts, offers opportunities for creative endeavor, the difficulty and angst of which James, for one, does not appreciate. Life and democracy find common ground in tragedy.

Democratic politics, at its best, inspires a tragic appreciation of life because of the cruelties that it habitually produces. Laws passed, policies enacted, principles embodied, interests promoted, campaigns waged entail exclusions, by-products, remainders, violences, and resentments that need to be addressed and redressed. The recognition that politics cannot be conducted without tragic procedures and outcomes does not occasion resignation or, as with patriotism, resentment; rather it fosters an obligation, as well as a pragmatic need, to attend to what comes next. Tragedy lives in the aftermaths that it engenders. I would argue that it points to the need for a democratic tithing, a kind of gifting or largess. Not in the name of sacrifice, with its intimations of life and death, command and imposition, but as a tribute to life's flows and energies. To refuse a patriotic ethos thus involves re-covering certain of its aspects after it's been dismantled. It is possible to appreciate the past and one's forebears and still approach the future without punishing and crippling the present by means of self-imposed debt. What greater challenge could there be than to recognize that a political vision realized inflicts wounds and engenders opposition, that these are the sure markers of achievement? What greater challenge could there be than to know, in advance, that the greatest of successes leads to distinct failures, themselves in need of tending, precisely because things went as planned? Tragedy thereby acts as a spur to possibilities previously unknown.

Patriotism, I believe, denies and thereby discloses tragic dynamics: patriotism as a reaction to tragedy's lived presence. Patriotism betrays an anti-tragic outlook, envisioning a romanticized world of redemption, salvation, and transcendence. Even so, the actualities to which patriotism is a response can become prods to greatness in its absence. Tragedy as constitutive of democratic citizenship suggests neither retreat nor surrender to the fates. Rather, tragedy encourages an ethos of self-overcoming civic generosity. Imagine a system of democratic tithing in which life-affirming production, reflective of democracy's mode of being in the world, namely its will to surpass the bounty of prior civic contributions, replaces life-denying sacrifice. Democratic tithing as benefaction, a gift from the surplus democracy generates as it unfolds. Once institutionalized, it induces similarly inclined contributions which themselves inspire a logic of emulation that redounds to common benefit.

If democracy requires self-affirming political projects, a tragic perspective cultivates a taste for initiatives launched, chances taken, risks assumed, wagers accepted, and—by implication—mistakes (even terrible mistakes) made. It also presupposes attentiveness and therefore answerability as key dispositions. Politics that specialize and take pride in assigning responsibility and blame, fomenting vilification and victimization, nursing ressentiment and reaction might decline in the new climate as they are squeezed from civic and cultural space. The patriotic politics of David Brooks would recede before the tragic joy to be discerned, say, in the story of a Springsteen tune.

In love everything is only illusion. I admit it . . . it is the work of our errors. So, what of it?—JEAN-JACQUES ROUSSEAU, *Émile*

I have never . . . "loved" any people or collective—neither the German people, nor the French, nor the American, nor the working class or anything of that sort. I indeed love "only" my friends and the only kind of love I know of and believe in is the love of persons.
—HANNAH ARENDT, *The Jew as Pariah*

At what point then is the approach of danger to be expected? I answer, if it ever reach us, it must spring up amongst us. It cannot come from abroad. If destruction be our lot, we must ourselves be its author and finisher. As a nation of freemen, we must live through all time, or die by suicide.—ABRAHAM LINCOLN, "Address before the Young Men's Lyceum"

This Patriotism
Which Is Not One

Patriotism sports impressive theoretical friends. Contemporaries include Charles Taylor, Richard Rorty, Maurizio Viroli, Ben Barber, Hilary Putnam, Robert Pinsky, Mary Dietz, Alasdair MacIntyre, Wendy Brown, and John Schaar. "We cannot do without patriotism in the modern world" (Taylor). "National pride is to countries what self-respect is to individuals: a necessary condition for self-improvement" (Rorty). "Patriotism well understood is . . . the foundation of a healthy, dynamic, open, liberal society" (Viroli). "What we require are healthy, democratic forms of . . . civic patriotism" (Barber). "The best kind of patriotism—loyalty to what is best in the traditions one has inherited—is indispensable" (Putnam). We must "respect the nature of patriotism and similar forms of love" (Pinsky). "Patriotism as a particular 'way-of-being' in the world . . . is nearly lost to us, and the damages that result from this . . . are not negligible" (Dietz). "Patriotism and those loyalties cognate to it are not just virtues but central virtues"

(MacIntyre). Patriotism is "a love of country oriented toward a thoughtful and empowered ... citizenry, a love of democratic traditions and practices rather than nation-state power" (Brown). And Schaar writes, regretfully: "We have lost patriotism. ... I believe the loss is great."[1]

These champions of patriotism command attention not only because they pursue and defend versions tailored to democratic political forms. They command attention because they assume the complicated, problematic, even dangerous nature of the ethic they propose and evince intent to avoid its ugliness, cruelty, and violence. In short, none of these theorists suffer from naïveté as they articulate patriotisms at their finest.[2]

Thus patriotism can lay claim to a renaissance—a development that predates the catalytic events of late summer 2001. Though I do not privilege America's contemporary war-driven patriotism to further the analysis, I abstain because I believe patriotism to be profoundly implicated in a complex of death—not just war. Moreover, I am concerned with patriotic visions, practices, and sensibilities that both involve and exceed contingent social and political events, affective intensity notwithstanding. Thus I am concerned with the patterns that myriad conceptions of patriotism display across time and place. I suspect that patriotism constitutes a permanent possibility more or less lodged in the human social predicament. As such, perhaps patriotism can be understood by exploring its conviction, voiced or quiet, that social and political life would secure its rightful form and achieve necessary unity and power if only patriotic dicta were experienced and affirmed in their moments of truth.

This is where things get interesting. To secure itself, patriotism resorts to promises and payoffs that resist articulation. Patriotic encomiums, that is, routinely point beyond the immediately political to something else. And it is this something else, whether the nature of things, the way of the world, or the foundations of life, to which patriotism aspires and from which it draws sustenance. This accounts for patriotism's liminal aspects. Ostensibly the most material of projects, it often turns out to be the most immaterial of affairs. Patriotism's open secret: it must infuse itself (and politics) with contestable truths that if stated openly might collapse upon delivery. Intimations of transcendent support done well, however, can provide much needed sustenance. If patriotism cannot compel solely on its merits, it may be able to win over through other means.

Transcendent entanglement, I believe, makes the project of patriotism doubly hazardous to democratic forms of life. It raises the patriotic above the mundane world of party or interest politics to a plateau from which it can look down, pronounce, and issue life-and-death edicts. Thus the love that it names invests contingent political schemes and arrangements with a status they would otherwise lack. It effectively ontologizes them, and they it. But this is a symbiotic operation shrouded in nuance and dissemination. The influence of the ontological dimension makes it tricky to contest patriotic narratives, for they circulate in important respects outside their explicit terms of discourse.

Exploring the ontological dimension may help to illuminate another problematic, paradoxical feature of patriotic discourse, namely its tendency toward narcissism. Patriotism's self-love is allied with affective exceptionalism, the conviction-cum-insistence that your country sets the standard for all that is deemed worthy of love. Patriotism does not so much require you to love your country regardless of its performance in attaining the standard that it sets. Patriotic love means that your country necessarily meets the standard despite any discrepancy (by definition nominal) between self-conception and life. Patriotism, in short, provides for a country that is always and forever what it claims to be. Well versed in the art of storytelling, patriotism owes its success to narrative creativity—a deft combination of political matter-of-factness, selective memory, indispensable forgetting, interpretive legerdemain, self-conscious repetition, and moral energy. The combination is critical because patriotism's love, paradoxically, precedes its entrance into the world. Insofar as patriotism means that true citizens always already love their country, patriotic love can only be confirmed and consolidated by the "empirical" phenomena it encounters.

Patriotism places the world at its imaginary disposal, transforming it into a blank sheet awaiting scriptural imprint. Patriotism's literary narcissism posits a world narratively reducible to a country's virtuous identity and good moral standing. Patriotism at its storytelling best does not deny the cruelty, ugliness, and horror endemic to politics. If it did, that would transform history into fairy tale, and the elimination of complexity or ambiguity might compromise believability. Rather, patriotism solidifies and consolidates the internal truth that it bears by folding missteps and misdeeds into a larger affirmative narration presupposing and revealing the country's virtue. Thus even when the country appears to do wrong, there is always a larger good at work to take care of it. Thus patriotism possesses self-overcoming properties thanks to the stories that it tells. If anything, discrepancies call attention to the goodness from which the country may regrettably depart. According to Rorty, for example, America admittedly makes mistakes. Through carefully crafted acknowledgment, though, America's goodness enhances itself. Patriotism means that the country never fails to become what it already is. No event (too horrific), no incident (too heinous), no cause (too dubious) can subvert, much less reverse, patriotism's expression of its inner truth.

The inner logic of patriotism thus tends to engender a politics concerned principally with itself more than with the purported objects of its care. Eventually patriotism cares for little but its own bona fides. The solipsistic logic can illuminate the insistent and imperatival character of patriotic discourses, as well as many of its destructive dimensions. Patriotism must be one with the world and the world with it. To attribute the resurgence and revitalization of patriotic ideas and inclinations to this or that political, economic, or cultural development would therefore miss the larger philosophical impulse that nourishes both the lament over the loss of patriotism and the drive to recover it.

Despite the contestable ontological underpinnings and political morality of patriotism, advocates cannot be dismissed as mere nostalgics or homesick romantics longing for a lost world. Patriotism is considered indispensable to the maintenance and flourishing of modern democracy, which must be able to draw upon a deep reservoir of civic ties, public commitment, and affective bonds to keep the common enterprise going. Discipline and sacrifice, necessities of any political order, must be self-imposed rather than coerced.[3] If people focus exclusively on their own affairs, a world according to Hobbes prevails.

Yet the democracy that patriotism supposedly serves might want to pause here. Patriotic discourses tend to deify and thereby immunize from examination (not to mention from challenge) certain fundamental matters—whether the core values of the republic, the way of life of a people, or the identity of the nation as a perpetual project.[4] MacIntyre concedes: "Because patriotism has to be a loyalty that is in some respects unconditional, so just in those respects rational criticism is ruled out."[5] That which is considered basic, essential, and foundational must be placed beyond reach. Moreover, nothing but complete compliance with this requirement can redeem privileging it. This reality may help to illuminate patriotism's curious affective insistence. For patriotism demands both emotional guarantees and behavioral assurances crippling to the democratic character of the political order that it ostensibly reveres. It wants in advance, before the fact, what ought to be the result of a robust way of life.[6] In short, you are supposed to love your country—always, already. Love does not need to be earned, as it were. You must love your country so that one day, having long been committed to its well-being, you will love your country. Love presupposes and engenders itself. Or, patriotism names a love that is in love with itself.

I suggest, however, that an estimable social and political order, in which norms of justice and practices of freedom predominate, artlessly engenders the civic devotion that it requires to sustain itself. My suspicion is that where patriotism becomes an explicit, determined object of cultivation, its artificiality—and thus its impossibility—have thereby announced themselves. Perhaps a political order that must make a point of fostering patriotism does not deserve the love it represents; conversely, perhaps an order that could deserve love has no need to concern itself with cultivation and would not pursue it. In light of the contextual paradoxes that it faces, pleas for patriotism ring hollow, for if commitment has to be arranged isn't it a sign that the order of things cannot generate the commitment on its own? This may explain Taylor's penchant for insisting on the necessity of patriotism while issuing simultaneous warnings about democracy's fate in its obvious and deserved absence. When it comes to patriotism, we must have it: "we have no choice."[7] Thus patriotism comes to possess remarkable powers: it can cure any ill because it can assume the shape it needs to become the remedy to the ill that it has identified.

Indeed, democracy requires citizenship. It calls for, I believe, a tragic ethos characterized by a commitment to pluralism and faith in constitutional principles themselves immune from cult-like obedience to an original fount. And if it is true to itself, the ethos will draw sustenance from a multitude of final sources. These would include different conceptions of God, gratitude for life in a world without a god, reverence for the diversity of human being, appreciation for and cultivation of the mysteries of life, belief in the sufficiency of reason, assumptions about the contingencies of science, and so on. This ethos is not built on love as a predominant passion but encompasses a multitude of possible dispositions and inclinations that skirt the demand for final vindication and have an appreciation of distance and difference built into their very constitution. With an abundant democratic ethos, the affective dimension need not be defined or settled before its enactment. Nevertheless, while citizens would be well advised to engage the political world, they need not announce, applaud, or celebrate their efforts nor devote to them the most precious and prized of all emotional investments.[8] Patriotism, alas, seems to suffer from a self-conscious self-consciousness. As it attends to social and political life, it ineluctably turns inward and fixes on self-generated preoccupations: us and them, loyalty and enmity, fidelity and betrayal.

Patriotism's problems beset even singular incarnations. I treat Rorty's and Schaar's patriotic translations as exemplars. They care passionately about America. Immersed in the country's history, they relate with pride its achievements and heroes. To express love of country, for them, is an act of civic responsibility. With political debts happily paid, remembrance becomes coin of the realm. Further, they commit themselves to critique and not mere celebration; love must be combined with overcoming. They think of America as a work of art in the making. Each possesses a strong faith in American exceptionalism: as the country goes, so goes the world. Rorty and Schaar know how to love.

Heeding William James's advice, I examine Rorty's and Schaar's theoretical endeavors as well as Norman Podhoretz's incendiary memoir. The patriotism that each articulates, at times compelling, moves inexorably toward self-subversion, violating its alleged reason for being. Because they seem not to appreciate this dynamic, I turn Rorty's, Schaar's, and Podhoretz's own words against them. I re-present their patriotisms from a new angle of vision, perhaps with but one degree of separation, to be seen as if for the first time. This may prove a risky interpretive strategy, since the commentary and critique that I fold into the re-presentation concede their contestability. Nevertheless, if patriotism is to be placed in a position to confront itself, it must be able to experience itself anew. The strategy here parallels that of the analyst who finds himself compelled to break silence and ask the analysand: Did you hear what you just said? The question, if timed well, can elicit surprise, confusion, shock, perhaps horror, and ultimately recognition of an inadvertent revelation. What if, for patriotism to carve out a place for itself in the late modern political world, it must not affirm itself as such, let alone fashion and advertise a catalogue of fundamental elements? What if it must be a self-abnegating, pluralized patriotism, a patriotism that is not one?

Richard Rorty relishes a good fight. Taking on the American left, especially the academic left, Rorty's patriotic jeremiad, *Achieving Our Country*, sounds a call for a left patriotism to restore and redeem political life in the United States. According to Rorty, despite our unprecedented wealth and power there is much to be ashamed of in contemporary America. Never has a country in a position to do so much actually done so little— self-image aside. In short, social justice has dropped from the lexicon of American political discourse, and it is up to the left, the party of hope, to intervene if America is to be all it can.[9]

Rorty, tone derisive, even Rousseauvian, does not mince words. His polemic stings—it's an attack from within. He decries "the vast inequalities within American society," where "economic inequality and economic insecurity have steadily increased"; he prophesies that "the new economic cosmopolitanism presages a future in which . . . we are likely to wind up with an America divided into hereditary social castes"; and he salutes the unions for having "prevented America from becoming the property of the rich and greedy."[10] He notes a pitiful silence: "It is as if the distribution of income and wealth [were] too scary . . . for any American politician— much less any sitting president—ever to mention."[11]

Rorty would reunite the American left.[12] To be one, the left must turn to the nation's past and make it present—that is, felt and lived. It can become viable and vital only with a foundation in the American yesteryear. Rorty's politics thus define, in part, a narrative endeavor of considerable magnitude. Visions of what America might become gain credence when linked to earlier episodes in the country's history. The logic is straightforward, the emotional appeal enticing. Considering what America has previously accomplished, especially in the twentieth century, there is no telling what we might do now as we strive to build a common future on increasingly just terms.[13]

For Rorty the left must be a self-conscious story-telling party. It must cite and celebrate uniquely American heroes and heroines who have been able to envision and effect a better America. Rorty's admittedly controversial list of great American leftists includes Woodrow Wilson, Franklin

Roosevelt, and Lyndon Johnson. While their administrations were profoundly flawed, each nonetheless made significant contributions to the cause of social justice to earn a place in Rorty's pantheon.[14]

Rorty defines the left broadly. He does so not just to ensure that his patriotic narrative can be rich and varied, capable of inspiring new generations of citizens to political action. He also wants to eliminate what he sees as a dangerously puritanical element within the left, especially in its revolutionary wing. The puritanical left, according to Rorty, defines itself by rejecting outright the social and political order that it denounces. It has no interest in mundane politics, because politics serve merely to legitimize a system rotten to its core and ripe for destruction: condemnation, yes, collaboration, no. For Rorty an obsession with purity makes politics impossible, since life in a pluralist democratic order requires negotiating deals and reaching compromises with avowed enemies. According to Rorty, the path of purity is a road to nowhere.

 Hence Rorty's patriotic ethos. For the left's politics to reach beyond the converted, it must concern itself not just with specific recommendations. It must also attend to its own self-constitution. The left must forge an all-American identity. It must possess genuine national pride and be able to communicate it effectively. Politics will be impoverished until pride is prominent in political discourse. Lacking affective commitment, national dialogue and deliberation will be listless, impotent. Only through profound emotional involvement and attachment can an image worthy of the idea of America first be postulated and then become an active object of political aspiration. Rorty thus considers the absence of inspiring imagery to be a hallmark—and failure—of contemporary political life.

Rorty's narrative regime is not, strictly speaking, historical. He is not concerned with an accurate account of America's history, whatever that might mean. Idealization, not truth, animates Rorty. He dreams of left and right locked in narrative combat over what America might be—based on what each imagines it might well once have been. He rejects the claim that a selective or revisionist approach to American history is ideological or mythical. Such an accusatory description presupposes access to an objective truth unavailable to us. Rorty's dialogical struggle over the moral identity of the nation would represent politics at its democratic best. Each party would offer a vision of America with its own distinct episodes, revered figures, dramatic events, and stirring moments. Politics would become a rhetorical exercise designed to establish the moral parameters within which questions of national legislation and policy might then proceed.

Rorty's recommendation elevates "politics" to a central place in American life. He emphasizes the experimental, open-ended, and contingent character of national self-creation. What we are today can never be fully satisfactory, because there is always more work to be done in the name of the image that brought us here. Moreover, the image that inspires generations will eventually wither and die, to be supplanted by an alternative account that seizes the nation's fancy. The dialectic of dissolution and replacement thrills and scintillates. We can make of ourselves whatever we will. Invoking the genius of Whitman and Dewey, Rorty insists there is no external authority to which we must answer, God or anything else. We need only please ourselves.

Rorty's vision desacralizes the political. There is no overarching Truth to which we must yield or bend. Thus the cruelty and sadism that shadow political schemes rooted in a knowledge of God's will for humankind might well dim in his hands. Yet Rorty's logistics of national self-creation suggest that the divine is still on the move and well armed. Europe, the Old World suffering from theistic battle fatigue, may find itself reborn in the New World, in America, Hegel's "country of the future."[15] Rorty writes of the United States: "We are the greatest poem because we put ourselves in the place of God: our essence is our existence, and our existence is in the future. Other nations thought of themselves as hymns to the glory of God. We redefine God as our future selves."[16]

Rorty thus redivinizes the world through creative projection. Once God has been driven from its place of privilege, the American nation self-consciously reoccupies its sacred space, as humanity grapples with its cosmic aloneness. Center stage with the whole world watching, what is America to do with this singular opportunity? Apparently, whatever it wants. Flirting with an ethic of creation ex nihilo, Rorty's America can invent and reinvent itself at will. Self-sufficient, self-subsistent, self-fashioning, "Americans [are] to take pride in what America might, *all by itself and by its own lights, make of itself.*"[17]

The stories we tell about ourselves must be worthy of our divine expropriation. They must lift and exalt us. America is sui generis, "the vanguard of humanity." Granted, once divine providence in human affairs has dissipated, the shape of things to come is radically unknown. Even the best plans may go awry, and Rorty concedes that America "may lose its way, and perhaps lead our species over a cliff." Moreover, he boasts that America alone will sit in judgment of itself, for America defines what it means to be human. And while Rorty's candor about the implications of his patriotic intervention can be disarming, candor does not lessen the danger involved. "To say that the United States themselves are essentially the greatest poem is to say that America will create the taste by which it will be judged. It is to envisage our nation-state as both self-creating poet and self-created poem." Circling eternally alone in unending worlds of our own making, our self-divinization is complete as we sing songs to the glory of ourselves.[18]

We are also to sing of victory. Rorty's poetic agon, otherwise known as politics, showcases contending forms of life engaged in discursive contestation. While he would prefer that the dialectical process unfold peacefully, Rorty does not lament the resort to violence when it becomes necessary (as in 1861). Rorty's Hegelian ethic—composure bordering on complacency—presumes the productivity of discordance: collision and conflict as prelude to newfound resolution and harmony. The dictates of "endless diversity" guarantee, however, that achievements will be temporary, ultimately "torn to shreds," and replaced by an even greater achievement, in a sort of creative destruction redux. Thus the promise that the future represents is always preserved.[19]

Rorty may reject the notion of obedience to a nonhuman authority, but that does not prevent him from gently offering a new "unconditional object of desire" before which human beings can stand in awe: America as a succession of utopian visions.[20] The desire to serve God and realize his will on earth is replaced by the desire to experience "ever more novel, ever richer, forms of human happiness." The political project of construction and reconstruction stretches from here to history's theoretical end. Rorty supplants God's authority with a democratically achieved consensus seeking perpetual expansion in order to incorporate more and more elements of society based on agreement as to "how things are." This all-too-human authority is to become increasingly irresistible as it pursues an expanding resolution through political means.[21]

Rorty insists that the United States, given God's exile in the world, has no alternative to self-creation and self-judgment. Yet he does not seriously consider whether it is ethically ready to install itself on God's vacant throne and arrogate a divine-like status with historical license to do what it pleases, when it chooses. It is no coincidence that America mimics God's dubious reign. Rorty may move hesitantly, but the logic of his patriotism carries him swiftly in the direction of a common, secular god. Thus, having taken God's place, America responds predictably to frustration and failure in the absence of divine wisdom and patience. In view of his democratic agenda, Rorty's silence regarding the dangers of a self-anointed God angry and dissatisfied with the results of its own creative self-expression disconcerts.[22]

Rorty regards his patriotic enterprise as safe for the world in that human beings will now look forward to the future rather than upward to the past. But he has described a situation in which these dispositions creatively combine. With America as God, citizens look upward to the future. Rorty does not reject "the religious impulse" itself, merely what he calls the childish need for security.[23] And while Rorty's valorization of contingent creation suggests that he has put away childish things in the name of temporalization, he may not live up to his own this-worldly billing. Rorty wants to tap into and mine the religious impulse. Thus his narrative gestures to something beyond the mundane world of politics— to something which has been awaiting the arrival of the United States and which the United States in turn has made possible. Rorty writes: "Because the United States is the first country founded in the hope of a new kind of human fraternity, it would be the place where *the promise of the ages* would first be *realized*."[24]

America represents the culmination, at long last, of a potential for freedom and diversity waiting to be realized in history. And despite Rorty's rejection of teleological conceptions of history, à la Whitman he describes the United States as "the *fulfillment* of the *human past*." For Rorty it was not necessary that this end be achieved, but its actual achievement is self-vindicating in a way that suggests affinities with a teleological view of the world. Humanity can now definitively define itself in America's wake. And it is with this trans-historical movement or trajectory that patriotic discourse is to be in alignment.[25] Thus it seems that Rorty's commitment to patriotism draws him toward an ontological commitment that he must not articulate as a Rortyan, because a politics of cruelty lurks in it.

Thus consider Rorty's rejection of the discourse of sin. Ostensibly opposed to political moralization, Rorty too theorizes purity—political purity. He insists that to participate in American politics means to offer specific programs for change. Rorty proposes a People's Charter, a political vision which privileges the nation-state as the site of politics and offers legislative as well as policy initiatives. Accordingly, Rorty shoves into the exile of illegitimacy those elements on the left convinced that the American experiment cannot be redeemed within the extant constitutional framework. They are said to have no interest in shaping a common future. Indulging the luxury of idle moral righteousness, they supposedly reject the opportunities for action that American citizenship entails.[26] They do nothing but distract, disrupt, and destroy. By definition they cannot be patriots.[27] Rorty's enmity is troubling. "Leftists in the academy have permitted cultural politics to supplant *real* politics, and have *collaborated* with the Right in making cultural issues central to public debate."[28] Both parties betray the spirit, if not the letter, of the republic and its hallowed political traditions.[29] They feel un-American. Rorty's commitment to patriotism tends to make him define those who celebrate a pluralism of respectful engagement as if they were mere purveyors of "difference." This keys their dismissal. Here Rorty's apparent candor fails him; it becomes mere caricature. Exactly what pressures are operative in his patriotic politics that require him to misrepresent his avowed enemies? What do the misrepresentations intimate about the patriotism that he proposes?

Rorty's patriotism displays other infelicities. National pride may suffer damage, but it can always be restored and the nation redeemed through self-creation. Nothing is written in stone, and original sins cannot be acquired. While Rorty knows the accusation that awaits him (Is there nothing incompatible with his understanding of patriotism?), he sees it as a relic of a discredited theological past. Again his candor raises suspicions. Rorty does not deny, per se, America's criminal past. Rather, he weaves transgression into his narrative, as if the act of acknowledging offenses committed in the past can be a point of pride in and of itself. For example, America can remember "that we expanded our boundaries by massacring the tribes which blocked our way, that we broke the word we had pledged at the Treaty of Guadalupe Hidalgo, and that we caused the death of a million Vietnamese out of sheer macho arrogance."[30] Yet Rorty's remembrance—not to be confused with accountability—deploys descriptive terms which make acknowledgment an easy project to recommend—in part because it is partial, in part because the events "we" are to "own" can be formulated in exculpatory language. Thus: because the boundaries that we expanded were ours and the tribes did block our way, the act of usurpation can be overlooked and responsibility shared by those who obstructed us. Thus: though we broke "the" word we had pledged in this treaty (not "our" word), it was an isolated incident and in the realm of international politics traditional moral considerations do not necessarily apply or need to be taken at face value. Thus: though we may have "caused the death" (how unfortunate this happening happened to be) of one million Vietnamese, the war was a stupid mistake that we could have avoided; therefore this war does not define us and can be safely considered incidental.[31] Rorty's language suggests the need for rapid forgiveness and forgetting of these violences. Is this because the very ideal of the nation prized by Rorty requires the violence that he himself regrets? Is it because these violences were necessary to achieving the nation? It is unclear. What is clear is that Rorty's narrative disposition finds ample support throughout American political culture. It dominates the storytelling motifs on the Mall in Washington, for example, which subsequent chapters explore.

Given Rorty's political privileging of the nation-state, given his conversion of the world into America's ontological playground, the violence that by Rorty's admission may on occasion be necessary now seems ineluctable or even calculated. As America enacts its democratic drama at home and abroad, the world profits from our experimentation. We define what it means, or what it can mean, to be human.[32] Violence necessitated itself in 1861; the cold war required it too. Future conflicts may not be so noble either, but for every atrocity that America might commit, it can learn a valuable lesson in its existential journey. In fact, unless allowed—repeatedly—to take missteps, America cannot progress and the world cannot prosper. Poets don't stop writing after the first draft of a poem.

Progress aside, has Rorty's America left behind the European past and its obsession with absolutes and certainties, as he claims? There is room for doubt. Rorty, it seems to me, manages to tame the terror of contingency by offering America a boundless future in which it can create and recreate itself at its discretion. History leaves open the possibility of redemption, which means any prior act rightfully subject to condemnation can be overcome. Self-respect trumps shame as pride can be restored—just wait long enough. Thus even where an instance of shame is supposedly permanent, as with Vietnam, it loses its sting once the factors occasioning it have been properly contextualized. With regard to Rorty's Vietnam, victory in the cold war becomes the larger, more important truth—for America, anyway. Here pride already animates shame. Thus Rorty's admission that America, self-willed, self-elected vanguard of humanity, "may lose its way, and perhaps lead our species over a cliff" seems glib and disingenuous. For time truly is on our side—even if in the meantime we "prove the most tremendous failure."[33] Every day is Easter dawn in America, country of the future. With an unlimited number of second chances, destruction on the world stage perpetually amounts at best to collateral damage and disappears. Poetry has its price.

Achieving Our Country may have succeeded beyond Rorty's keen ambitions, since George Bush, it could be argued, enacts the Rortyan tradition in the twenty-first century. In an essay published in the *Nation* in late 2002, Rorty presents a trenchant critique of Bush's war-making politics and the dangers that they pose to American democracy.[34] Bush, according to Rorty, covers fundamental ignorance with displays of military bravado as he seeks to place the world at America's mercy. He argues that Republicans have a number of vested political, economic, and electoral interests in the creation of perpetual war. The conquest of Iraq is imminent, and Rorty fears that the political fallout is likely to prove Orwellian.

For all his criticism of Bush, however, Rorty's own patriotic politics sanction Bush's broad response to the events of September 2001. It's not just that Rorty leaves open the possibility of making a case for regime change in Iraq (a case he thinks Bush has not even tried to make). If one accepts Rorty's claim that the United States is not only vulnerable but also impotent in the face of "our new enemies," Bush's apocalyptic musings about the dire threats facing America, threats that require immediate and overwhelming response, could be read as necessary fictions, critical elements of a great American success story yet to come. Since the outcome of Bush's adventurism cannot be known in advance, the possibility cannot be dismissed. America at its best does not capitulate without a fight. Nor can it stand by just because existing categories, practices, and institutions seem ill fitted to the current threat matrix, as Rorty claims. Rorty, in short, lives in fear as much as Bush does. He even deploys with unthinking repetition the 9/11 mantra, his own rhetorical contribution to the rationale for a war that he may or may not oppose. If anything, Bush self-consciously engages America in the kind of epic project that lends itself to the heroic mythmaking celebrated by Rorty. Rorty's differences with Bush, in the end, may amount to a patriotic family disagreement. Affinities overcome divergences as Bush's global crusade for freedom (and simultaneous war on terror) succeed Rorty's like-minded cold war cause. Bush has Iraq, Rorty Vietnam.

Perhaps I have it all wrong. Rorty insists that unless actualized on the world stage, America must remain incomplete, a mere idea. The world may not appreciate America's unique destiny, but could there be any greater confirmation of its exceptionalism?[35] Yet which peoples or nations would second the idea that America, with its willingness to experiment, suffers on the cross of history and should be applauded for its sacrifices? While Rorty conceives certain actions as absolutely forbidden (what he calls "tragedies"), should they nevertheless be committed he recommends that America conduct itself "so as never to do such a thing again." He realizes, therefore, that tragedy is not only possible but inevitable. Rather than explore how shame or self-disgust might reduce the possibility of future tragedies, however, Rorty prefers to secure agency from potential passivity or spectatorship. [36] The opposition that he forges between pointless self-flagellation and purposeful self-assertion makes the latter the morally mature, responsible option. The world thus remains at America's disposal. It would be unworthy of a secular deity to obsess over limitations.[37] Even where we gods fail to please ourselves, even when we gallop over a cliff, the fault (and thus the power) are still ours. The world did not stop us. We stopped ourselves. Even in failure, we remain godlike. Rorty desires a civic religion, a religion of pride and love. Well, *Achieving Our Country* perfects national love. We are gods adoring our selves in the reflection of what we make. At long last, we are in love with ourselves, our achieving country.

RORTY'S PATRIOTIC FRONT

Rorty's patriotism, including its flaws, bears a strong family resemblance to William Galston's account of the necessity of civic education in America. The crux of Galston's concern is that liberal democracies cannot generate the commitment and allegiance they need from citizens through purely rational means. If they are to flourish, they must concern themselves with producing character, namely developing people who know how to meaningfully support the larger political order and are inclined to do so. Children, accordingly, require "a pedagogy that is far more rhetorical than rational." Taking America's dubious historical legacy for granted, Galston concedes that scholarship dedicated to its retrieval would divulge its constitutive nature. This could compromise the possibilities of affective attachment for citizens. Enter civic education and its "nobler, moralizing history." Its aim is to enable people to embrace the polity with appropriate fervor, thanks to the self-evident legitimacy of founding institutions and the certain moral example of political heroes.[38]

Galston's project has produced its share of critics. Eamonn Callan, while sympathetic, suspects that Galston's "sentimental" approach will self-destruct. It cannot produce the kind of citizens that liberal democracies require. Among other things, citizens require critical capacities to render difficult judgments, and sentimentality subverts these capacities.[39] Nevertheless Callan, inspired by Rorty's example, also insists upon the indispensability of patriotism to liberal democracy. It—and it alone—can generate the emotion that will bind citizen to order. He thus proposes "an emotional and interpretive generosity" toward the past.[40] This approach enables him to mine America's past and isolate the best of its traditions. The best may or may not be dominant historically speaking, but for Callan instrumentalism reigns. This approach also means that he does not have to deny objectionable features of America's complicated history; he takes only what he needs.

Callan may, however, fall victim to his own success. His position derives much of its attraction from its call for moderation and reasonableness. Rejecting extremes, Callan charts a political course midway between Galston's citizen-crippling sentimentality and an unflinching critical ethos that would invariably produce political alienation. Yet Callan's third way compels only to the extent that you share his belief about the indispensability of patriotism to the liberal polity. Moreover, with Callan's patriotic intervention—as with Rorty's—among the dispositions that citizens might adopt toward their countries, love cannot be one of them.

Consider Callan's account of slavery. Those who would use America's racial history to condemn it and challenge the very possibility of patriotism receive short shrift. Righteous innocents, they fail to take context into account. This amounts to "a failure to imagine a historical context for judgement in which what is morally obvious and compelling to us would not be so to others, or where the social costs of acknowledging certain moral truths may be more burdensome than they are for us."[41] Does Callan's approach represent critical patriotism successfully trumping civic sentimentality and ahistorical moralism, or little more than sheer patriotic insistence? Unfortunately for Callan, America's founders knew slavery to be evil. At the Constitutional Convention, for example, James Madison called it "the most oppressive dominion ever exercised by man over man."[42] In addition, the question of "burdensome social costs" ought to be irrelevant from not just a moral but a patriotic point of view. Jefferson, for one, exposed consequentialist thinking as one of slavery's many self-perpetuating corruptions. It cannot be used to defend the evil institution that deployed it. Finally, the founders made no effort to eliminate an undeniable wrong. If they had tried and failed to eradicate slavery, Callan's position might have some merit. Since they did not, another point needs airing. America secured its freedom through slavery. It's not as if slavery were an unfortunate but incidental part of the founding equation. Slavery made America possible.[43] The founders also left the country with a legacy that would lead to civil war and a long reign of segregation. Slavery defined the self-repeating "civic gift." Callan's imaginative and emotional generosity, mimicking Rorty's treatment of Vietnam, converts love of country into self-excusing narcissism.

Callan likewise enjoys allies. Walter Berns has issued a self-styled primer entitled *Making Patriots* enunciating a hagiographic version of American history.[44] Though democracy and patriotism are wonderfully fitted for one another, you are not born loving your country. This love can and must be taught, nurtured, cultivated, weeded, pruned, and repeated. For Berns, with war no longer a viable school of virtue, civic education must supplant it. Stories of America's past loom critical to patriotic citizenship. People must learn of America's superiority to other countries if they are to make sacrifices on its behalf. American history is defined by epic achievements, great triumphs, stunning successes. Such episodes are to be the centerpiece of school curricula, folded into celebratory public architecture and made the occasion of national holidays. Love flows from awe, which then induces reverence.[45] For Berns, best of all, ardent love of America operates not in the realm of interpretation, which is contestable, but moral fact, which is irresistible and final.[46]

Berns tells the story of America's founding. The American republic embodies God's will for human beings on earth. The abstract principles of political right, given voice in the Declaration of Independence, for example, disdain geopolitical boundaries. The United States may provide them with unique expression, but as universal edicts they first and foremost represent God's gift to one and all.[47] Thus American patriotism does not suffer from willful parochialism. In short, America's founding defines its finest moment. Though subsequent generations would be required to perfect constitutional republicanism, the founders laid the cornerstones.

Like Rorty and Callan, Berns notes potential objections to his own narrative and addresses them. Thus while it is true that the Founding vouchsafed slavery, the bargain flowed from provisional necessity.[48] Slavery simply could not survive in America—not in the long run. As a result, those who disparage or dismiss the founding and its legacy make themselves politically suspect. Berns, accordingly, commends the founders for paying the initial price of union, namely an accommodation with slavery demanded by the southern states.[49] Yet here Berns's story begins to subvert itself. By his own admission, the founders made a deal "out of what they thought was necessity." The phrase intrigues. Was the founders' political assessment astute, or was it invoked to justify a decision already made not to deal with slavery? Would the southern states actually have refused union? Berns takes an empirical question that can't be answered and converts it into self-evident truth. Most of the founders understood slavery to be morally indefensible, but they were in Philadelphia to make a constitution, or so they said. This suggests that they possessed the requisite moral knowledge but lacked the moral will to eliminate slavery. Again, what is problematic is that the founders made no attempt to eradicate an obvious evil. The founding moment may have been America's single greatest opportunity to destroy slavery before Lincoln's election. Forcing the issue may have led one, two, or possibly three southern states to balk at union, but post-ratification they would have experienced enormous pressure to return. Would they have preferred, for example, to handle alone the European imperial powers and Indian nations on their borders? Berns's patriotic narrative does not permit such questions. His account also suggests a disturbing possibility: for him no price of union would have been too high. Thus Berns may inadvertently reveal the patriot's logic: substantial sacrifice, even destruction of the nation, can invariably be justified in the name of protecting or saving it. One senses that this is enough to prove patriotism's love to be true.

Enter Frederick Douglass. Required to buttress his argument, vindicate the founders, and celebrate America, Berns credits Douglass with an appreciation of the country's origins worthy of the fathers themselves.[50] Negotiating a complex situation verging on collapse, the founders crafted documents containing principles that could be turned against their own flawed institutional realization. The potential for self-overcoming adhered to the founding genius. Douglass, recall, proclaimed "no love for America, as such"; he had "no country," thus "no patriotism."[51] According to Berns, however, once America fulfilled the promise of its birth, Douglass could reverse field and affirm what he previously but provisionally denied. In the interim, in anticipation of the great day to come, he called on his fellow blacks to join the Union army and demonstrate the capacity for republican citizenship that one day would be theirs.[52] With the Civil War, Lincoln rises to the occasion as America's savior, re-founds the nation, and redeems Douglass's latent patriotism.[53]

If you don't share Berns's patriotic faith, you may balk at his Rortyesque recapitulation. Berns gladly takes Douglass's sacrifice and appropriates it for narrative patriotic purposes that effectively deny the history, Douglass's history, according to which patriotism and love of country would be made impossible, even obscene. The Constitution can be amended to redress formally its prior shortcomings, but one cannot thereby retroactively vindicate the crimes that the nation's founding brought about and facilitated. Patriotism's literary narcissism, courtesy of Berns, would have you believe otherwise. Not my country right or wrong; my country always, in the end, right.

Rorty's distinctiveness notwithstanding, nearly thirty years ago John Schaar wrote a similar paean to patriotism with similarly ambitious reach. I turn to Schaar to explore whether the problematic features of Rorty's patriotic project might be attributed to the freewheeling affirmations characterizing Rorty's ethic of national self-creation. Schaar's communitarian vision, however, cannot save patriotism from itself. Schaar matches Rorty's blindness to the implications of his patriotic ethos.

Contrary to Rorty's Hegelian pronouncements, Schaar offers musings reminiscent of Lincoln on the American political condition. He calls for the long overdue recovery of a covenanted republic to restore the natural political order of things. He confidently articulates an ontological politics that Rorty resists acknowledging because of its contestability and potential for moral mischief. What's more, the role that enmity plays in a patriotic ethos also finds undeniable, if subtle, expression in Schaar's communal vision. Enmity animates his conception of a participatory politics to be conducted on terms that work to drain democracy of contingency and unpredictability. Not surprisingly, Schaar's embrace and enactment of life as debt reveal a troubling ressentiment floating around in Rorty's version too. When the political world does not cooperate with the will to better it, patriotism amounts to a cure more problematic than the (alleged) malady.

Framed by the specters of Vietnam and Watergate, Schaar makes a self-conscious "plea for patriotism." He begins by attending to the question of definition. A complex of significations must be employed to capture adequately the essence of patriotism. "At its core, patriotism means love of one's homeplace, and of the familiar things and scenes associated with the homeplace."[54] "Homeplace." Schaar doubles the attachment to the politics of place. Patriotic politics means that you feel there is one territorial site where you really belong, a place that must feel like home to participants.[55] For Schaar, the love that patriotism names flows from the basic facts of life—it is as natural as anything can be. "We become devoted to the people, places, and ways that nurture us, and what is familiar and nurturing seems also natural and right. This is the root of patriotism."[56] For Schaar the feeling is so powerful that what seems natural and right effectively becomes so—which is why he can write confidently that the word springs from life itself. Patriotism therefore is not something imposed on the world.

Schaar's patriotism of attunement issues a series of promises to sustain itself. Though Schaar willingly concedes that traditional forms of patriotism "cannot be ours," a uniquely American incarnation can be realized. Here Schaar turns to Lincoln, veritable divine messenger bearing the Word, to develop a notion of covenanted patriotism. According to Lincoln, America's diversity prevented unity by race or blood, culture or religion, territory or tradition. The one bond available was a political idea. Schaar writes: "We are a nation formed by a covenant, by dedication to a set of principles and by an exchange of promises to uphold and advance certain commitments among ourselves and throughout the world. Those principles and commitments are the core of the American identity, the soul of the body politic." Should the commitments fail or the promises fade, political death results. For the commitments and the promises make us what we are.[57]

Schaar, like Rorty, appeals to history—not just for inspiration, but because it is the source of political life. He stresses the narrative character of the nation. It is through the telling of tales that the nation exists in the first place.[58] At every opportunity political education must be pursued. Start with the Founding: articulate the principles discovered; recount the sacrifices made; revisit the scenes of triumph and tribulation; guarantee that nothing is forgotten; remember well. Only if the Founding lives in the hearts and minds of citizens can the covenant be preserved. This patriotism defines life in terms of debt.[59] Citizens enter life responsible to and for a legacy publicly bequeathed. Obligation is part and parcel of life—whether one likes it or not. The gifts left are abundant: land, people, language, memories, customs, gods.[60] The debt is deep, of lifelong duration. It must be acknowledged. Patriotism involves great insistence, as legacies impose identities. They make us who we are. They constitute us. We ought to be grateful. The patriot is.[61] Patriotism proffers a unifying vision that at its best transcends national differences. Truly political in character, it eschews parochial forms of identification—such as those based on blood or race.

Yet there is something disconcerting about Schaar's republican patriotic imaginary. Even at its most inspiring, Schaar admits that patriotism begets conflict. What unites and binds simultaneously divides and rends. Patriotism shares this with other forms of human devotion. Thus patriotism is "inherently ambivalent."[62] And the ambivalence cannot be denied or wished away. Yet Schaar's candor, like Rorty's, may conceal as much as it reveals. Displaying the literary narcissism characteristic of patriotism, Schaar writes as if his vision of American political life, once correctly presented and properly received, can convert one and all to its truth, if not now then ultimately; in the meantime, indifference and opposition represent little more than forms of ignorance and willful refusal, each to be overcome. All children—that is, all future citizens—must be taught basic truths, and there is always a learning process. Schaar enacts Lincoln's conviction "that the articles of the political covenant are both perfectly clear and grounded in the firmest authority."[63] Schaar's pedagogical insistence intensifies to the extent to which patriotic politics gravitates to the moment of birth, to how things were "in the beginning." Founding myths, bordering on the miraculous, animate the formation of Schaar's idealized citizen, "the conscious patriot," whose mode of being in the world involves acknowledgment and commitment, suspicion and militance. "The conscious patriot is one who feels deeply indebted for those gifts, grateful to the people and places through which they came, and determined to defend the legacy against enemies and pass it on unspoiled to those who will come after."[64] Here Schaar describes an affective movement in citizens that begins with appreciation and gratitude and concludes with vigilant enmity and hyperprotectiveness.[65]

With conflict and even violence inevitable, what is to prevent politics from becoming a medium for the exercise of thinly veiled wars of faith? Schaar elevates his patriotism to a civic religion, and the purity of this religion requires inoculation so that it can be transmitted untainted to posterity. Yet politics so understood tends to breed internecine battle; adherents to one or another sect seek to assign the mantle of truth to their understanding and deny it to rivals. Schaar's conscious patriot cannot see that the legacy he would defend is susceptible to multiple interpretations. That is, it is inherently political. Both the effort to secure a single legacy and the effort to "pass it on unspoiled" engender enemies. Thus the conscious patriot will never run out of enemies, of which he is the tireless production source. Unable to understand his role and responsibility in the production process, patriotism turns dangerous and deadly, as it confronts those who threaten the legacy and its future.

Consider Schaar's return to "our" roots. Granted, Puritan nostalgia may be for him an idealization capable of reminding America of what community can be, but what is the price of that community? There is reason to suspect that it cannot be realized—conceding to it the harmony, belonging, and fulfillment promised by it—without disciplining and punishing whatever deviates from its privileged (yet contestable) norms. Schaar invokes the Puritan practice of combining a profession of faith with proof of the sincerity of that profession through public practices monitored by the covenant's guardians. Listen to Schaar's inspirational account of history, offered in mellifluous tones, as he tries to recover the American covenantal communal tradition: "The Puritan Commonwealth of New England was exactly such a community. Individuals became members of the community only upon acceptance of certain articles of religious faith and morals. That acceptance had to be proved in practice, and to the satisfaction of the guardians of the covenant. Social institutions were designed to encourage performance of the covenant. The Puritans discouraged the formation of isolated, private farmsteads and tried to keep all persons in the towns, in sight of each other, and with life centered in the meeting-house. In sum, membership was not a right of birth. It had to be earned, and was the reward of choice and effort. Institutions were designed to encourage the choice and supervise the effort."[66] Schaar's depiction of life in the Puritan community features its favored values: commonality, membership, freedom, choice, sincerity, authority, generosity, participation, assistance, belonging, and requital.

Back to the present: Schaar issues a call to action, and the struggle he would like to commence promises to be a long one. But it may be "the most worthy struggle of our time." The cure for homelessness, heartlessness, and tribelessness lies precisely here.[67] In the course of struggle itself, the life-giving force of patriotism can be revived. Without national revitalization, all of us, according to Schaar, will continue to suffer dissonance and displacement—whether we know it or not, whether we can identify it or not. Remember that it is unnecessary to have actually possessed something to feel its loss.[68] Patriotism can save us from our fallen condition.[69]

Without denying Schaar's appeal to those for whom his ideal community represents a life well worth living, a democratic order also needs to concern itself with the remainder. For others, life takes on a different aspect. Consider enforcement of the covenant in the face of opposition and resistance. Schaar's Puritan encouragement becomes coercion and supervision tantamount to surveillance. The Puritan commonwealth that Schaar prizes was thus rooted not just in reward for choice and effort but in retribution for the wrongful exercise of each. One cannot be without the other. This is the logic of Schaar's community as he presents it.

State of emergency)

end of Chapter 2

Sacrifice in the name of love

Schaar's account thus proves troubling, in that the communal vision rehearsed by him names a univocal experience with one legitimate public expression.

If every moral and political order generates its own forms of resistance, how it responds to its own creations offers one means of assessing that order. Notwithstanding Schaar's disconcerting fondness for the Puritan world, what might life look like in his debt-laden republic? Schaar's would-be order, determined to avoid a pedestrian life long after the glorious days of the founding have passed, doggedly tries to recreate and recapture them. Should these efforts meet with repeated obstacles and obstruction, this means only that they need to be doubled and trebled. For Schaar's patriotism works to guarantee the republic is clear to the eye, close to the body, dear to the soul, and present to the heart. Indifference and self-induced amnesia are enemies.[70] While Schaar offers an empathic account of a fully realized Puritan community, he is silent about the official response to disobedience and disruption when the terms of the covenant are challenged or denied rather than promised or performed. The suspicion arises that there is an underside to community harmony.

To contemporize the question, take Schaar's narrative treatment of his fellow citizens regarding civic duty during wartime. Schaar expresses admiration for those young men who refused the Vietnam draft on the grounds that the war made a mockery of American principles—at least for those who also *"publicly resisted and publicly paid the penalties of resistance."*[71] Accordingly he expresses contempt for those young men who refused the war by leaving the country (they fled), turning to the underground (they hid), or manipulating the law (they prevaricated). Thus only select resisters, those who submitted themselves to the state and went to jail, become part of the dissident tradition that made possible both America's birth and long life. Other resisters, those who denied the state altogether or outmaneuvered it, enjoy no political substance or standing. For Schaar only certain forms of public action merit recognition, let alone respect. Thus Schaar's recommended conversational ethos draws its inclusive power in part from its exclusions. Schaar speaks only to those who reflect him himself. Yet he does not consider the possibility that those whom he scorns may have been making both a great sacrifice and an effective public statement about the war (I elaborate on this below). The claim here is not that Schaar lacks an argument. It is that he has usurped and monopolized the terms of political criticism. Thus he has not earned—because he has not justified—his moral and political disdain. Nevertheless, Schaar's moral judgment aggressively pursues its targets. Through censure he punishes some citizens a second time for their decisions. That is, his prescriptions add a dose of shame and humiliation to lives already damaged and lost. If punishment is to be proportional, Schaar would have to impose even greater penalties on these citizen imposters who—on his reading—merely play at resistance. They play insofar as they will not publicly pay "the penalties of resistance."

Schaar recognizes the inevitability of conflict and violence for a patriotism-driven politics. And yet he does not address what is to be done when its "dark force" is encountered. It seems as if admitting violence's inevitability amounts to accepting its irresistibility. For Schaar, violence is not so much a regrettable and remediable phenomenon as one inherent in his patriotic republic. Enemies represent more than a lamentable by-product that could in theory disappear with time and education. Schaar's patriotism identifies enemies to enable and energize the political order.

SCHAAR'S CHILD

Perhaps the character of Schaar's patriotic community can be clarified by one of his theoretical targets turned admirers after September 2001. Todd Gitlin takes the occasion to offer a confessional narrative in which he reassesses (his) citizenship.[72] In the immediate aftermath of the attacks, he recounts his experiences on the streets of New York City. Much to his surprise, Gitlin found both a people and an attachment to them.[73] The solidarity that he saw displayed around the city, whether substantive or symbolic, coupled with the spontaneous assault on the cockpit of flight 93 over Pennsylvania, reinvented patriotism for him: "patriotism was the sum of such acts." This is what Gitlin will refer to as true, genuine, liberal, lived, or deep patriotism.[74] A few days later a flag flew on his terrace. No announcement accompanied the "plain affirmation of membership."[75]

Gitlin's essay, both memoir and meditation, is confession as well as damning self-criticism. He uses the September attacks to rethink the account of patriotism offered by Schaar and, bathed in its cleansing light, to revisit the fighting of the Vietnam War in America. Accordingly, Gitlin adopts wholesale Schaar's stinging rebuke of the New Left. It is one thing to criticize your country, perhaps especially during wartime, for the greater good of the republic. It is quite another to renounce your country altogether, if you are infused with a self-righteous venom that spares nothing and no one. Gitlin places his earlier convictions into the latter camp: "I am not speaking of my ideas here, but of feelings, deep feelings . . . I was choking on the Vietnam War. It felt to me that the fight against the war had become my life. The war went on so long and so destructively . . . My country must have been revealing some fundamental core of wrongness by going on, and on, with an indefensible war. . . . You can hate your country in such a way that the hatred becomes fundamental. A hatred so clear and intense came to feel like a cleansing flame."[76] Having won the war—that is, the fight to end the war—the New Left lost the peace. The New Left became the "anti-American Left." According to Gitlin, echoing Rorty, it preferred the pleasure of censure to the project of reconstruction. By eschewing America it effectively committed suicide.[77]

At the time Gitlin was undisturbed by losing "the patrium" and the "title to patriotism" that went with it.[78] Yet after September 2001 he altered his judgment. He saw that Schaar was right when he argued, following Lincoln, that America was unique. This is a land of ideas, of political principles, a place where citizens debate what it means to be an American and to belong to America. Blood does not bind the nation; instead commitment to basic ideas does. If this is lost, all is lost. It is everything, politically speaking.[79]

Gitlin proceeds carefully; he knows that patriotism has a flip side. Thus Gitlin emphasizes patriotism of deed, of sacrifice, of civic action. This patriotism stands in contrast to merely symbolic patriotism, patriotism of gesture, of posture. Gitlin also recognizes how the distinction between the two can easily become collapsed. After all, patriotism "is a self-declaration."[80] Gitlin nevertheless insists that words alone do not and cannot suffice. Professions of faith matter, dependent on the occasion, but they can also be cheap. There must be more to patriotism than ritual, ceremony, offering, and memory.[81] In sum, George Bush's macho bravado and pledges of allegiance must give way to "the exemplary patriots . . . who brought down Flight 93."[82]

Like Eamonn Callan's appeal, Gitlin's flows from his efforts to establish a third way. His patriotism navigates between what he deems the reflexive anti-Americanism of the left and the knee-jerk, chauvinistic flag waving of the right. Though Gitlin desires to distance himself from one without becoming the other, what price success? After the attacks in 2001 Gitlin construes his emotional experiences in patriotic terms. Yet this approach to life and politics amounts to a narrative decision; it does not spring from the experiences themselves. Gitlin thus counts on readers to identify "instinctively" with his narration rather than subject it to scrutiny.[83] Consider in this light Gitlin's patriotic commandments. He articulates both what a left patriotism must do and how it must conduct itself. In short, it proceeds from "the inside" and keeps everything in the family.[84] Patriotism's politics of hope, of modest critique, of reform appears to be nonnegotiable. Simultaneously, Gitlin offers advice on dealing with America's history. As the two combine, his account, like Rorty's, begins to subvert itself. He admonishes the left to come to terms with "the strange dualities of America." He describes one part of the duality as "the awful dark heart of darkness."[85] Here Gitlin recalls America's imperial history, including Manifest Destiny. Yet Vietnam names the decisive experience for his generation.[86] Having recently rejected the position that Vietnam revealed "some fundamental core of wrongness" about America, has Gitlin adopted the alternative view that the war represented nothing more than a "wrongheaded policy"?[87] He does not say, though the conclusion seems hard to resist. Otherwise, you wonder why the seemingly willful effort to fight "an indefensible war," Rorty's feared genocide, does not make love of country a sheer impossibility.[88] The impossibility: to love the unspeakable. Such love in turn presupposes and encourages the fictions that enhance patriotism's dubiousness.

Gitlin apparently cannot see that he may have traded a condescending anti-Americanism for a disdainful patriotism. It is disdainful of those who would feel tainted by it (that is, his comrades from the 1960s).[89] It is also disdainful of those, like George Bush, who would understand differently the mission that American patriotism assigns and the sacrifices that it commands.[90] True, according to Gitlin's version of patriotism America is the "nation that invites anxiety about what it means to belong."[91] Yet he acknowledges that patriotism "is imperious about its imperatives."[92] It might surprise Gitlin to learn that he and Bush, despite differences, agree that life names the ultimate form of sacrifice for your country.[93] For both, death governs patriotic experience. Long after the Vietnam War, Gitlin rethinks his position on the draft. He ultimately embraces the virtues of conscription. Though Bush would second Gitlin's ideal of service to country, he would not agree that the country needs a draft. Bush lauds American soldiers as they fight on behalf of America abroad; Gitlin salutes America's homeland warriors who give their lives crashing airplanes to save fellow citizens. He thus makes a point of noting that Bush spent September 11 flying around the country rather than returning to Washington. For Gitlin, Bush's patriotism must be inauthentic; he treats Bush with scorn sufficient to erase him.[94] But the scorn itself establishes Bush's allegedly false patriotic credentials. If America's distinctive characteristic is self-contestation, how can Gitlin deny Bush inclusion in his rhetorical republic? Bush's summary treatment gives the lie to patriotism's famous "indignation born of family feeling." Gitlin refuses intimacy of any kind with Bush. There is no familial membership to be shared with small-minded cowards.[95] Gitlin's newfound commitment to death would re-cover America's lethal history and forge a new chapter in contemporary American political life. Gitlin may not possess the monopoly on civic virtue to which he aspires, but he knows true patriotism's enemy when he sees it. It must be vanquished, because patriotism "moves only in one of two directions," backward and chauvinistic, or forward and democratic.[96] Gitlin's telos leads straight to John Schaar.

LOVING AMERICA TO DEATH

Moving from the world of theory to autobiography, Norman Podhoretz, longtime editor of *Commentary* and neoconservative polemicist, represents one version of the patriotic ethos that Rorty and Schaar extol. Podhoretz's *My Love Affair with America* enacts the very patriotism that he celebrates and commends. As he recapitulates his life of civic engagement from prepubescent Second World War enthusiast to "reluctant" senior citizen as cultural and political warrior, the text is a patriotic performance. While Rorty and Schaar might well find Podhoretz's love of country unattractive or dangerous, Podhoretz's candor, conviction, and contempt draw me to a consideration of his short treatise. Not only do I wonder if Podhoretz has the courage to declare—often violently—what Rorty, Schaar, and others cannot or will not admit regarding the foundations of patriotism, America, Vietnam, or political opponents, but I suspect that Podhoretz's love of America fulfills—and in so doing dissolves—the patriotic sensibility they celebrate. This, anyway, is the story I wish to tell, and given Podhoretz's militant Americanism, it may well prove parabolic.

Podhoretz feels compelled to relate his life story from a sense of profound gratitude to America. While not denying that he enjoyed considerable native abilities, worked diligently throughout his life, and possessed a keen sense of ambition, Podhoretz insists that he would not have made it, that he would not have lived such a deeply satisfying life, were it not for America. America delivered the goods to Norman. From inconspicuous origins in Brooklyn to stardom in Manhattan and eventually nationwide, *My Love Affair with America* tells of Podhoretz's rise, "fall," and redemption.

Podhoretz loves to tell stories. His is the tale of an admittedly angry seventy-year-old who must—reluctantly, he protests—do battle with America haters. Anti-Americanism runs loose in the land, and the country's lovers must lend it assistance. Podhoretz finds it hard to believe that he's in this position, again, at his age. But the right—not the left—turned on America. Hence Norman's recall to active duty and assignment to the front lines. (The military metaphors are his.) Podhoretz's love expresses not just affection for what he esteems but anger and rage at what he cannot abide, what he loathes. Following Rorty and Berns, *My Love Affair with America* teems with enemies. Hate for others not only kindles Norman's love, it makes it incandescent. Accordingly, Podhoretz will tell us how and why he loves America and simultaneously deal with its foes. The tasks are symbiotic. Patriotism, love of country, leads to destruction and death.[97]

MR. PODHORETZ'S WARS

Though Podhoretz's love affair begins with his early years in Brooklyn's public schools, the Second World War proves foundational for his mature patriotism. America represented good; the country went to war to defend not only itself but the entire planet against the apostles of evil. What could be as ennobling, as enlivening as a Manichean struggle for the world's soul? The war transformed America. At this moment in world history it became one with itself. Pockets of dissent dissolved. As of December 7, 1941, the isolationists had been routed, then redeemed (Lindbergh signed up to fly in the Pacific). Even the pacifists joined the cause while nonetheless sticking to their principles; or else they went peacefully to jail so as not to be a bother. Who could imagine a greater display of unity and solidarity? Podhoretz recalls that he never heard a single discouraging word. Just the opposite: he learned the lyrics to the war anthems of all of the military branches.[98] Service would amount to a prayer answered. Podhoretz was ready to depart for Montezuma, Tripoli, or the wild blue yonder. He took enormous pride in American military success, especially the decisive Battle of Midway. The turning point of the war in the Pacific, it "became our revenge for Pearl Harbor." Filled with martial fervor, Podhoretz experienced a tinge of regret at war's end because he was only fifteen and had missed the action. A true patriot's lament: "Now I would never get a chance to find out what it was like to be a soldier fighting for my country and whether I was man enough to take it."[99]

Podhoretz's narrative then jumps forward to 1950. Thanks to a Columbia University fellowship, he sets sail to Cambridge, England. Flush with success, Podhoretz has also won a Fulbright Scholarship courtesy of the U.S. government. There is one problem, however: the Korean War, which erupts as Podhoretz embarks. Once again missing frontline action, Norman soon encounters discursive conflict in Europe. Over the next three years, Podhoretz wages defensive political warfare against the left, both English and French. He cannot stand the political and cultural attacks against America and leaves his enemies in disarray. His is a reasoned patriotism: he combines passion with argument, while his opponents have nothing but knee-jerk ideology at their disposal. Disgusted by European ingratitude and stupidity, Podhoretz sees his love for America intensify. Only the unthinking could compare the United States to the Soviet Union, McCarthyism or not.

Vietnam takes center stage in the next decisive period in Podhoretz's patriotic odyssey, the 1960s. Podhoretz's account of the war at home and abroad reiterates the war he fought in Europe in the 1950s. Here, though, Podhoretz's interlocutors are American citizens, including many close intellectual friends, even so-called fellow radicals. The scene is set for political fratricide. While in England, Podhoretz missed Korea; so Vietnam offered him the prospect of redemption. He would aid America in its time of rhetorical need. Having dispensed with America's polemical enemies in Europe, who better than Podhoretz to fight the good metaphorical fight at home?

Like Rorty, Podhoretz locates Vietnam in a cold war context. Just as the United States had crushed Nazi totalitarianism, it would stand up to the "more insidious" Soviet strain. America sacrificed blood and bounty to win "the two main challenges . . . in the twentieth century."[100] Vietnam's status as "the wrong war in the wrong place at the wrong time" ultimately subsides. While the logic of containment defied translation to Asia, the United States successfully checked the Soviet Union in Europe.

Podhoretz's own narrative raises challenges to it. If Podhoretz is filled with love for America, what makes him so angry as he expresses it? Podhoretz insists that he is cheerful, but his love is not marked by generosity, forbearance, understanding, or forgiveness (some of the possible signs of cheerfulness). Why does he feel compelled to denounce and dismiss any rendering of America not in accord with his vision? How to explain the textual enemies endlessly present?

Clues abound in Podhoretz's life story. The end of the Second World War and the beginning of the Korean War seem critical. Podhoretz describes a scene where he and fellow Fulbright scholars discuss the Asian war and its ramifications for them: "As the ship sets sail . . . a charmingly roguish character from New Mexico . . . comes up with a pungent expression of the general mood: 'I don't mind *di*arrhea, and I don't mind *pyor*rhea, but I don't want none of that *Korea*.' I laugh along with everyone else, but unlike everyone else's, mine is an uneasy laugh. Certainly I would not wish to be drafted now, just when I am about to be launched on a great adventure of another kind. Not that there is any danger of being drafted: as a student, I enjoy an exemption, and unless the rules should change, I will continue to be exempt for the three years at Cambridge that my two fellowships have given me, and as many after that as it takes for me to complete the Ph.D. I am planning to get. By then the war will surely be over anyway."[101]

Three years later, in 1953, Podhoretz decides to return to America and make himself "available to the draft." This even though he had been invited to stay in England. The longing to be in uniform and test his manhood still lives in Podhoretz—but only to some extent, as he acknowledges. He does not volunteer for military duty, which would result in immediate induction and last for at least three years. Rather, Podhoretz submits himself to the draft board. Here the timing is uncertain; if called, he would serve only two years of active duty and six months in the reserves. Podhoretz takes delight in telling us that both school officials in England and draft board members in the United States express incredulity at his decision. With regard to the latter: "Perhaps that is why they take nearly six months before calling me up, by which point an armistice has been signed. When I am inducted into the army in December, then, there is no longer any prospect that I will wind up in combat. I am a little disappointed, but also, and again sheepishly, relieved at having gotten it both ways: becoming a soldier but spared the risks of actually having to fight and maybe even being killed." [102]

Podhoretz seems candid recounting his flirtation with Korea. He does not try to conceal his ambivalence. Yet his adamant professions of love for country would seem to dictate a different outcome. This is a matter not only of his passion and feeling, but also of principle. Recall that he claims to have experienced some regret at the close of the Second World War at *never* having had a *chance* to fight for America and confirm his masculinity. Yet that is precisely what he did get with Korea—twice, in fact. Still, he declined both opportunities, if in different ways. First, he decided to go to England, putting his education and career ahead of his country. Thus when he writes, "Certainly I would not wish to be drafted now," there is nothing certain about this. Given what he's said previously about the Second World War, he should want to be drafted. Nonetheless, when Podhoretz could no longer live with his decision and submitted himself to his draft board, he again put his life ahead of his country and refused to volunteer. He proceeds to assign responsibility, subtly, to the draft board for denying him his war. Rather than protect him through their delay, they should have called him up immediately. Again, he was ready to go. And he wants credit for it. The war unfolds around him. He does not control either the draft rules or the timing of induction. What could he do?

Thus Podhoretz's military career may illuminate the fundamentalism of his patriotic politics, for he cannot brook criticism of America in any form. Arriving at Cambridge, student leftists attack him over Korea and McCarthyism. Note (again) the passivity and self-pity in Podhoretz's description: "I (like every other American in Europe in those days) was called to account, and had to endure a constant barrage of challenges and even insults." [103] He had to endure challenges and even insults. This is unfair, Podhoretz informs us, because he was no supporter of McCarthy or McCarthyism. "Like all liberals, I was against the methods being employed by the congressional committees and embarrassed by them." [104] He was against McCarthy methods and embarrassed by them. Of course to Podhoretz, the problem with McCarthy was that he gave a good cause a bad name and thus did a disservice to the country he loved. But again, Podhoretz took no action despite his opposition as he understood it.

Aside from Podhoretz's benign reading of McCarthyism, what makes him dismissive of political criticism? For one thing, he equates those leveling it with Soviet agents ("not for nothing had Cambridge been the breeding ground of the Soviet spy ring in the 1930s"); for another, he does not understand himself to be engaged in a conflict of ideas at all. Podhoretz possesses the truth about America. He defends it, but does not take seriously the opposition that he faces. He will not accord ignorance-driven insults and bigotry the status of alternative political visions.[105] Perhaps Podhoretz, having failed America militarily during the Korean War by privileging his own "great adventure," must defend the country with sufficient rhetorical militancy to make amends. America's generosity and munificence are such that even during wartime it allows would-be recruits like Podhoretz to live their lives while it literally fights for its own. What better proof could there be of American goodness and the bankruptcy of its detractors? As Podhoretz acknowledges, "In the end, I suppose, it all comes down to gratitude."[106]

In short, Podhoretz's lifelong commitment to himself maps patriotism's narcissism. The great personal success and, ultimately, political influence that Podhoretz achieves require that he knowingly, routinely fail his beloved country. He will sacrifice it for himself. If anything, the imbalance between debt and payment enhances Podhoretz's gratitude and affection for country. Ironically, America not only forgives him his inability or refusal to match word and deed. It rewards him. It rewards him for the surfeit of words that he offers in compensation. Countries relish cheerleaders, those who stay on the sidelines and offer encouragement, support, and loyalty with exceptional vigor. (Perhaps only those so removed can attain the patriotic intensity that countries cherish.) Apparently the political truths that patriotism presumes achieve self-vindication through the encomia offered to it by devotees such as Podhoretz.

NEXT YEAR VIETNAM

Podhoretz's patriotism can be illuminated further thanks to his confession. He tells us that his love affair with America was marked by betrayal. Even though he himself never came to hate his country, others did. The anti-American pathology spread far and wide in the postwar world. Podhoretz feels tormented by his share of the responsibility for this nasty political disease. What were the origins of the ideological affliction? In a word: utopianism.[107]

Utopianism, as Podhoretz defines it, is a profound dissatisfaction with extant social and political life. Self-consciously informed by a set of ideals, utopianism presumes that the world can be brought into alignment with its ideals, as flaws and failings are identified and eliminated. This restless political vision can "even present itself as a higher form of patriotism." It seems so all-American. After all, who would not want to see the United States finally live up to its political ideals as articulated in its founding documents?

Podhoretz confesses his utopianism. He fastened onto America's blemishes and sought to right them. Unfortunately, utopia's noble vision belies its intrinsically lethal aspects. The logic of utopianism is sharp, precise, and compelling. It promises much. Yet what can it deliver? What has it delivered? What is to be done, moreover, when the world does not co-operate with it and politics falters or, worse, fails outright? The road to fanaticism is littered with good intentions. This, according to Podhoretz, is the psycho-logic of utopianism. Disappointment leads to anger and bitterness. These then seek targets—which they invariably find. Disasters result.

Hence Podhoretz explains the radical left's reaction to Vietnam. The America that the left denounced had disappointed it. Not because of anything America might actually have done; but because the America loved by the left, assuming that it loved America at all, lived only in its fevered imaginings.[108] The utopian ideal created excessive expectations that once unrealized fostered a corresponding condemnation. Tragically, the blindness inherent to utopianism means that the self-fulfilling dynamic cannot be discerned.

Like Gitlin's, Podhoretz's patriotism mimics the logic that he discloses—and denounces—in utopianism. Beholden to an ideal of America both vivid and visceral, Podhoretz rages at those who point out and especially act on discrepancies between ideal and reality. Podhoretz claims that they obsess about what *little may* be wrong with America (which is either "inescapable" or due to "the nature of things itself") while ignoring the gigantic good that it embodies and performs.[109] Anger turns into fury as

America haters refuse to see reason, and as they privilege ideology at the expense of fact and argument. Fury then deteriorates into "self-righteous hatred" with the rejection of Podhoretz's dream world—America as a veritable "Kingdom of God on earth." Thus *My Love Affair with America* is a kind of enemies list as Podhoretz names his names.

Podhoretz, ironically, describes himself. The America he loves exists only in his mind. It spills onto the printed page in *My Love Affair with America*, but what he believes he is merely reporting and describing he is actually concocting. Podhoretz's America is a discursive production. In the process of deliberately celebrating America, Podhoretz loses sight of the product of his linguistic labors. Otherwise, Podhoretz might be able to pierce the patriotic veil that he throws over America and its history. Consider his account of the Vietnam War. Podhoretz reacts with disgust and disdain to the charge that America committed war crimes. Podhoretz assumes that "we" simply do not do such things. We are not Nazi Germany, after all; therefore the accusation must be false. Here is one of Podhoretz's rebuttals: "The charge of genocide was especially bizarre, since the population of North Vietnam, which we were allegedly trying to wipe out, actually *grew* during the course of the war."[110] Here I would remind Podhoretz not that Vietnam was fought principally as a counter-insurgency war waged against the people themselves, nor that Vietnamese casualties—even on Rorty's account—totaled one million dead, but that Podhoretz himself broke with the war. As he acknowledges, he could no longer support Nixon and continued bombing of the North once the war's futility became obvious. Hear Podhoretz's words: "I had come to the conclusion that the sole alternative to a defeat was now a continuation of the war, and that such a continuation would be a *futile exercise in pointless destruction*."[111] According to Podhoretz, this happened "only toward the end" of the war, in late 1972 or early 1973. Yet Podhoretz's preferred interpretation of Vietnam, that it was the wrong war at the wrong place at the wrong time, disputes his own claim. In addition, Podhoretz ignores the consequences to the Vietnamese as the United States deployed its awesome military power imprudently and wastefully (Podhoretz's words) on "a foolishly chosen political and military field."[112] Unless self-regard exhausts morality, Podhoretz should be horrified by his own account. America's good intent, presumed by Podhoretz, must surrender to America's effect on Vietnam.[113]

Insofar as Podhoretz's patriotism is fueled by his own acknowledged betrayals, he cannot see that what he labels betrayal (his utopianism and the radical changes in American life that it required) is nothing of the sort. Too busy blaming himself for the outbreak of the anti-Americanism that he deplores, Podhoretz misses the upshot of his retrospective critique of his critique of America. Speaking of his radical political vision, he writes: "Obviously such a program [utopianism] implied a vast dissatisfaction with America as it then existed and really was. It bore, as I now see, the seeds of the anti-Americanism by which I would later be repelled. But it simultaneously embodies a limitless faith in the perfectibility of this country, and as such did not force the breakup of my love affair with it."[114] Thus it might be asked: Where is the so-called infidelity? Podhoretz's critique embodies not only faith but "love" as well. What kind of love of country turns away from the serious problems facing the country? Is not giving up on your country the real betrayal? Unable to negotiate the permanent tension that love and dissatisfaction entail, Podhoretz converts serious problems into unavoidable imperfections of little consequence and dismisses them. To do anything other than celebrate America in toto is to succumb to anti-Americanism. But perhaps it is Podhoretz who hates America, because it does not—cannot—conform to his narrative conjuring of it.

WHAT'S LOVE GOT TO DO WITH IT?

Rorty, Schaar, and Podhoretz love America. Love of America in turn encompasses love of the world. If love is indispensable to politics, however, it also proves inimical. This is patriotism's secret and the time has come to tell it, for democracy might be better off if Rorty, Schaar, Podhoretz, and other patriots loved a little less—or not at all.

Not surprisingly, patriotic discourse has underthematized love itself. Assuming strong bonds of affection and civic attachment to be critical for a democratic political order, what makes love of country the appropriate sensibility to fill the need? Maurizio Viroli has written an impassioned treatise on behalf of patriotism. He considers its resuscitation valuable in and of itself. No political community that prizes its own brand of freedom can truly thrive in its absence. Viroli also regards patriotism as critical, since it alone can contest one of the most dangerous and deadly forces of our time, nationalism. Here patriotism finds a new reason for being. Viroli believes that patriotism is best suited to counter nationalism, because like nationalism it is a form of particularity. It can thus engage nationalism on equal terms, matching it passion for passion.[115] Viroli thus ups the ante, as he recommends unleashing political love on the world in order to save it from itself.[116]

Viroli concedes the danger inherent in his project: "Civic virtue has to be particularistic to be possible and yet we do not want it to be dangerous or repugnant." He believes that a "solution to this dilemma" is at hand. To preempt misunderstanding, Viroli reiterates his position early and often. "I must emphasize that I do not mean love of the republic in general or attachment to an impersonal republic based on universal values of liberty and justice. I mean the attachment to a particular republic with its particular way of living in freedom."[117] Yet Rorty's brand of patriotism fits well within Viroli's definition, especially when it comes to a people with a particular history living its freedom. Rorty's America lives in freedom through experimentation on the world stage. It is the sole venue worthy of American exceptionalism. America creates and recreates itself perpetually in an agonistic display of will to power. Pace Viroli, with Rorty the problem is precisely that love of liberty extends beyond national boundaries and presents itself as an act of solidarity. If the world is not at America's disposal, and Rorty cannot prove that it is, then his patriotic ethos becomes dangerously self-regarding and self-indulgent. Despite some talk of taking responsibility for American fits of virtuosity, it remains just talk.[118] Rorty's patriotism induces blindness—or perhaps a calculated indifference—when it comes to consequences. He might prefer to call it tough love, of course, but he and Schaar tend to privilege love's intent over its effects and thereby gloss over the experience of (some of) its unhappy recipients.

Perhaps Rousseau can be of assistance. In the second *Discourse* he delineates the ambiguity inherent in love. On the one hand, love as a moral notion can remove a person from his or her narrow world of self-regard. Love can transform. Thanks to its unique powers, people become capable of amazing feats. A parent will trade his own life for a child. A spouse will do likewise for her partner. A patriot will die for the good of the republic. No sacrifice appears too great in the name of love. Love thus inspires and ennobles human beings. At its best it allows us to partake of another realm. The world would be a dark and dreary place without it.

Yet the flip side of love is equally bleak. Exclusivity coupled with generosity makes love special. Should it fade, transfer, die, or be rejected, love becomes capable of the most horrendous crimes. Thus love is intrinsically bound up with the intense passions of jealousy and indignation. If these reign, pity anyone who stands between someone and his beloved. Once again, no sacrifice is too great in the name of love. As Rousseau argues, the two aspects of love cannot be separated. To enjoy one is to live with the permanent possibility of the other. It cannot be otherwise. The noble, with but a slight change of circumstance, becomes the ignoble, and vice versa.[119]

Thus patriotic love seems perpetually poised to bring about the ruin of the republic that it is supposed to guarantee.[120] Any achievement appears within reach, but so simultaneously does self-destruction. One induces the sensation of dizziness, the other of despair. As patriotism forges bonds of solidarity, it foments corresponding divisions, as enemies to the republic are identified, located, and targeted. I offer this particular formulation precisely because Rorty, Schaar, and Viroli would be unlikely to see things exactly this way.

Concerns multiply. Because of love's imperatives, patriotic political life readily becomes heavy-handed and moralizing. Take the question of debt, one of patriotism's keystones. To the extent that a community folds recognition and repayment of debt into structures of law and habits of life, it tends toward the nostalgic. Those who acknowledge and affirm debt are bound to resent those who dispute, ignore, or refuse it. Yet a community's democratic credentials are jeopardized to the extent that one generation is able to govern succeeding generations through a debt that cannot in the end be repaid—except in perpetuity. Permanent debt does not lead to bankruptcy, but to abject dependency. Such debt can kill what it once brought to life.

Schaar's treatment of "the radicals of the 1960s" again becomes pertinent.[121] He insists that they failed the love test. And thus were not patriots. (They may even have been un-American.) They failed, in short, "to persuade their fellow-Americans . . . that they genuinely cared for and shared a country with them."[122] In Schaar's patriotic community, selected citizens need to prove themselves to the rest before being granted permission to engage in politics. The irony here is that the politically active minority had to convince the passive majority. Apparently, laying one's life on the line for civil rights justice or peace in Vietnam did not amount to genuine love of country. Perhaps Schaar cannot allow himself to consider the possibility that radicals in the 1960s were indeed patriots and that their "contempt" for fellow citizens does not disprove but discloses, however imperfectly, their political commitment. Perhaps Schaar's persuasion deficit can be attributed to the ressentiment of citizens who discovered that their own commitment paled by comparison. In any case, leaving the country or living underground was an act of resistance. Certainly they involved sacrifice. People gave up the lives, attachments, commitments, and loves that gave them meaning and purpose. Exile, abroad or internal, may well feel like a kind of prison. Paradoxically, their acts were also highly visible public acts. Ponder for a moment the attention, the criticism they received. Furthermore, travel to Canada kept alive the moral and political issues surrounding the war long after it was formally over, since the question of whether exiles should be allowed to return meant that these issues were continually being revisited.

Schaar ultimately seems more concerned about professions of republican faith and ritual performances of the covenant than about treating with generosity—an integral element of patriotism—fellow citizens whose conduct he finds problematic. He stresses the formation of citizen identity—the making of good patriots—such that the promises of American life begin to fade before its burdens; the indebtedness that he champions threatens to become the "static legacy" that he eschews in Rousseau, whose republic merely "induce[s] the individual to venerate the nation."[123] In short, Schaar's instantiation of Lincoln's ethos collapses from the weight of its own accounting practices. An order that devotes a preponderance of its civic resources to perpetual public education centered on foundational political truths rather than the lived practice of democratic politics has already wounded itself. Here the problem of patriotism comes to the fore. The pre- and extra-political formation of citizens designed to secure bonds of unity, both normative and affective, shapes the character of the polity in ways that may compromise its democratic aspirations and perhaps its identity. More specifically, the patriotic project renders dubious an understanding of politics as an art of engagement and contest conducted—sometimes with gratitude and forbearance, sometimes with venom and vitriol—between enemies locked permanently and perpetually in this or that fundamental disagreement. It makes no sense within its frame. Schaar reduces the antagonism at the heart of politics to a "lovers' quarrel" and thereby preemptively folds resolution into discord. If you are patriotic, there is nothing that cannot be resolved: hence Schaar's condemnation of the radicals of the 1960s. If they had behaved as proper patriots, they would not have taken to the streets or the campus quads in the manner they did. (I doubt Schaar would prefer to live with the silent majority that dutifully attended Memorial Day ceremonies and reflexively supported the bombing of North Vietnam through the end of the war. To say nothing about keeping company with the Teamsters, who publicly opposed war demonstrations, assaulted war protestors, and were prepared to pay public costs for their violence.) That the radicals of the 1960s ended the war abroad but not also the one at home—and home has not been the same since—may be their greatest offense. The public commitment that was supposed to bind, heal, and elevate instead divided, wounded, and exhausted. Rather than restore the world to oneness, politics revealed its dissonance.

Finally, Schaar promotes and exports American patriotism as ambitiously as Rorty does. The world can profit from America's brand of patriotism, whether or not it recognizes that it can do so. America's exceptionalism flows from having recognized this truth first. Schaar's inclusive ethic "decisively transcends the parochial and primitive fraternities of blood and race, for it calls kin all who accept the authority of the covenant."[124] Bonds formed by ideas float over and above national borders, and the fate of kin calls for action. Schaar thus affirms Lincoln's historical mission for America, a nation "uniquely valuable" to other nations. America does not reduce politics to biology. This is what makes the new world new and valuable. America's mission, godlike in its embrace, neither condescends nor threatens its beneficiaries. Acceptance of the Word becomes the sole criterion of belonging. The self-appointed teaching mission works by example, says Schaar, where America presents itself to the world and the world then responds as it sees fit. Lack of formal invitation aside, exemplarity does not easily recognize, much less impose, limitation in the classroom of global power politics. Self-display can take any of a number of forms, some more demonstrative and expansive than others. The shining city on the hill periodically brings the light that others need directly to them. Accordingly, Vietnam could be interpreted as an instance of American idealism exported to a land and people who were "forced to be free" in the American mold. Thus Schaar's claim that "patriots do not comfortably support wars of expansion or wars of 'principle'" fails to supply the reassurance it is meant to induce,[125] for they do support these wars, if uncomfortably. Part of paying debts requires sharing the wealth with others.

Patriotism insists, demands, enjoins—whether theorizing the identity of the republic or the proper relationship of the citizen to the order. Only a responsible love that declares and defends itself suffices. The love that patriotism expresses would thus contribute to its irresistibility. What's more, given the nature of its love, it must be returned in kind. Self-same confirmation means everything to patriotism. Schaar insists that he wrote his patriotic plea out of respect and affection for other citizens, "and from [his] wish to *see them even more respectable than they are*."[126] But when patriotism cannot make over the world in its own image, it blames and punishes the world while it retreats behind professions of love.[127] As Nietzsche advises, this is an old stratagem that ought to sound alarms. Schaar, recall, condemned war resisters who left the country rather than accept the legal consequences of their refusal to be drafted. Yet his judgment is premature and incomplete. For one thing, he apparently failed to explore what these resisters did once they made it to, say, Canada. What kind of lives did they lead? Many continued to oppose the war; they did not simply retire to private preoccupations. They led public political lives.[128] Not perhaps as Schaar would have preferred (or as Socrates believed possible), but consistently with his committed citizen ethos. They remained dedicated to America—from abroad. If anything, to oppose the war publicly from a foreign land risked the wrath of a scorned nation that would neither forget nor forgive its alleged betrayers. This is hardly cowardly. Of course, by leaving the country war resisters called into question not just the war but America itself. Departure suggests that they had no choice but to leave home. It could even be argued that they placed on the defensive those who stayed. To patriots like Schaar, on this reading, citizens' willingness to go to jail can provide reassurance. It suggests that America, our "homeplace," remains much the same, political turmoil notwithstanding. The lives of expatriates in Canada complicate Schaar's easy judgment of the radicals of the 1960s, condemned for having "contempt for others." Curiously, Schaar returned them the favor.[129]

Rorty may provide an explanation for Schaar's derision. As he tries to broker a contemporary political peace agreement, Rorty revisits the civil war between Old and New Lefts. The New Left, Rorty concedes, did the country an incalculable good service: "It ended the Vietnam War."[130] Its rage brought to conclusion a war that might otherwise have dragged on endlessly—with more lives lost. The New Left rightly opposed American intervention in Vietnam, Rorty admits, but wrongly condemned America itself. The cold war continued the crusade against totalitarianism that the Second World War inaugurated, as Stalin became Hitler's successor in evil. The sequence is critical to understanding Vietnam. Opposing monstrosity, tragically, can lead to blindness and excess, which must then be interpreted rather than self-righteously condemned. For one thing, it does not erase the debt owed to cold war liberals who were freedom fighters, not scum.[131] Thus the New Left failed to understand that "America is not a morally pure country. No country ever has been or ever will be."[132] Starting with a presumption of purity, however, the New Left ultimately came to hate its homeland for its errant ways. According to Rorty, it needs to jettison such theistic notions.

Yet Rorty's generosity feels parsimonious, as if he cannot forgive the New Left its perspicacity. Perhaps he cannot stomach the notion that since the New Left captured the Vietnam War, it might have been right about the cold war too. What, then, of the rest of America's history? Where would critique stop? Apparently Rorty fears what Podhoretz already understands, namely that America as the thought of a possibility might not survive the falling narrative dominoes. Thus for Rorty, when critique exceeds the limits of good political taste—if, that is, it hinders patriotic politics—it becomes tantamount to moral fanaticism, to America-hating. In other words, it exposes itself as nothing more than self-indulgent, self-destructive nihilism. The New Left, in other words, should have quit with success. If it loved America, it would have known when to be quiet. Love entails discretion.

Ultimately Rorty's patriotism ends up trapped in a circle of self-affirmation: We must love America and we love America by being in love with it. For Rorty this means that America always is what we would like it to be at its best. Patriotism's literary narcissism sees to it. Yet the accompanying ethical price is steep—to others, to us. Thus, notwithstanding Benjamin Barber, rather than make patriotism safe for the world, what if patriotism were to make the ultimate sacrifice for the world: itself? For love of country, love that anchors itself in either republican truths, truths of the republic, or truths of the self also inspires a fatal politics of hate. Witness Schaar, Rorty, and Podhoretz.

Besides, Socrates, I do not think that what you are doing is right, to give up your life when you can save it, and to hasten your fate as your enemies would hasten it, and indeed have hastened it in their wish to destroy you . . . You seem to me to choose the easiest path . . . I feel ashamed on your behalf . . .—PLATO, *Crito*

I only regret that I have but one life to lose for my country.
—NATHAN HALE

It's nothing. It's good to die for our country.
—YOSEF TRUMPLEDOR

Iconic Drama I:
The Mortal Logic of Enmity

From Rousseau to Rorty, theorists place serious expectations and demands on democracy's citizens. They must participate, contribute, serve, pledge, commit, learn, love, die, kill. Without these, democracy is condemned to nominal existence. Patriotism, as a result, becomes democracy's sine qua non, supplying the affective commitment and political energy upon which a robust democratic order must be able to draw unthinkingly. Democracies must stock themselves with awe-inspiring stories, self-sacrificing heroes, all-too-clever enemies, and death-courting deeds—the standard equipment of patriotism, which induces people to stand up to tyranny and risk life and happiness to oppose evil. The stories that peoples tell about themselves set examples, inspire emulation, give confidence, offer hope, and confirm belief. They also incite anger, outrage, even hate. Laced with familiar themes and reassuring outcomes, they both describe and create the world they present. Such stories work best if ready-made, on call for deployment, obvious without being transparent.

Yet democracies suffer routine, predictable failures. During war, for example, unity is presumed, criticism condemned; loyalty mandated, opposition denied; sacrifice extracted, scapegoats sought; solidarity demanded, difference vilified; support coerced, dissent silenced. Those who practice the democratic arts during wartime are rarely if ever honored and celebrated by the broader community—just the opposite. They are all too often threatened, marginalized, jailed, and worse. War, it seems, exceeds action on a battlefield. There is also a domestic front, with home implicated. Insofar as war or crisis reveals the seriousness of a polity's commitment to its basic principles, war, politically speaking, tends to bring out the worst in a democracy. Democracy's aspiration fails in part because war's existential threat calls home into question; it also fails because the politics accompanying war make the identity of home a question, and war is considered no time for questions, no time for democracy to be at odds with itself.

Thus democracy's greatest threat arises from within.[1] Danger affords opportunities to tame, domesticate, and subvert democracy in the name of democracy. From Socrates to John Schaar and beyond, democracy suffers grievous harm from those sincerely well disposed to it, from acts taken on its behalf. Danger's lethal flavor prepares the ground for democracy's permanent transmogrification; practices essential to democracy become subject to restriction (or worse) and rendered ancillary to democracy itself. As democracy's foundations are shuffled successfully to the margins, they lose their constitutive status. Changes advertised as temporary thus become permanent.

How to explain democracy's self-induced collapse? Patriotism composes the threat that explains democracy's self-destructive paradox—that is, patriotism exercised as a singular loyalty to country, rooted in love, which trumps all. Loyalty, moreover, brings out patriotism's narcissism. More specifically, what I call patriotism's literary narcissism manifests a tendency toward calculated, gratuitous self-display—making a point of moral virtue or goodness, going to extraordinary lengths to do so, and then calling attention to it. The idea is not just to articulate an idealized self-image that sets a standard for love and adoration; the idea is to show the world that it must acknowledge the accuracy and rightness of your self-assessment and self-affection. Patriotism, in other words, insists that others subscribe to its self-image and indicate their agreement. External confirmation becomes vital in that patriotism understands, because of the internal contradictions and violence it suffers, that you cannot love a country, any country, including your own. If to make the case for patriotism, to make the case for why you must love your country, also means to make the case for why you cannot and should not love your country, the love that patriotism names becomes something like a volitional act.[2] Patriots like Rorty reflexively become their own nemeses—they provide the dispositive evidence against their own position—and they know it. The will to love defeats any other consideration, real or potential. The will to patriotism, willing what amounts to an impossibility, becomes consumed with itself as it experiences disagreement, opposition, skepticism, and doubt as deliberate, intentional, and laced with malice aforethought. It cannot live with the idea of resistance. It must seek it out, expose it, account for it. The world must be made to reflect the narrative image projected upon it.

Whence the origins of patriotism's cross-examinational style? Patriotism's structure lends itself to mischief. Love of country suffers from many of the problems that afflict romantic love. It can wither, alter, relocate, or die. Love, which longs for permanence, defines the ephemeral. Politically, love's transience engenders a thorny question. How do you know if citizens love their country? Because they declare that they love it? Anyone, sincere or not, can say the words. By matching their declaration to deeds? What are the criteria by which to judge an alleged fit? Patriotism's response to uncertainty is an exercise in paradoxical genius. Love of country can be demonstrated by exposing those who do not love it. The patriot insists that he is willing to die for his country; he insists that you must be willing to die as well. If not, by disclosing such cravenness, cowardice, or corruption, patriotic love can establish itself negatively. Your love becomes transparent thanks to the failings of others to likewise love. Thus if you are willing to risk or, better, sacrifice, life for country, not only must you be right, you must love it as well.

Patriotism's comportment to the world thus holds neutrality to be a moral and political inconceivability. It proceeds through life in Manichean fashion. You are either a patriot or you are not one—that is, you are unpatriotic. For the patriot extant political conditions, fortunately, tend to favor identification of us and them. Names can be named. If founding principles crumble, wars flounder, vital laws fail, key policies unravel, or dangers go unanswered, responsibility can be pinpointed and assigned. If you locate those who lack faith, question truth, resist commitment, spurn obligation, or, worst of all, harbor sympathy (or even love) for the enemy, you can preempt the problems that they pose. Alas, since the world never quite conforms to the patriot's heart's desire, enemies always remain among us. And since no exposé produces a full and accurate accounting, the search for the unpatriotic invariably continues. Patriotism thereby possesses an interrogative, even inquisitional logic and sensibility that borders not just on the self-destructive but on the indecent. The presence of this bent in patriotism's finest expressions, namely the presentation of heroes, displays another aspect of its narcissism.

Thanks to patriotism and the melodramas that sustain it, however, democracy can be re-imagined—despite itself. The patriotic threat, through the logic of its unfolding, ultimately reveals a remedy for the ill that it communicates. The greatest stories ever told, approached on a bias, perform their own undoing; they become agents of their own destruction. In this chapter, Socrates speaks. In the next, *High Noon* and *Saving Private Ryan* dominate the action. Each of these life-and-death dramas provides an unusual cautionary tale. Film's distinctive abilities to speak to the visceral register of being proves revelatory—Plato's rhetorical playwriting skills notwithstanding. Patriotism encompasses not only commitment to a set of principles (or dedication to a way of life) but a particular manner of holding them. Patriotism defines itself not just by what it believes but also by how it believes it.[3]

Initially I focus on Socrates. The *Apology* and *Crito* figure as epic political confrontations conducted in the aftermath of Athens's humiliating defeat in the Peloponnesian War. I take Socrates's trial to be a continuation and extension of war by other means. Athens needs a scapegoat to restore its good name and self-image. Nevertheless, if it's true that Athens wages war against Socrates, Socrates reciprocates, ostensibly for Athens's greater good. The mortal conflict of contending patriotisms nevertheless fashions only Pyrrhic victories.[4] Or, better, death alone emerges victorious.

SOCRATIC CITIZENSHIP

Socrates rarely fails to inspire. Independent of thought; steadfast against the corruptions of power; ready to risk life for the city in war or the courts; inveterate seeker of knowledge and critic of convention; resolute not to commit injustice; serene as he lives a contrapuntal life—Socrates defines exemplarity, combining individual and civic virtuosity. Dana Villa praises Socrates's moral contribution to politics: "Socrates invented a form of philosophical or dissident citizenship which puts . . . well-worn nostrums in doubt . . . Socrates can be said to put intellectual doubt at the heart of moral reflection; he makes such doubt the duty of any conscientious citizenship. Indeed, he can be described as the inventor of 'conscientious citizenship.'"[5] Peter Euben praises Socrates's "critical patriotism": "Socrates turns the accusations leveled against him against his accusers by claiming that he is the one true patriot, the one genuinely pious man, and the one true Athenian."[6] Again: "Socrates . . . denies that he corrupts the young . . . It is he . . . who is the true patriot and true Athenian."[7]

I too find myself inspired by Socrates. Yet pace Villa and Euben, I do not posit a Socrates that begins and ends with moral or political tribute.[8] Rather, I try to examine Socrates as he examined others. I explore aporetic moments, even failings, in his life and thought. The point is not to expose Socrates but to capitalize fully on his contributions, knowing and otherwise. I suspect that Socrates did not know himself as well as claimed.[9] Nor did he fully appreciate the ethical and political possibilities he had forged. I would argue, despite appearances, that Socrates was no Athenian. His way of life, I believe, anticipated as much as it exemplified: a life at once philosophic, democratic, skeptical; thus restless, homeless, exilic, foreign. The ethos that he styled through a distinct way of being in the world had agonistic, disruptive, transgressive, itinerant, boundless, and prophetic elements. Even so: I argue that Socrates at key moments refused his philosophical vocation, political principles, and way of life and that his legacy needs to be contested.[10] I believe Crito essentially right when he intimated that Socrates capitulated to and collaborated with Athens. Rather than dismiss exile, Socrates might have chosen life, relocated Athens in his thought, and continued his self-appointed vocation. A principled death may or may not establish your integrity and conscience. Either way, Socrates enjoyed another, admirable option, one I believe to be implicit in and fully consistent with the best of his life and teachings. Accordingly, what Villa refers to as Socrates's "relentless questioning and ferocious intellectual honesty" deserts him in the end.[11] If anything, Socrates's love of Athens loved him to death.

The *Apology* presents one of literature's great juridical mismatches. Even with conclusion foregone, Socrates delivers a terse, tense drama that has a surprise ending. He leaves destruction (of enemies) and silence (of friends) in his wake: a patriotic masterpiece for the ages.

Early in his defense, Socrates points to its peculiar difficulty. He has been subject to rumor, misrepresentation, and slander for most of his life. People do not understand him. His judges have been exposed to these lies since they were children. They imbibed what they heard, accepted what they were told. To uproot long-held, deeply rooted prejudices poses a monumental task under any circumstances; to do so at trial, in less than a day, becomes Herculean. Even though biases tend to operate beyond the realm of evidence and refutation, Socrates expresses hope: "I wish this may happen . . . and that my defense may be successful" (19). Because of the seriousness of the charges, because Socrates is on trial for his life, his remark seems unremarkable. Yet what does success mean to him? Can it be assumed that Socrates seeks acquittal?

If Socrates wishes to defend himself, he faces a devilish dilemma. With corrupt accusers, how can a corruption charge be fought? To the extent that Socrates's mission in life has been to induce the people of Athens to care for their souls rather than the trivialities with which they preoccupy themselves (power, wealth, reputation), what kind of defense is plausible? He does not share their values. They scorn his. On Athens's terms, guilt seems beyond doubt. My suspicion is that for Socrates success means not just a guilty verdict but death, death fashioned on his terms. From commencement Socrates's approach to his defense perplexes. He insists that it is Athens, his accusers, who corrupt the young, not he. How can such a strategy work? After all, occlusion is one of the byproducts of corruption. The corrupt cannot see, still less understand, their corruption. It is thus inherently self-protective and self-perpetuating. In addition, to reverse the corruption charge may only further antagonize them. Socrates must do more than declare the Athenians corrupt if he is to convince them of the truth of what he says. He must ask them to think thoughts that for them border on the unthinkable. He must get them to turn on themselves and pursue their own internal examinations. They must be made to see what they have made (of) themselves. But since they have also made the cognitive and perceptual tools with which this exercise must be carried out, how can it succeed? Since Socrates leaves the paradox unarticulated, he relieves the Athenians of a considerable burden. Though he exhorts his judges, "concentrate your attention on whether what I say is just or not, for the excellence of a judge lies in this" (18), he offers them no insight or practical guidance into how they might actually achieve excellence. Listening alone cannot suffice. Congenitally corrupt, Athenians somehow have to overcome it at trial. Socrates fails, however, to prepare his judges for the defense he supposedly plans to make.[12]

After his frustrating encounter with Euthyphro, perhaps Socrates concluded that his trial could not be won. This possibility may account for the unexpected character of his defense, which feels more like a prolonged attack, a series of insults and provocations masquerading as a defense. Socrates's broadside feels designed not to secure an acquittal but to guarantee a guilty verdict followed by a death sentence. Consider his opening moves.

Socrates believes that he knows one source of his troubles. He proceeds to tell a story involving the Oracle at Delphi. Anticipating the reaction to it, he urges his listeners not to make a commotion as he speaks—thus encouraging them to disturbance. Chairephon, a friend since childhood, visited the Oracle and asked if anyone were wiser than Socrates. The reply was that no one was wiser. Incredulous, Socrates sought a solution to this mystery.

Socrates first probed Athens's public men. Surely the politicians would be the wisest in Athens. They ruled the city. But Socrates, after pointed inquiry, learned that these so-called wise men were not wise at all, not fit to govern. The exposé generated great anger. (Socrates does not name names at his trial, but as he points out, there is no need to do so.) Having failed with the politicians, Socrates systematically examined the rest of the city. He would question the poets, the craftsmen, anyone and everyone who might be wise. While it is true, he says, that he met many men who knew many things, they possessed at best limited wisdom. Among other things, they assumed that knowledge in one area of life translated into expertise in other areas—including the most important areas of life. Socrates did not hesitate to deflate these pretenders. What's worse, he did this to fathers in front of their sons, who then imitated the Socratic art and likewise questioned those with pretensions to wisdom. Socrates was assigned responsibility for their familial and civic impertinence.

Though Socrates tells his story to identify one source of slander against him, he has simultaneously reenacted—in the law court, before the entire city—the humiliation that he visited upon the best and the brightest, the rich and powerful, the vain and ambitious of Athens. Socrates sums up his service: "I go around seeking out anyone, citizen or stranger, whom I think wise. Then if I do not think he is wise, I come to the assistance of the god and show him that he is not wise. Because of this occupation, I do not have the leisure to engage in public affairs to any extent, nor indeed to look after my own, but I live in great poverty because of my service to the god" (23b–c). Thus not only does Socrates invoke the god to legitimize his vocation; he informs Athens that he has done so at expense to himself. He has suffered as a result of his obligations. Unlike the Athenians, he pays a price for his life. With life and death at stake, Socrates's rehearsal of his life's mission in Athens is likely to do nothing but exacerbate the prejudice against him. He started his defense by mocking his prosecutors as Sophists who nearly succeeded in convincing him of the truth of their lies. Now he has humiliated many of Athens's leading citizens as they sit in lethal judgment. He has reopened old wounds and forged new ones. "I know well enough that this very conduct makes me unpopular" (24).

CONTENDING PATRIOTISMS

Socrates, having dispensed with ancient prejudices by deepening them, turns to contemporary enemies. As he addresses Meletus's accusations, he challenges, among other things, Meletus's patriotic self-conception and would-be reputation (24b–c). Some may presume that Meletus acts in the best interests of Athens, but the truth is otherwise. A summary consideration of the charges and a quick glance at the affidavit proves it. Meletus insists that while all of Athens works to make the young good, Socrates alone corrupts them. The absurd attribution of power aside, Socrates wonders why he would pursue such a project, since he would thereby injure himself, which no man wishes to do. For this Meletus has no answer. In addition, the recital of charges leads Meletus to argue that Socrates both does and does not believe in the gods. Faced with an embarrassing contradiction, Meletus again has no response. Socrates thus accuses Meletus of acting in bad faith—that is, with insolence, recklessness, violence, irresponsibility, and frivolity. The man is no patriot.

Socrates disposes of Meletus with deliberate, mocking speed. Yet he is not finished speaking—far from it. Though he insists that he has dealt sufficiently with the charges against him (28), he has just begun to address Athens. Revealing familiarity with the law courts after all, Socrates composes a series of hypothetical questions to teach Athens necessary moral and political lessons. He thus puts the city on trial for its own good: Athens must defend itself. Governed by a patriotic ethos, he becomes the most Athenian of Athenians.

Athens may assume that Socrates lives the life of a philosopher because it suits him, because he has a gift for it, because he can make a living at it, because it pleases him. Yet this is not the case. Socrates has lived the life of a philosopher, a life estranged—from family and city alike—for Athens. The god placed him in the city for its own good. He has thus lived an itinerant life of poverty while neglecting his own affairs; Athens's needs transcend his own. Socrates endeavors to make appearance and reality harmonize: Athens is the "greatest city with the greatest reputation for both wisdom and power" (29d–e). He rebukes his fellow citizens because they devote their lives to inferior matters and neglect "the most important things" (30). He demands to know how Athenians can worship wealth, honor, and reputation at the expense of truth, wisdom, the soul. You must give an account of yourself, he tells them. You must defend your way of life. This questioning, if successful, benefits both the witnesses interrogated and the city itself. The two are inseparable. It is only the soul's health and well-being that foster a general good: "excellence brings about wealth and all the other public and private blessings for men" (30b).

Socrates's best hope might be to persuade Athens without convincing it. Thus he establishes his civic credentials to anchor his defense. Invoking the judicial death that faces him, he neatly introduces his war record. It is well known that he distinguished himself on the battlefields of Potidaea, Amphipolis, and Delium. It is the duty of a soldier to remain at his post as ordered by superiors rather than flee in the face of death. Socrates remained steady even though he had been ordered by the god to live a philosophic life. When you can, you must do the right thing. Considerations of life and death would violate morality itself. Thus Socrates has been consistent throughout his life. Whether serving Athens as a citizen-soldier or philosopher, he acts the best he can, which he must do, regardless of consequences, even if those consequences entail death. He thus acts no differently from how his fellow citizens would act at their best.

What they claim to value in public or military life, he does too. Even if he were offered an acquittal on condition of silence, he would of course refuse it (29d).

Euben notes the relentless character of Socrates's critique of Athens. Socrates highlights the disjuncture between Athenian ideals and practices; he also subjects their ideals to withering scrutiny and attack. Given the depth of Athens's corruption, the city is in no position to respond. Socrates thus conceives of himself as providing invaluable ethical and political service to the city in which his life and death, his mode of being in the world, play a central role. Euben observes: "aretē becomes detached from the heroic ethic and reassigned to philosophical activity." Thus the latter is "parallel to but even more significant than his military service, because this enemy was more dangerous to collective life."[13] Euben's assessment may be an indiscretion. Insofar as Athens has been re-presented as an enemy, a deadly enemy, the warrior ethos still appears operational, part and parcel of philosophy itself. In light of Socrates's aggressive posture in the law court, he seems determined to vanquish his foes. Yet how is it that military service has acquired such significance for Socrates? How did it become the model for his political comportment? Military service negates dialogue. It suggests not just a mind made up, but a mind shut down. What's more, Athenian "ideals" led directly to wars of glory, ambition, conquest, and domination. Socrates's role, which Euben lauds, problematizes his moral authority. While serving your city in time of war may be admirable, does the status accorded to it depend on the nature of that war? Athens fancied itself an imperial power bent on expansion and conquest. Does the domination of others raise the specter of injustice? Socrates rejects prison as an alternative punishment partly because he cannot subject himself to enslavement. Rather than subject others, why did he not stay home when required to fight? (He had a history of refusing orders.) Apparently, unable to conceive of life without Athens, he would reflexively serve the city in time of war when by definition its very life was at risk (even if Athens incited the danger). With Athens taken to be the condition of possibility of life, it must be served even when its own actions threaten it. Hence the vicious circle of patriotic logic that Socrates leaves unexamined. Dissenting from his beloved city's wars named the unthinkable; dissenting from judicial imprisonment and death reiterated it. Reflexive obedience to orders in the military prefigured unthinking acquiescence in a judicial verdict. The first paved the way for the second, which in turn ratified the first. Socrates nevertheless insists that willingness to stand fast and die measures one's commitment to political principle—just as a soldier remains at his military post. From war to politics: Socrates's analogical insistence slides into the legal conversation without full articulation, much less defense. How has death been installed as *the* sign of authentic conviction? How have death and slavish cowardice become the sole linked alternatives? Socrates's silence enables Hegel to moralize, "We should expect nothing else of Socrates than that he should go to meet his death in the most calm and manly fashion."[14]

Socrates's self-appointed vocation enables him to anticipate a possible retort. If he possesses such extraordinary concern for Athens, why has he not dedicated himself to politics? Why has he shunned the assembly and the law courts? Why has he eschewed traditional public life in Athens? Why has he lived on the margins of city business? Socrates explains the distance he has kept by introducing the specter of death, a rhetorical move that simultaneously makes death now more likely. That is to say, Socrates's answer to his own question cannot do anything but insult, antagonize, and inflame. He insists that the just man must shun public affairs if he is to survive. No one who works for truth and justice without hesitation or opposes Athens can expect anything other than death. The accusation masquerading as defense provides a new twist on the depth of Athenian corruption and borders on slander. The logic of escalation, a logic culminating in death, governs Socrates's "defense."

Nevertheless, Socrates did publicly serve Athens. What might account for his involvement with the city? Hegel insists: "Though Socrates himself continued to perform his duties as a citizen, it was not the actual State and its religion, but the world of Thought that was his true home."[15] I would like to break down the distinction that Hegel posits. Patriotism, I believe, informs Socrates's selective interventions. His love of Athens leads him to imagine a city that transmogrifies itself, that might some day take shape in the world. As such, it entails dedicating his life, as much as he can, to the city's moral health and welfare.[16] Nevertheless, he cannot necessarily avoid all public service. When called, he responds. Thus his conduct can be questioned. Socrates's love of his imaginary Athens, the Athens of his dreams, means that he cannot refuse service when its earthly counterpart calls. Patriotism thus involves both elevation and descent. Consider

Hegel's reading of events. Hegel's tragic interpretation of the trial depends on fixing Socrates's identity. Hegel takes it for granted that Socrates represents "the principle of subjective reflection," that he was a moral man possessed of "the consciousness of what he was doing." This sets up the conflict with Athens as "two opposed rights com[ing] into collision, and the one destroys the other. Thus both suffer loss and yet both are mutually justified; it is not as if the one alone were right and the other wrong." I would reverse Hegel's analysis and argue that the trial represents not so much a tragic conflict but, to quote Hegel: a "crime . . . that the spirit of the people committed against itself." The sources of the crime were two kinds of unthinking patriotism, namely that of Socrates and that of Athens. Thus Hegel's presumption that "Socrates—in assigning to insight, to conviction, the determination of men's actions—posited the Individual as capable of a final moral decision, in contraposition to Country and Customary Morality" strikes me as overly generous. Although Hegel and I part company, we can agree that "[Athens and Socrates] must be pronounced guilty or innocent" together—that is, they both loved and died through unexamined first principles. As Hegel notes, "we may dispute with the Athenians about this." This I am doing.[17]

Contra Hegel and Euben, I believe that patriotism operates as Socrates's unthought. While it would seem to be a powerful source of Socrates's vaunted courage and integrity, it also triggers his undoing. The generosity, care, doubt, skepticism, and inquisitiveness that bear his name disappear at both trial and sentencing. It's not just that Socrates says: Here I stand, I can do no other. He says: Here I stand, I can *think* no other. Moreover, after the death penalty is imposed, Socrates's thinking turns imperatival as he rushes to consolidate the death sentence he needs. With death, Socrates simultaneously abandons Athens at its greatest moment and brands it forever. If anything, Athens's determination to kill Socrates discloses his necessity not just to Athens but to democracy. Alas, Socrates's patriotic love, tinged with ressentiment, traps him within its conceptual confines. As Socrates's death ensures his legend it also harms Athens, perfecting the city's moral and political failings. Socrates becomes complicit in Athenian self-destructiveness.

In sum, for Socrates life must prove itself through death. For death confers meaning on life—not living the life. Death must become constitutive of it. Hegel insists that it is the individual who is vanquished, not the principle, and since the ephemeral cannot compete with the eternal, principle trumps individual life.[18] This logic makes sense within a patriotic frame, but I believe that it does violence to democratic modes of being in the world.

DEATH, WHAT IS IT GOOD FOR?

Crito has not fared well in the history of political thought. James Boyd White believes that he must have been a grave disappointment to Socrates. As Crito urges Socrates to escape, his arguments not only fail but articulate precisely the amoral ruthlessness that Socrates deplores. He seems to believe that justice means helping your friends and harming your enemies. Doesn't Socrates deserve better in his last hours?

I would like to redeem Crito; I would like to revisit the question of exile. Or, better, I would like to make exile a question, for Socrates gave it short shrift. Socrates's readers tend to do the same. James Colaiaco, for example, writes: "Finally, Socrates considers exile." This is precisely what I argue Socrates does not—cannot—do. Colaiaco continues: "But for Socrates to submit to exile would legitimate the indictment and be interpreted as an admission of guilt . . . There was another, unstated reason why Socrates rejected exile. The ancient city was regarded not only as a dwelling place but also as the vital matrix from which an individual sprung . . . If Socrates accepted exile, he would become *apolis*, without a city, *even more alien than he was as a philosopher* in Athens. The most pathetic figure, for the Greeks, is the stateless person."[19] Here Colaiaco's account of Socrates's identity contains—and works to resolve—the same political and practical tensions that Socrates cannot negotiate, or fully recognize, on the question of his fate. Thus both succumb to the apparent inexorability of dominant Athenian norms and traditions—including patriotic loyalty.

I am not arguing for the soundness of Crito's reasoning. Rather, Crito's intuition-cum-insistence on exile corresponds to fugitive elements in Socrates's life and thought—which means that Socrates might well have reached the conclusion that Crito urged upon him. Yet from the moment when Socrates first broaches exile in the *Apology*, he displays uncharacteristic thoughtlessness. He turns rhetorical, dogmatic, and cursory, a tendency which peaks in the conversation he concocts with the Laws of Athens to vindicate the death sentence he has maneuvered. What, then, might account for Socrates's refusal to subject exile to the same scrutiny that other dominant conventions received? How has Socrates forsaken his renowned ways? The short answer: patriotism. Socrates's love of Athens means that he cannot imagine a life elsewhere, and therefore death is folded into the core of his thought, antagonizing and militarizing it. Death provides a cognitive and affective frame that fixes certain philosophical positions and effectively preempts alternatives.

When Socrates first "considered" exile as an alternative to death, he dismissed it as impossible. Pragmatically speaking, it would not work; it thus held little or no appeal (37d). No thought, however, was given to Athens, real or ideal. Socrates drew a grim picture of exile. What kind of life might he enjoy? Well, if the citizens of Athens found him intolerable, how would strangers treat him? He prophesied a life on the run, being driven from city to city. Either the young would report him to their fathers once they had heard him, or else the fathers would learn of his presence themselves and evict him to protect their children. Regardless, the result would be the same. On Socrates's account, all cities become Athens. Wanted nowhere, he has nowhere to go.

Crito applies pressure to Socrates's eloquence. Socrates has, Crito informs him, friends in other cities, friends who will not only take him in and protect him but welcome his company and conversation. Socrates can live *his* life outside Athens. Socrates is a subject of desire, not pity. His friends do not deem him compromised. Athens's injustice creates an opportunity. Socrates has options. Thus Crito poses a threat to be neutralized. Socrates accordingly brings to life an idealized Athens, the Laws, to speak on the city's behalf. The Laws reduce Crito to quiet compliance with Socrates's original decision to die. Plato may not allow Crito to contest Socrates's patriotic legerdemain, but it can be contested. Socrates, especially Socrates, is not entitled to the benefit of the doubt.[20]

Socrates's Laws make several angry speeches. How can Socrates consider escape when escape would mean the city's destruction? No city can survive if its citizens decide they can break the law at their discretion. The Laws wonder if Socrates understands the ramifications here. The city and its laws are the conditions of possibility of life. The debt that he owes— that all citizens owe—defies calculation.[21] Yet Socrates plans to repay the city with betrayal? Think of the city's generous terms of membership. People may live in Athens as long as they obey the laws. They can leave at will if it does not suit them. They may take their worldly goods. In case of conflict between citizen and city, methods exist to resolve it. Either obey the laws or persuade the city to change them. But if persuasion fails, obedience follows. Citizens agree to this arrangement when they live in Athens. Socrates's own life indicates acceptance. For seventy years he has not left Athens—except for military service. He has never traveled to another city, not even to visit friends or attend a festival. The way he has lived his life communicates his consent to Athenian arrangements and understandings. He cannot be contemplating exile. In any event, no city would want a man so lacking in respect for law. He would be considered an enemy. Any city that would welcome him would be undesirable. Either way, his life as he knows it would be over (50–54).[22]

Socrates makes these declarations in rapid-fire succession. They arrive as ready-made truths rather than considered judgments, and command attention because of their conviction. When he makes the Laws speak, they speak through imperatives. He presents the Laws as entitled to the last word: "Is your wisdom such as not to realize that your country is to be honoured more than your mother, your father, and all your ancestors, that it is more to be revered and more sacred, and that it counts for more among the gods and sensible men, that you must worship it, yield to it and placate its anger more than your father's? You must . . . endure in silence whatever it instructs you to endure, whether blows or bonds, and if it leads you into war to be wounded or killed, you must obey. To do so is right" (51b–c).

Colaiaco claims that Socrates resorts to the Laws because Crito cannot understand the philosophical arguments in play. "Asked by Socrates whether he would be committing an injustice and violating a just agreement if, without first persuading the state, he decides to flee Athens, Crito effectively bows out of the conversation: 'I cannot tell Socrates; for I do not know.'"[23] Yet Colaiaco does not scrutinize Socrates's argument that led to this position. He writes in the imperative form: "He must accept conviction and the death penalty, even though unjust, because they resulted from a legitimate legal process and because he made a just agreement to respect the principle of the rule of law. The only recourse he would have had, he says, was to persuade the state to permit him to leave. Not having done this, he must submit to authority and obey the legal verdict . . . To consent to Crito's plan, Socrates would not be committing civil disobedience, but engaging in a cowardly evasion and subversion of the principle of the rule of law."[24] Yet what if the legitimate legal process was a show trial or, better, a Socratic morality tale with the verdict a foregone conclusion? What if Athens needed a scapegoat or Socrates sought martyrdom for its obvious decline?[25] Acting on behalf of a better Athens, might this not account for Socrates's angry provocations in court? Socrates's positions would then reflect nothing so much as pre-given patriotic command (30b). Moreover, even if Socrates conjures the Laws so that Crito can understand the issues, this doesn't necessarily make the position taken ironic. Socrates can believe it too. Colaiaco is right that "Socrates the philosopher never says that the speech he gives for the Laws represents his own views," but if you read Socrates as patriotic in the *Apology*, you don't need to deny his patriotism in the *Crito*.[26] But if you identify Socrates as a philosopher, you will need to distance him from this patriotic position. And what if Crito cannot bring himself to affirm Socrates's philosophical argument? Colaiaco writes: "having assented to the initial propositions of Socrates, Crito, facing the prospect of his friend's imminent death, allowed his sentiments to overwhelm his reason. He could not bring himself to draw the obvious conclusion, even though based upon premises he and Socrates had agreed upon in the past. Crito was in conflict."[27] If, however, Crito's prior assent was tainted because Socrates did not make the case against exile, Crito's conflict reflects Socrates's own capitulation to sentiment. Crito's argument, furthermore, does not explain why Socrates would abandon his pedagogical ethos and resort to an argument that he did not believe simply because Crito was supposedly overwhelmed. His usual practice was to start again. Does Socrates want his last conversation with Crito to be an insulting self-betrayal? Is this how friends treat one another? Or is it that Socrates is frustrated with Crito for another reason, namely Crito's intuitive resistance to concede Socrates's initial argument on exile, itself informed and animated by patriotic affect? The conversation with the Laws may be philosophical, but it resembles Socrates's relationship to Athens. That is, Socrates may not openly embrace the Laws' monologue, but the tone and substance resonate with his invocation of military service where he unquestioningly serves Athens's imperial military machine.

Patriotism is thus the unthought that leads Socrates to subvert his highest philosophic ideal and drop his art of critical investigation. Hence I would deny a fundamental tension between the *Apology* and *Crito*. Patriotism links them. At times, Socrates performs without question what he imagines Athens demands of him, in the process contriving arguments that make it seem necessary.

SOCRATES IN EXILE

When Socrates is speaking the Laws, his disposition subtends his life-long conversational practice. His insistence, I believe, expresses a patriotic unthought, suggesting that responsibility rests with the life of exile he nominally, but vehemently, rejects. That is, Socrates resorts to rhetorical drama because of his philosophical and affective vulnerability. It's not just that citizens can respect and benefit their city by disobeying an unjust law. Disobedience might be the only way to move the city to do what it would, upon reflection and at a better moment, want to do: namely, live up to its ideals. The presumption that disobedience equals destruction seems not only unwarranted but also convenient. Colaiaco argues that the moral legitimacy of civil disobedience depends on its open performance, coupled with the acceptance of consequent penalties. Accordingly, if Socrates were to escape, he would be evading the laws, in cowardly fashion. This reading strikes me as self-serving (for Socrates) for a number of reasons. First, Socrates's refusal to escape is parasitic on his prior refusal to consider the question of exile. How can Socrates be given credit for moral consistency when it rests on thoughtlessness? His consistency consists of never giving a thought to exile. Second, Socrates cannot escape prison without Athens's connivance (read: consent). If he were to leave, it would be under the city's watchful gaze and witnessed by every citizen, as it were. Cowardice requires stealth. Besides, seventy-year-old war heroes do not make good cowards. Third, exile involves serious consequences. For Socrates exile might not entail the utter humiliation of Athenian legend, but it would entail disruption, loss, and anguish. Again, this is hardly cowardly. Furthermore, to reconsider an ill-considered public decision would require lonely civic courage. If the unexamined life is not worth living, why not challenge the official terms of political discourse on exile? Why not challenge standard understandings of law, (dis)obedience, punishment, death, and patriotism? Fourth, Socrates might have announced a different alternative "punishment": he could have imposed exile on himself and named a return date. He would then have been liable for his actions upon return.[28] And what a return it would be. Given his riveting "defense," how does Socrates's theatrical imagination fail him here?

Socrates, recall, counters Meletus's death sentence by suggesting that he be feted daily at the Prytaneum at city expense, which would enable him to continue living his life as before. The suggestion allows him to celebrate his critical role to the city, supplanting its traditional military heroes. Indeed Socrates refuses to offer an alternative punishment since, as far as he is concerned, he deserves none. His actions make the city better. In addition, to propose a punishment would be to commit an injustice, here against him, which is something he never does willingly or knowingly.[29] Socrates's Dionysian provocation, it should be noted, means that he would like to continue his life's work. He would continue if, per impossibile, the city agreed to reward him for it. He would "continue" if, more likely, the city killed him. Thus Socrates's recommendation can't but offend Athens's patriotic sensibilities. And inasmuch as he implies that he is the true patriot, his fellow (false) patriots become obligated to kill him. Socrates may not know much; he does know death.

I believe that Socrates, following Crito's advice, could have proposed exile and continued to practice his art. That exile was disgrace according to convention cannot have mattered to Socrates; common opinion did not concern him. If anything, it ought to have led to reconsideration.[30] As the corruption charge actually compliments Socrates, so exile could honor him. Yet when it comes to exile, Socrates suddenly knows. And he knows exile so well that he not only rejects it outright; he fails to consider it. What happened to Socrates's fabled profession of ignorance? Save for participation in dubious imperial warfare, Socrates, a true and proud provincial, has never left Athens. He has known but one home his entire life. He rejects a (way of) life based on ignorance of it. Thus he imagines a life in exile convenient to his rejection of it. Or perhaps his patriotism operates on him viscerally to the point where thought becomes disabled. Regardless, he seems to ape his fellow Athenians for whom banishment equals disgrace. It means separation from the institutions and opportunities through which Athenians define themselves and achieve greatness. For them, exile as horror makes sense. Yet Socrates rejects dominant Athenian ways. How, then, does he cling to his own version of their understanding of exile? It's as if he mimics the opinion of the many. Though

Socrates scolds Crito for adopting such opinions, he apparently exempts himself.

Before issuing a final judgment on exile, perhaps Socrates needs to take a closer look at his life. First, his self-invoked military heroism (at Delium) consisted of leading a hasty retreat (without orders) under enemy onslaught. Socrates remained calm and saved lives. He did not hold his ground no matter what and die for Athens, as ordered, as required by duty. No good could come from death. For Athens's sake, he fled and lived to do battle another day.[31] Second, Socrates's mission, assigned by the god, was to seek out reputedly wise men and engage them in conversation. The god had said that *no man* was wiser than Socrates. To fulfill his mission, Socrates traveled to and fro in Athens, speaking to citizen and stranger alike. The mission knows no inherent boundaries since man knows no such boundaries. (The god did not say that no Athenian was wiser than Socrates.) Thus to go into exile would be to continue the god's mission elsewhere. Athens is not the only city that needs Socrates's talents. Most people do not care for the most important things in life. If anything, Socrates has spent enough of his energies on Athens. True, Socrates feels a kindred connection to the people of Athens, but he feels it for others too (30). And while Athens may have provided a world conducive to Socrates's peripatetic philosophizing, it is not strictly speaking a precondition for it. Socrates fosters the space in which he conducts his art. This means that other places, even if they are not as hospitable as Athens might be, can be made hospitable. He could even continue to work on Athens from exile.[32] Borders are fluid. His friends would visit him. Other Athenians would seek him out. More might pursue him because of the trial and its outcome. They would insist that he give an account of himself. The political possibilities explode.

And though Socrates hailed from Athens, birth obscures the fundamental foreignness of his life in it. Socrates may have spoken and acted like a patriot; the best of his lived life suggests "resident alien." His moral and political sensibilities ran counter to the city's own; he rejected the material and moral values that governed Athens and by which it defined its greatness. Where Athens's leading citizens pursued power and self-aggrandizement, where they presumed truth and certainty, Socrates tended to self-abnegation and skepticism. When Socrates insists that a just man cannot participate in politics—because he cannot remain both true to his convictions and alive—he implicitly claims that Athenian institutions cannot deliver the justice they promise to citizens. This is more than moral censure. It amounts to declaring that Athens is not self-sufficient, let alone self-same. Socrates founds a new political space in the city. It irrupts wherever he goes, as does the fight for justice. Not just because Athenian institutions are corrupt, but also because they are Athenian—meaning necessarily perspectival, partial, and limited. They cannot generate critical insight because, among other things, they cannot secure the angle of vision that criticism requires. The only limit to criticism would therefore be Socrates's travels. Famously, Socrates never articulated a systematic philosophy of his own. Perhaps his silence was unavoidable, for he could not articulate what was impossible to conceive within the confines of a single city. Athens did not—no city could—provide sufficient resources for a comprehensive philosophy. For Socrates, other worlds, other ways of life, were required—just as Athens required Socrates's foreignness for its transformation. Perhaps Socrates wandered the streets of Athens because what he was looking for could not ultimately be found in the city. This might illuminate why he never stopped moving. Perhaps he could feel it even if he did not explicitly theorize it. To prefer death to exile curtails his investigations and denies to the world the critical homeless ethos that Socrates embodied and enacted. This ethos may have emerged in Athens, but it also pointed beyond it. No wonder Athens found it threatening, for Socrates's ways implicitly suggest that no one city can or should be the unquestioned site of identification, or of loyalty and allegiance.

For reasons potentially patriotic, James Boyd White also argues that Socrates must stay. Contra the Laws, Socrates's life does not embody a binding agreement between Socrates and Athens. Rather there subsists between them an intimate relationship. To escape would be to abandon the relationship, thus himself and his life. Execution, paradoxically, does not require that Socrates surrender the principal "purpose of his life," namely "to establish the value of thinking and talking about" the moral identity of the polity by posing such central questions as: Who are we to be? What ought we to do? Socrates has worked diligently "to establish . . . the legitimacy of discourse about the nature of the just community." Socratic purpose points to a larger concern: that while people matter as individuals, they are—or can be—more than individuals. Should Socrates escape, White claims, he could pursue the question of justice only in theory. He would lack the existential engagement that makes the quest real. On White's account, Socrates has converted Athens into an "idealized dialogic partner," an active moral creature, and he would die before denying his fictive creation, which he can bring fully to life through his death. Death names a "fitting end" for Socrates.[33]

White's argument compels assent. Like Socrates, however, White presupposes the indispensability of a homeland, a territorially defined order. For the just community to be a subject of fundamental concern, people must be able to imagine themselves as more than individuals contingently located in the same place. They have to imagine a "we," think of themselves "as a larger polity, as a city or nation or society that has a moral life and career of its own of which we can ask, Is it just?"[34] Socrates thus routinely compares Athens to an idealized conception of it and issues judgments. White claims that Socrates's escape would be tantamount to denying the possibility of this discourse. Yet why does conversation about the just community, in this case Athens, necessarily have to occur in one place? Crito's friends in Megara, Thessaly, and Thebes believe otherwise. They wish Socrates to join them so that he can continue his philosophic work. They do not privilege Athens as the site of discourse. Nor do they presuppose that unless you are willing to put your life on the line, you are not to be taken seriously. (Tyrannies can induce conformity; they cannot compel belief or define character.) Socrates's concerns transcend Athenian boundaries—not just despite his love for the city, but because of it. To repeat, Socrates seems incapable of re-covering exile, turning it into a good. After a temporary departure, Socrates could practice his art and plan a return to Athens—with newfound influence, a new twist on his claim that Athens would assist him in its own unjust way (38d). Exile might lack the immediate drama of death, but the specter of return could prove haunting. Vietnam War protestors, recall, moved to Canada, where they continued to participate in American politics. If anything, expatriate dissent provoked greater outrage in America than domestic antiwar politics did. Politics don't stop just because you leave home. And imagine Socrates returning to Athens after banishment and conducting conversations on his trial and punishment. Crowds would flock to hear him. Imagine Socrates pursuing a "public career" to prosecute Meletus for his crimes against Athenian democracy. More crowds. Possibilities multiply; Socrates shrinks from them.

White's account thus mimics the tensions in Socrates's thought. On the one hand he insists that "Athens is [Socrates's] city: both the actual polis and, equally important, the vision of what it could become if it were to define itself by a concern for justice . . . This is what he cannot leave without abandoning himself." At the same time, White notes that Socrates does not greatly admire Athens in many respects. "He is profoundly separated, in attitude and value, from those who dominate his culture."[35] In light of Athens's state, what does it mean to say that the city is his? Socrates's foreignness means that he cannot live the ordinary life of a citizen—for fear of death. This may be another reason why he does not stay in place but remains an internal refugee, one step ahead of the authorities. Socrates and his interlocutors make up a fugitive community in, around, and across Athens. With its borders fluid, mobile and porous, you need but an open mind for membership. As a community, it is decidedly un-Athenian. Socrates may be said to have left behind Athens long ago.

LONG LIVE DEATH

To conclude the chapter, Nietzsche's diagnosis of Socrates may illuminate the reign of death that he consolidates. Nietzsche credits Socrates with having invented an agon where he perfected his "monstrous" craft on Athens's youth. Yet he scolds Socrates for linguistic indiscretion with death imminent: "whether it was death or the poison or piety or malice—something loosened his tongue at that moment and he said: 'O Crito, I owe Asclepius a rooster.' This ridiculous and terrible 'last word' means for those who have ears: 'O Crito, *life is a disease*.'"[36] The source of Socrates's insult may be a mystery to Nietzsche, but I think it flows from his patriotic reverence for Athens. Consider love the disease that Socrates intimates. To the extent that patriotism creates a gap between ideal and actuality, the ideal operates not so much as an object of aspiration but as a fount of anger and resentment. The imperfections that bedevil any order, rather than provide a reason for modesty or caution, fuel an insistence on fidelity to the ideal. With the ideal just beyond reach, failure can be assigned to readily identifiable corruption with those responsible known. Rage finds itself built into the patriotic fabric of things—because the gap by definition cannot be sealed. If anything, the ideal is animated by the gap itself.

Here Socrates's thoughtlessness resurfaces. At trial he insists that it is

Athens—not he—that is at risk of harm. "I am far from making a defense now on my own behalf, as might be thought, but on yours, to prevent you from wrongdoing" (30d–e). With verdict delivered, Socrates returns to Athens's self-endangerment: "It is for the sake of a short time, gentlemen of the jury, that you will acquire the reputation and guilt, in the eyes of those who want to denigrate the city, of having killed Socrates" (38c). He parts from the jury with the following prophecy: "I leave you now, condemned to death by you, but they are condemned by truth to wickedness and injustice" (39b–c). Here Socrates concentrates on the affect of his absence on Athens. The city stands to lose its most provocative and productive critic. Socrates deems himself indispensable to the city—which explains why he cannot leave. He presumes the city incapable of effective moral agency in his absence. Athens amounts to nothing without him. [37]

Yet Socrates did not address Athens's fate should it kill him. True, Socrates refers to Athens's future reputation in the eyes of its enemies, but ordinarily he regards this as unimportant. He does not consider what might happen to Athens in the wake of his execution from the execution itself. How might his killing affect the soul of the city? Can Athens survive "a man executed unjustly" (30d)? Perhaps Socrates's willingness to let Athens be "condemned by truth to wickedness" reveals something about his principles? Does Socrates's need to teach Athens a lesson overwhelm his ethical imperative to consider the ramifications of decisions? Socrates's persistent invocation of military service, symptomatic of his preoccupation with death, suggests an overweening love for Athens, a love that has not been reciprocated. Socrates feels entitled to impose on Athens a lesson—whether it can benefit from the lesson or not. What's more, Socrates posits a pair of false options to narrow the conversational field. He would rather die having given his defense than beg for his life; he would rather stand his ground than do or say anything to avoid death. "Neither I nor any other man should, on trial or in war, contrive to avoid death at any cost" (39). Socrates seems, however, to be in no danger of avoiding death at any cost. Rather, without the meaningful consideration of alternatives, his position means that death alone vindicates principle. Inasmuch as trial and war become collapsed in the *Apology*, the pressures involved militate against thought. Thus Socrates will do *nothing* at all that *might* make it *seem* as if he is trying to avoid death.

Though Socrates has quit the agon that he reinvented, he wages war on Athens to the very end of his life. After sentencing, he again invokes his exemplary war service and rebukes the Athenians for the unmanly stunts to which they resort to escape their fates (39). He accepts death like a soldier. What does Socrates hope to accomplish with his noble death? Much, apparently: Socrates would remake Athens. Though Athens suffers the "indignity of wickedness and injustice," perhaps Socrates's approval of his own execution can redeem the city. It would be his last service to Athens. If he is willing to die for the city, it must be worth dying for—if not now, then later; if not in fact, then in theory. Yet Socrates's gesture has to be more than a sign of hope. Athens's potential must be latent. Otherwise, the gesture would be futile. This is why it is allegedly better for Socrates to die than depart (41d). Perhaps he wants to save Athens from itself and undo some of the harm that it means to self-inflict. Thus he will make a point, a patriotic point, of staying. Yet the very fact that Athens would "let" Socrates die suggests that it is in no position to be saved. Death thus serves nothing more than an ideal of patriotism.

Nietzsche would have Socrates remain silent. The slip of the tongue about Asclepius suggests that Socrates can no longer abide Athens's corruption. Euben argues that Socrates was the one true Athenian patriot. He may be right, but what kind of patriot makes a point of displaying his patriotism and then insisting on it? Here such self-identification becomes the first step on the road to a "noble" death. Athenian patriotism, I believe, has compromised Socrates as well. As he stares down the city that he holds in contempt, a life supposedly lived free of injustice dissolves. With exile Athens would have enjoyed the luxury of one day changing its mind and correcting its gross injustice: better wrong than infamous. Death makes this impossible. As Socrates's death secures his legend it also harms Athens, perfecting the city's moral and political failings. Socrates becomes complicit in Athens's infamous moral self-destruction. Socrates closes his lifelong investigations with a performance of patriotic loyalty that eternalizes his encounter with Athens. He and Athens thus live on, one immortal, the other infamous, both thanks to his unforgettable death.[38]

If Socrates's death cannot redeem, perhaps he should have left "home" instead: exile as a cure for the diseased life of an Athenian patriot. Socrates's life might have been difficult in exile, but think of it as the eternal return of the same. Locked in perpetual struggle with Athens, Socrates's life may have given the appearance of enchantment, but ressentiment ultimately infected it and exhausted him. Socrates gave so much to Athens and received so little in return that he cannot consider exile—that is, life after Athens—which also means that the patriotic life remains unexamined. The irony is that it needlessly costs him his lifelong commitment to philosophy and permanently scars the city he claims to love.

Indeed Socrates challenges traditional ideas of citizenship, including a patriotic sensibility and its corresponding intuitions of home. And his very life points the way to an alternative homeless democratic ethos and politics. At the same time, Socrates does not resist or fully appreciate the patriotic pull of home. Militarizing his philosophical convictions, he writes: "wherever a man has taken a position that he believes to be best, or has been placed by his commander, there he must I think remain and face danger, without a thought for death or anything else" (28e). Socrates's insistence that he not give death a thought forms the patriotic mantra of the *Apology*. Yet it seems that death already informs and animates the position he is bound and determined to defend, a position that cannot be vindicated, we are led to believe, except through death. Death may be placed outside the bounds of formal consideration, but this leaves its original position inside his thinking not only uncontested but also fortified. Thus when Socrates remarks (32b–c), "I thought I should run any risk," this may be read as willing embrace rather than candid recognition or mild lament. In short, Socrates's life discloses new possibilities, yet he does not pursue them, thanks to an unthinking patriotism, itself enthralled to a politics of death. Patriotism kills Socrates; through it he kills himself. Ironically, however, patriotism's self-defeating, self-destructive bent points to the need for a broader sensibility and practice that challenges death's will to power. Long live Socratic life.

Westerns at their best constitute a powerful anthology of political philosophy.—BERNARD WILLIAMS, *Truth and Truthfulness*

Those who are so absorbed by the world of the movie—by its images, gestures, and words—that they are unable to supply what really makes it a world, do not have to dwell on particular points of its mechanics during a screening . . . they react automatically.
—MAX HORKHEIMER AND THEODOR ADORNO, *Dialectic of Enlightenment*

It's the most un-American thing I've ever seen in my whole life. The last thing in the picture [*High Noon*] is ol' Coop [Gary Cooper] putting the United States marshal's badge under his foot and stepping on it.—JOHN WAYNE, *Playboy*

Iconic Drama II:

The Socratic Way of Death

John Schaar, as we saw in chapter 2, issued a plea for patriotism in 1973 and doubted its prospects.[1] He cited Tocqueville for the argument that "instinctive" patriotism belonged to a world dead and gone, the world, say, of Socrates and the Laws.[2] He may have conceded too much. Even as intrinsic connections to land dissipate, the connections themselves can be augmented and replaced. Thus despite differences in political affiliations, in modes of production, in ethical vocabularies, and in ways of being in the world that mark off contemporary Americans from "the Greeks and the Navaho," the instincts themselves, so to speak, may be intact and operational.[3]

Schaar feels his way in and around the universe of patriotism with considerable acuity. He describes patriotism as a "basic urge" flowing from "primary experiences." Endemic not to the laboratory but to life, it relies on an "immense power of habit."[4] A sentiment long in the making, it rests on what is familiar and nurturing, which also feels natural and right.

Patriotism may dry up intermittently, but its springs can be refreshed and "the real thing" restored.[5]

Nothwithstanding Schaar's observations, even if patriotism looks to be in decline in modernity, the surface world of deed and expression is belied by a rich affective dimension below the threshold of visibility. Though Schaar firmly concludes that "instinctive patriotism . . . cannot be ours," he turns to a version designed specifically for America. Following Lincoln, Schaar invokes a patriotism built on ideas, a core set of political principles and commitments capable of binding the nation in mutual promises.[6] Schaar articulates the means and mechanisms by which this patriotism can be inculcated. He is a theorist of patriotic practices. While covenanted patriotism admittedly differs from the patriotisms of old, I argue that it names a complex potentially no less "instinctive" than previous forms. It can be as affectively rich as its ancient predecessors.

Schaar, Rorty, and Berns extol the virtues of storytelling precisely because of the affective attachments it can induce. In the remainder of the chapter I explore, though for different reasons, what I call patriotic cinema. Film not only tells stories; it tells them in ways that speak to what William E. Connolly refers to as the visceral register of being.[7] Connolly argues that instincts cannot be reduced to a nature both determinate and irresistible. "Instincts are proto-thoughts situated in culturally formed moods, affects, and situations . . . [They] are thought-imbued intensities moving below linguistic sophistication, consciousness, and reflective judgment as well as through them."[8] Thus John Wayne's outrage at *High Noon* led him in the *Playboy* interview quoted in the epigraph to unknowingly rewrite the film's conclusion. Will Kane (played by Gary Cooper) flicks his marshal's badge to the ground with calm disgust, but he then climbs into a waiting buckboard and leaves town with his new wife. His feet are otherwise inactive, though the downward thrust of the camera lens may seem to drive the badge into the dirt. What's more, Wayne's revisions spilled out of the theater. He came to believe (mistakenly) that he had helped drive Carl Foreman, the screenplay's blacklisted author, from the United States.[9] Apparently movies, like Western Union, do send messages.[10] For Wayne, the director of *The Green Berets*, not even the anti–Vietnam War demonstrations of the 1960s compete with the power of Gary Cooper on screen. Patriotism lives deeply in culture.

To honor Wayne, as it were, I explore two films in which America itself stars: *High Noon* and *Saving Private Ryan*. I have selected these classics in part because they defy placement on a liberal-conservative spectrum: when it comes to representation, politics apparently stops at the screening room door. I also selected these films because they can illuminate the character and logic of patriotism.[11] Again following James's advice on horror, I take iconic films with familiar themes and rework the details without the patriotic gloss. I turn their own words, deeds, sights, and sounds against them, forcing them to reflect back on themselves. In short, the Americas portrayed here, thanks to the brilliance of the productions, ultimately defeat themselves. The very effort to secure an authoritative moral identity results in its subversion. The need for enemies borders on insatiable. Enemies, though, can always be secured. Moreover, the love revealed in these films feels narcissistic and cancerous. Extravagant self-regard coupled with transcendent inspiration and purpose constitutes and compromises the patriotic love that these films purport to embody. Patriotism proves inimical to itself precisely because it insists on declaring and proving itself right. If anything, patriotism seems to suffer from self-induced success. I hope to elucidate this dynamic below through dramas that are nothing if not Socratic.

YOU MUST GO ON, I CAN'T GO ON, I'LL GO ON

High Noon represents what Robert Warshow termed a "social drama" and André Bazin the "superwestern." Thus *High Noon* is not really a western at all. It pursues interests external to the genre. More specifically, the film is a cold war parable; and because it lends itself to complementary, if contending, readings, I argue that it's a parable for patriots.[12] Consider two possibilities. First, as Marshal Kane discovers that no one—friend, neighbor, fellow lawman—possesses the courage or conviction to face down the Miller bunch, *High Noon* warns of the insidious character of the Mc-Carthy menace (the threat from within). Second, as Marshal Kane discovers that no one understands the nature of the threat posed by the arrival of the Miller bunch, *High Noon* warns of the inexorable communist peril (the threat from without). In each case, people supposedly reliable turn their backs on you in the face of danger. I suggest a third reading, one agnostic toward the telling of contemporary moral and political tales. I read the film as illustrative, if inadvertently, of the self-destructive dynamic of patriotism. Neither the complacency nor the cowardice of the town, nor the violence and depravity of the Millers, poses a threat to Hadleyville. Rather Kane himself, the town marshal, its nominal protector and self-appointed savior, endangers Hadleyville.[13]

The moral mission of *High Noon* can be seductive; it would seem to fulfill Rorty's injunction that American politics requires inspirational stories well told. The considerable pleasures of succumbing notwithstanding, I believe that the audience has been entrapped. The combination of economical structure, relentless recourse to time, and cinematography rooted in Civil War photography provides satisfactions such that awareness may prove difficult. The film tells a story, of course, but audience affect names its reason for being. Success means identification with Will Kane and the moral outrage and self-righteous indignation that accompany it. To break the spell that *High Noon* casts, I propose to relive the film from a new angle of vision, on the diagonal. Freed from Gary Cooper's optic, doing so enables a fresh look, a film as if seen for the first time. Because patriotism relies on obviousness, the film must be made unfamiliar, foreign, discrepant. At the same time, to render salient the self-indulgent violence and horror of the film, it must participate in its own undoing. It is important, à la James, to enter deeply into the film and let it speak in close proximity to its own words and images. Stories lie in the details.

High Noon takes place in Hadleyville, a small, peaceful, God-fearing town. From his first scene, Kane, an aging marshal whose wedding outside the town's church coincides with his forced retirement, needs to rewrite his life—and thus the film's ending—before it unfolds. The town, symbolized by the wedding, has figuratively rejected him and his ethos. The only life he has known, the one life he can live, has thus ended. The rejection must be answered, and Frank Miller, the film's absent villain, becomes the occasion, the excuse, for Kane to vindicate himself. Thus *High Noon* frustrates claims to civic virtue or the greater good. Because of Kane's imperatives, pace Garry Wills, the action is not forced upon him; Kane forces it upon the town to stamp his identity on it and secure his legacy.[14] Yet whence the imperative to which Kane responds? Rejecting the pleas of spouse, the advice of colleagues, and the good wishes of friends, Kane stays. Unable to take no for an answer, unable to articulate a reason even to himself, he stays. Kane may not be his own man after all. If so, Hadleyville becomes the scene of a larger metaphysic working itself out with Kane as the focal point of its expression. There is to be but one truth in the film.

From the opening frame, *High Noon* stacks the emotional deck. As the opening credits roll, three men meet in the middle of nowhere. They exude menace. Tex Ritter's somber, melancholy voice sings the dread of abandonment ("Do not forsake me . . ."), the anguish of which obscures the song's sense of mission. As they enter the small town of Hadleyville, people take notice; a few react with alarm. It is Sunday morning. The first sound of life: church bells. Parishioners gather. A steady stream enters the church. The three ride past, unmindful of it. The men ride by the marshal's office. One of them rears his horse before it. They have business with the law. Because most of the town remains ignorant of these events, the audience must take responsibility for the danger that has arrived. *High Noon* performs every scene for our benefit.

Move to a judge's office next door: a wedding. It looks to be a happy occasion. Conducted by a justice of the peace, the vows are swift and serious. Will Kane and Amy Fowler marry. After the coterie of friends assembled offer their congratulations, the justice of the peace commences a second ceremony. Marshal Kane must cede his badge (having already surrendered his gun). In view of Fowler's religious convictions, disarmament makes marriage possible. Yet Kane hesitates—three times. Nevertheless, he finally pins the badge to his holster. Kane is now a civilian. The defrocking fades before subsequent developments but remains critical nonetheless, for nothing Kane does later can claim the mantle of law. He soon retakes the badge, but he performs the pinning ceremony himself. Kane becomes his own law.

Though surrounded by smiles and congratulations, Kane's ambivalence resounds. His new life rests on the death of his previous life. Reinvention here may be equivalent to spiritual death, involving a loss of everything Kane holds dear: authority, status, pride, masculinity. The new beginning also means relocating. Why? Can't (or won't) the town support his store? Perhaps he's leaving for other reasons?

The telegraph operator arrives with a message for the marshal. Kane reads it, though he has just retired. No one notices the arrogation, let alone objects. The would-be happy ending evaporates in the face of news that distant politicians, for reasons unknown, have pardoned Frank Miller, convicted murderer. The revelation explains the presence of the three armed men who moments earlier arrived in town. Kane once again states that he should stay. As they urge Kane to leave, his friends fear for him— but not for themselves. The danger is his not theirs. Kane wants to stay. The best man suggests that he think about Amy instead. He agrees. As Kane sits down on the buckboard his predecessor slaps one of the horses and sends the newlyweds on their way. Kane's exit feels reluctant, rushed, and forced. The film ought to end, a truth that the remainder works hard to deny. For *High Noon* cannot admit Kane's responsibility for the violence to come; it would be tantamount to admitting its gratuity.

Kane's narcissism erupts outside town. He speaks through moral imperatives. "It's no good. I've got to go back, Amy." He refuses to provide a reason, citing lack of time. When she protests, Kane, without noticing, changes rationales and invokes his manhood. Now he—not the town—is the issue. "No, I've been thinking. They're making me run. I've never run from anybody before." Self-focused, he has conveniently forgotten that they were to leave town after the ceremony. Kane's perception feels self-fulfilling. The crisis to come does not exist. Kane creates it with his return to Hadleyville. This is not the kind of story that Rorty and Berns envision. Kane's love for the town, an insistence on defending it where no need has been established, must display itself regardless of the consequences. Such love concerns itself first, though noble proclamations deflect the self-regard. Amy implores him not to return. He responds again with moral imperatives. "I've got to [return]. That's the whole thing." This is the first in a series of repetitions. Kane cannot articulate what makes staying or returning mandatory. Yet it holds him in place.

Kane's solipsism deepens with his first act upon return. Once in the office, he reclaims the badge—though no longer entitled to wear it. As Richard Slotkin observes, Kane effectively transforms himself into a vigilante.[15] Retired, ushered out of town, he can't even claim to be acting in the name of right in the town's absence. The town hasn't done anything yet one way or the other. There is no danger. Amy recognizes the arbitrariness of Kane's decision and continues to object. While Kane offers an abbreviated version of Miller's history, he fails repeatedly to heed her wishes or address her objections. They go back and forth. Amy counters effectively any assertion he makes. Yet this is lost on Kane. He alone knows what is best for the community he loves. Having made his "decision" the moment he learned of Miller's release, he searches for a justification. He will say anything to rationalize the decision. Sensing futility, Amy pleads with him to leave. He refuses: "I can't."

Kane's narcissism escalates as Amy moves close to the heart of the matter, not recognizing that her opposition feeds his determination. Perhaps Kane wants to play hero for her? The thought infuriates him. He then denies an accusation that has not been made: "If you think I like this, you're crazy." But he does like this. Kane has come alive; he has received his own stay of execution from civilian life. The prospects of violence and death prove not only energizing but life-saving. His badge and gun recovered, Kane restores the proprietary order of things with a patriot's projection: "Look, Amy, this is my town." Kane's usurpation entails the denial of his wedding vows and the dismissal of Amy's religious beliefs. With obligation unidirectional, only she can betray him. The narcissism is unthinking. He defines the terms of marriage. She, mere "fair-haired beauty," disappears. Though the film's title song sings of the conflict between love and duty, for Kane there is no conflict. He loves his duty and his duty is to his love—his town. Amy reminds him that they were just married, about to embark on a new life together. She wants to know if that means anything to him. What she doesn't realize is that their new life is not the answer; it's the problem. She refuses to wait around to see if he will live or die. Undaunted by her stand, Kane invokes his mantra: "I've got to stay." The marriage seems to be over on the morning it started. Kane, however, had prior commitments when he took his vows. For the true patriot, there is but one true love.

Nevertheless, *High Noon* would have you believe that Amy has abandoned Kane. Her decision triggers a chain reaction. If she will not stand by him, who will? At this juncture the film turns decidedly on the viewer. Sequence after sequence applies moral pressure in pursuit of total identification with Kane's truth. Yet the manipulation must be obscured. The judge who presided over Kane's wedding offers Kane a history and civics lesson that provides the film's official interpretation, its credibility assured because Kane does not provide it. In ancient Athens citizens welcomed a returning tyrant previously banished. Not only did they open the gates to welcome him, but they stood by while he executed their leaders. The judge experienced something similar in his own life eight years earlier. From ancient Greece and the age of Socrates to the Wild West, events happen fast and people cannot adjust. Patriotism's truths acquire time-lessness. The judge advises Kane to leave town while he has the chance, a piece of advice countered by Kane's claim to the contrary. Ultimately the judge realizes the pointlessness of arguing: Kane cannot hear a word he's saying.

Kane turns to the town. As Socrates looked for a man wiser than he and found fools, so Kane looks everywhere for one upright man. Like Socrates, Kane presumes to know what's best for the town, what it needs. He tries to help the people help themselves. They will have none of it. The scenes that follow enrage us. The judge's prediction means that we already know what will happen as Kane seeks support; with the element of surprise eliminated, we can concentrate on the cultivation of anger and enmity. In terms of patriotic discourse, a community under crisis defines itself by what it does—or does not do. Ambiguity disappears: You are on the side of either right or wrong.

First Kane's deputy abandons him in a childish fit of self-interest. Kane then heads over to the saloon. His appeal there is met with stony silence. You also learn that he once had six deputies, all first-rate gunmen. Yet what kind of small town needs such force at its disposal? Kane leaves to quiet laughter at his predicament. In each scene the performance is for our benefit. We're mad.

Despite Kane's "failures," the audience has yet to be fully implicated. The next scene remedies this deficit and conveys one of patriotism's core truths: the most insidious and therefore deadliest enemy is the one closest to you. Kane's odyssey converts each resident of Hadleyville into a col-laborator with evil. Kane walks to the house of Sam Fuller, one of his dear friends. As Kane approaches we see and hear what he cannot. Fuller cravenly orders that he be sheltered by his wife in his own house. While he cowers in the kitchen (where else?), Mrs. Fuller complies. Rather than expose her, Kane leaves. In the film's affective division of labor, his gentle-ness induces our outrage. With the audience emotionally primed (we're furious), Kane proceeds to the church where people have been gathering since the film's opening.

To demonstrate that Kane's initial recruitment efforts were more than isolated incidents, the town as a whole must account for itself. Kane's pleas for help culminate in a town meeting.[16] With Hadleyville at an im-passe, Jonas Henderson intervenes. Though he represents democracy's inherent potential for irresolution and weakness, Henderson ultimately zeroes in on the truth that Kane refuses to entertain. Henderson insists that if Miller returns, the town bears the responsibility to deal with him, not Kane. He concedes the potential gravity of the situation. But Henderson looks to the future. The fate of the town that its residents forged from nothing hinges on what happens next. But Henderson understands this differently from Kane. The town's growth is at a critical juncture. Capital is on the verge of flowing into Hadleyville to build stores and factories. This is the moment for which the townspeople have been waiting. Henderson does not deny Kane's role in making this possible, but reports of killing in the streets would brand the town wild and scare off investment.

Henderson, Kane's best man at the wedding, restates his appreciation for Kane. There is no doubt that Kane is owed a great debt and is a fine man. Henderson also points out that Kane did not have to return. Kane has thus put the town in an untenable position, with a "crisis" of Kane's making. Henderson refuses to be implicated in a situation that could have been avoided. Looking him in the eye, Henderson advises Kane to leave, both for his sake and for the sake of the town. After Henderson's speech the church falls silent. Henderson supposedly represents the ultimate betrayal, both calculated and self-interested. Kane has exposed Hadleyville as Socrates undressed Athens.[17] The scene feels interminable. With Kane's abandonment complete, our outrage has been perfected. Kane's refusal to rage at the town requires that we do it for him. If anything, his stoic silence exacerbates our sense of betrayal.[18]

Fred Zinnemann's neurotic camera pressures the audience as well. As he flip-flops among empty train tracks, Kane's perpetual motion, and hyperactive pendulum clocks, your imagination conjures the approaching evil that refuses escape. If Kane knows that time is short, you watch it race past, as if caught in the grip of an obsessive-compulsive disorder. Insofar as patriotism relies on death to nourish and sustain it, *High Noon* deploys time to announce death's remorseless arrival. The film's geography, ever narrowing, matches Kane's existential situation. He finds himself alone, streets empty, with no place to go but his claustrophobic office. At twelve o'clock high, if you allow it, you feel sweat dripping from Kane. *High Noon* is one of Hollywood's hottest films. Gary Cooper's temporal domination of the screen feels exhausting. You seem always to be with him, which leaves no time to think.[19] The audience tires with Kane. His screen isolation, however, enhances the audience's identification. Finally, tightly wound, you're itching to bolt from Kane's office, guns blazing, enemy engaged, and death scorned. With dissent disallowed, *High Noon* conditions total identification with every camera move, thereby mimicking patriotism's narcissism. You are one with Kane (and his truth) as you accompany him step by step to the train depot. The Miller bunch has no idea what awaits it.

TERRIBLE SWIFT SWORD; OR, A MYSTERY IN NEED OF A SOLUTION

With Kane's betrayal final, his earthly resources have been exhausted. In chapter 2, I discussed patriotism's oblique connection to something beyond itself. *High Noon* insinuates a transcendent gesture that provides clues to its power. As we have seen, Kane dismisses all advice to leave. Determined to execute Frank Miller's sentence in disregard of the workings of the legal machinery, Kane would act as Miller's ultimate judge. Yet Kane cannot invoke the law to justify his course. Despite a lifelong commitment to it, the law opposes him. The only authority available to Kane might be God. What other authority would enable him to scorn the express democratic will of Hadleyville? Throughout the film, Kane has been unable to articulate his reasons for staying. Yet with noon's arrival, Kane composes a last will and testament. He writes deliberately. It can't be the usual last will and testament. He has no estate. What little he owns is packed in a wagon. If Kane expresses the truth that has eluded him for the entire film, to whom does he write? Amy deserves an explanation for his stubborn refusal to leave, but she is an unlikely addressee. As far as Kane knows she is on the train to St. Louis and will never see it. Having sealed the envelope, Kane starts the short walk to the train depot—to his death.

But Kane does not die, and once the screen fades to black the film can be retraced—thanks in part to the composition of the shootout. The Miller bunch in the end offered little resistance and posed a minimal threat. Kane shoots Ben Miller dead in anything but a fair fight. Colby makes a suicidal rush on a stable where Kane had taken cover. Amy shoots Pierce in the back while he reloads, effectively murdering him. And thanks to Amy, Kane guns down Frank Miller while Miller does not get off a shot. With the dreaded Miller bunch vanquished by an aging marshal and his pacifist wife, Kane tosses his badge in the dirt and departs. Like the former Soviet Union, the bogeyman in *High Noon* departs history with a whimper rather than a bang.

Once faith in the film's unspoken truths fades, questions emerge about Frank Miller.[20] Consider this a patriot's litmus test. Though convicted of murder, the victim and the circumstances of the crime remain unknown. When Miller was scheduled to hang, politicians commuted his sentence to life and ultimately pardoned him. These judicial actions take place elsewhere, off screen. There is much talk about Miller. He is wild; he is crazy.[21] For the good people of Hadleyville, there is consensus about Miller, who has sworn revenge on Kane. Yet is it possible that Miller's ambition stems from wrongful conviction? Could this be why he was pardoned? Given the film's moral economy, how much confidence can be placed in the townspeople who prosecuted him? These are the same people who supposedly prove themselves cowardly, untrustworthy, and despicable.

Besides, there seems to me a moral subtext at work. It's not so much that Miller committed a brutal crime; it's that he represents a way of life at odds with the now predominant moral norms of Hadleyville. It looks to be a quiet, sleepy town where no one but the marshal wears a gun. Decency prevails. Not everyone desires to live under a regime of virtue, however. On Sunday morning the saloon rivals the church as a destination. Remember Kane's effort to enlist guns. The bar manager speculates on how long it will take Frank Miller to kill him. Enraged, Kane assaults him without warning (an odd recruitment tactic). From the floor, he objects that Kane hides behind his badge and gun. The incident not only offers insight into life in Hadleyville under Kane's rule; it bears on a remark made earlier by the hotel clerk. Waiting for the noon train in the lobby, Amy senses that the clerk does not like her husband and wants to know why. He obliges. For one thing, Kane's rule cost the hotel business. For another, many people think Kane due a comeuppance. To them Miller may even represent justice. Kane and his six deputies brought order to "anarchy" through their killer expertise. The citizens of Hadleyville paid him to employ overwhelming violence on behalf of society, which freed them to devote their time and energy to business and other matters, private matters. They conceded a critical part of civic life to professionals with guns and paid no heed to the remainders of their abdication.

If Kane's concluding violence requires legitimization, what can provide it? Amy may unlock the answer. Awaiting the results of the shootout in

Kane's office, she discovers and reads his last will and testament. Crafted with care, the contents are puzzling. Amy visibly breaks down after reading it. The resolve to oppose her husband that she had dissolves—she picks up a gun moments later. Amy placed herself in harm's way and then violated her most cherished conviction to save Kane's life. Of the two, she was the one who took her wedding vows seriously. She put him first, something he refused to do for her. What words could pack such force? [22]

Since Kane remains convinced until the end that he's right, the testament can't be a mea culpa. You assume that he finally articulates—to posterity—the truth that had previously been inchoate. Throughout the film, he could not name the imperative that had taken hold of him—though he had to bend to its trajectory. Nor could he articulate its character publicly. Perhaps the age in which he lives has witnessed too much change. Capital rules the affairs of men. Incipient industrialization confronts Hadleyville. Even he must join the world of commerce as the old world gives way to the new. This is no longer a world in which Kane's truths flourish. Which truths exactly? For Amy, they would have to be the highest truths.

The townspeople, ironically, assist with the answer to the Kane mystery. Ben Miller's quick death, a veritable execution, brings to mind an earlier scene. After the news about Miller erupts, we first see Hadleyville's residents singing in church. The choir booms with "The Battle Hymn of the Republic." It may be the loudest moment in the film, gunshots included. Verses one and four have been collapsed. They follow each other in rapid, furious sequence, as if to be deposited for later retrieval as the audience rehearses the story's details.

> Mine eyes have seen the glory
> Of the coming of the Lord;
> He is trampling out the vintage
> Where the grapes of wrath are stored
> He hath loosed the fateful lightning
> Of His terrible swift sword
> His truth is marching on.
> He has sounded forth the trumpet
> That shall never call retreat;
> He is sifting out the hearts of men
> Before His judgment seat

Oh, be swift, my soul, to answer Him;
Be jubilant, my feet
Our God is marching on.

The scene appears timely: churchgoers sing aggressive words coinciding with Miller's return. They do not know it, but they sing of Kane. What to them looms in an abstract future has taken concrete form in Hadleyville. The words they sing condemn themselves. God's truth marches on, but they sing in church. The words give meaning to Kane's itineration. His feet move to God's command. Apparently walking in circles of futility as he seeks the town's aid, he generates power with each step taken, the power the audience provides. The town's indifference fuels Kane's determination. Unlike Hadleyville, God knows men. He can see through to their hearts. We can't. We can only know men through their actions. Yet Kane's heart governs his actions. They are one. And thus he is one with God. Kane will pass judgment, as God's agent. Like Socrates with Athens, Kane acts for the town's own good. Unlike Socrates he does not publicly reveal his status as messenger. Kane had informed Amy (early on) that he is the same man with or without the badge. Now we know why. Kane sensed it all along. Perhaps he didn't know it fully until he started to write his last testament. Once Amy reads it, witnessed by God alone, she knows it too. He had a higher obligation that trumped his merely civil wedding contract.[23] She can now pick up a gun because God authorizes it, thus squaring it with her convictions. She did not originally support her husband because she did not recognize him as one of His servants. Amy insisted to Helen that a life with guns was no life at all. When Kane kills Frank Miller, the death sentence handed down five years earlier has been implemented. God's Law: Take life, lose yours. Violence, however, miraculously erases itself in its righteous exercise, or so the film would have you believe.

Kane's patriotic ethos gives new meaning to sacrifice. Consider the price imposed on Amy. Kane dismissed his marriage vows the minute he made them; he forced his wife to repudiate her principles to do his work. Though Kane drops his badge in the street, he takes his gun with them. Death and killing have marked their marriage. Kane's view of the world has refined Amy's. She (had) insisted that guns have no place in life. Having lost her brother and her father to violence, she sought a different kind of world. But the kind of life she pursued rested on certain presumptions, presumptions that the events in Hadleyville compromise. Kane can now "retire" in peace—not because Frank Miller is dead and he and Amy are safe, but because whatever differences they brought into their marriage have been overcome by a transcendent act of violence. Amy picked up the gun at the moment of truth; she cannot simply put it down now. Killing Pierce stained her hand. She murdered a man. Kane's view of the world is now hers too. He made it become hers. He could not convert the town, but he did convert her. They are now one. He can safely look into her eyes and see his own reflection. He can hand her the reins of the buckboard as they leave. Death marks them both.

Like Socrates, Kane too dismissed the possible consequences of his decisions. Having courted death, Kane retreats into his own universe—joined by Amy—and scorns the world around him. Right must establish its presence in the world, and the world provides it with the arena to do so. As the community on whose behalf Kane ostensibly acts is a mere prop, however, its fate ultimately does not concern him. Here Kane's story models Rorty's vision of America acting on the stage of history according to its divine discretion. Slotkin writes: "Instead of vindicating Kane discredits the community, which proves itself unworthy of the sacrifices he has made for it. At the end, Kane contemptuously drops his badge in the dust.... The people have been saved, but they have less value than the man who saved them."[24] I would alter the formulations slightly. If anything, Kane decided to make the town unworthy of the sacrifice he would impose on it. He staged a shootout with a paper tiger and converted it into an occasion for moral spectacle. The irony of the outcome is that Kane, as he consolidates his prior achievement with new death in the streets, exposes the founding fictions of Hadleyville. The invention of the Miller gang brought Hadleyville to life and concealed the violence that it required. The enmity was real; the enemy fictive. Regardless of what Slotkin writes, the people have not been saved. To Kane, moreover, they could not be saved; corrupt from the start, they were already lost. Kane drops the badge in the dirt, where he believes it belongs. Law, a thing of this world, involves ambiguities, complexities, and aporias. This Kane cannot abide. Now content, he retires to the truth of his self-fulfilling prophecy. He leaves town in silence. To speak—to censure—would invite challenge. Kane's action supposedly speaks for itself. It cannot persuade through ex post facto articulation. Kane's final silence reiterates his earlier reticence. If you need truth explained, you cannot understand it. What can you understand? That opposition to truth's irresistibility invites violent reprisal. In the name of deliverance, truth kills.

THE PRESENCE OF THE PATRIOTIC PAST

Steven Spielberg's cinematic monument to the Second World War, *Saving Private Ryan*, cries epic. Designed in the late 1990s as tribute to the war's veterans, the film nevertheless seems incongruous. Whence the need for a self-conscious salute to a war already immortalized in countless films, histories, novels, and documentaries? Do self-evident cultural truths need confirmation and consolidation? If the Second World War enjoyed status as the indisputably good war in the America imaginary, why make this movie?

Political context illuminates the film's origins. Spielberg reconstructs the war as the American Century comes to a close. Not only did the cold war conclude unobtrusively, but the sudden collapse of the Soviet empire called into question the nature of the threat that it allegedly posed. To understand the cold war as a cosmic face-off between good and evil might seem overblown. And now we call into question the war in Vietnam and the trauma with which the country lived in its aftermath. Perhaps the cold war amounted—at best—to a Pyrrhic victory? If you judge a polity by its enemies, what does the peaceful implosion of Soviet Russia say about the United States? As if mimicking Rorty's creative counsel, *Saving Private Ryan* looks to June 6, 1944, D-Day, as the defining moment not only of the twentieth century but of American history tout court. By rewriting the finish to the Second World War, closing it in the fields of France a year early rather than in Asia, Spielberg can simultaneously burnish its status as paradigmatic noble cause, remind the world of its debts to America, revive the century it made possible, and enhance the country's self-conception. Spielberg's Normandy, like Walter Berns's Founding and Rorty's Civil War, offers protean narrative possibilities.[25]

Yet *Saving Private Ryan* reflects more than contemporary political factors. It amounts to an inadvertent confession of patriotic will to truth. In the tradition of *High Noon*, the dominant story line renews and reaffirms the meaning of sacrifice. Spielberg's contribution to the war effort suggests a heroic tale of rescue: save a mother's sole surviving son before death claims him. As the European mission of mercy proceeds, however, the primary threat flows not from the German Army. Despite the stunning, sickening battle sequences, the Wehrmacht barely registers. Real danger wears an American uniform. As such, the film revolves around enmity, the key to the virtue of citizen-soldiers. Evidently patriotism must always be on the alert for new sources of support. To expose the enemy within, the Second World War can be reactivated. Death discloses identity; it makes patriots; it unmasks pretenders. In *Saving Private Ryan* patriotism's narcissistic cruelty ascends. Like the World War II Memorial on Washington's Mall, Spielberg's extravaganza specializes in gratuity. They form a perfect pair. Spielberg's film also forms part of a larger web of patriotic iterations. At once theory, story, film, monument, and history, patriotism presupposes, engenders, and expands itself.

THE COLDEST OF COLD MONSTERS

Saving Private Ryan opens at a French military cemetery. Normandy. Spielberg's camera locks on the eyes of an anonymous American, a veteran, on his knees, overcome by emotion. He stares. No blinking. Reliving the past, eyes wide open suggest that you will see the truth of war, at last. Assisted by the validation of flashback, this man will be our guide.[26]

Spielberg studied Defense Department footage to stage his rendering of Normandy. The beach sequence states the film's claim to authenticity, even though Spielberg insists that his is a pale facsimile of the invasion. Appalled by the euphemistic treatments that tend to characterize war in general and Normandy in particular, Spielberg reinvents both on film. Even if you share Spielberg's judgment of the antiseptic character of American films about the Second World War, it does not explain the making of *Saving Private Ryan*. Thanks to Oliver Stone and Stanley Kubrick, for example, the ontological superficiality of American war movies has long been known. Spielberg's representational ambition nonetheless presumes to bring the full truth of war to an innocent world in need of civic education. Hence the graphic, even sadistic, performance of *Saving Private Ryan* cannot be reduced to tribute alone. It is shock therapy designed for immediate results. Spielberg seizes an opportunity to implicate the American citizenry and induce a sense of indebtedness, and thus of attachment. With America a debtor nation to the so-called Greatest Generation, payment must be made. Given historical ignorance, the visceral dimension underlies his cinematographic intervention. You must see what American men at war experience; you must see what men at war do. Though no simulation of war can duplicate the lived experience of it, Spielberg has executed a cinematic coup in the name of patriotism.[27]

How, specifically, does Spielberg work his film's patriotic will? The invasion sequence forms a veritable film within the film. From an angle, you first see waves washing ashore past massive cement barricades. Yet what is most noticeable is the sound.[28] The ocean roars at you. Sound makes war into a closed universe. Hermetically sealed with primitive motions and movements, it is a world outside of which nothing exists. War constitutes a pre-moral, pre-linguistic space. The sound also displays vicious precision. At times it feels as if the fate of every bullet fired has been individually recorded. Their speed, intensity, and energy deconstruct not just bodies but psyches.[29]

Cut to a landing craft bouncing toward the beach. The strain of its overworked engines coupled with the sound of metal slamming on water assaults you. The pilot shouts instructions. Men look somber, grim. There is no banter here, none of the macho glibness of Hollywood war legend. It is physically impossible. You cannot even hear yourself think. The sound beats you. Spielberg's invasion sequence de-romanticizes war. Here men puke as they get closer to shore. One eruption triggers another. And another. Everyone wears it. You can smell it. More instruction—from Miller, an Army captain. In this context, however, instructions prove useless; nothing can be heard; no one listens.

As the landing craft opens, machine gun fire sprays its inhabitants. The sound escalates. Beach landing equals survival exercise. No heroics. Contingency is god. This is slaughter. Before every body aboard is massacred, the captain orders everyone over the sides. (Just do what everyone else does.) Water provides no safety. Bullets follow you underneath, piercing fluid with surgical precision. If bullets don't kill you, your pack drowns you. There is no escape. Sheer numbers: some survive—not everyone can be killed. When your country asks you to die for it, sometimes it means precisely and only that. Some bodies are killed so others won't be. Thousands are nothing more than dead bodies waiting to happen.[30]

On the beach, death mounts. You are treated to grisly scenes. With explosions omnipresent, bodies hurl through the air. A soldier loses the lower half of his right arm; then retrieves it. Miller pulls a wounded man out of the water—to discover the lower half blown off. He drops it. You do not see Rorty's would-be John Waynes. You see bodies dictated by necessity. To carry on names a feat in itself. In the safety of the theater, you want the invasion sequence to end—now. You hope you survive the awful experience of watching it.

The invasion sequence of *Saving Private Ryan* makes you watch as long as possible, as if to account for each cross in the Normandy cemetery. With the landing concluded, you marvel at its success. An irresistible force (America) supplanted an immovable object (Germany). The sentimental cemetery scene followed by the brutal beach action form the flip sides to the same patriotic apparatus. You identify with the first; the second makes it possible. America's exceptionalism presupposes America's vast military prowess. To love one is to love the other. Anything that potentially threatens the power that makes possible America's goodness invites a reactive, even reactionary, response. Spielberg's cinematizes what patriots already experience, the affirmation of whatever violence may be needed to guarantee the American way.[31]

The first thirty minutes of *Saving Private Ryan* form the cinematic counterpart to Friedrich St. Florian's super-sized World War II Memorial. In Normandy's immediate aftermath, American soldiers look down on the carnage and human debris; they agree it's "quite a site." Three days later, as Miller departs on his goodwill mission, the same site is reviewed again; order has supplanted chaos. Blue water, previously red, laps on shore. Corpses have been retrieved. Troops move in unison. Trucks haul freight. The Army is on the go. Nothing can stop it. Signs of the invasion have been erased. Nothing untidy remains. This is what American power, properly amassed, can do. Creative destruction perfected, it removes all traces of its exercise. Rorty would approve of its godlike aspect.

With Normandy secured, Miller receives new orders. After the horrors just witnessed, the film needs a redemptive story. Nausea must be converted to righteous anger and channeled. This is Spielberg's forte. The war, you learn, has taken a heavy toll on one particular family. Three of four brothers have been killed in a two-week period. Back in Washington the Army chief of staff, George Marshall, decides to extricate Private James Ryan and send him home before Mrs. Ryan loses all her boys. Individual life remains sacred, and the country must honor it by rescuing Ryan regardless of military necessity or logic. American generosity matches its military might. Rather than simply issue an order, Marshall turns to his bible, where he stores a letter that President Lincoln wrote to a northern mother who lost all five sons during the civil war. Professing the futility of solace, Lincoln nonetheless thanks her on behalf of the grateful republic they served and for which they died. Deftly mixing religion and politics, Lincoln intimates that comfort can be found in God, who must look charitably upon her sacrifice at "the altar of freedom," a sacrifice that Lincoln insists must be a source of "solemn pride." Primed to best Lincoln, Marshall, in a leap of faith, decides that Ryan is alive. Doing God's work, could he be anything else?

Thus patriotism demands the personal touch. American power, reduced and refined, now concentrates on the effort to rescue one boy for his mother. The true mark of greatness lies in the details. America is to be defined by the little things—like saving Ryan. The war to end "tyranny and oppression" thus pauses at a pivotal moment for an ethical task. It can spare a few good men. The mission can't be justified. Everyone from Marshall on down to Ryan himself knows it. And this is precisely the point. It is an act of grace. This war, Spielberg's Second World War, exudes unmerited goodness.

Saving Private Ryan, spectacular battle sequences notwithstanding, might be another run-of-the-mill patriotic encomium were it not for a disconcerting paradox. Private Ryan, more occasion than cause, is not the centerpiece of Spielberg's morality tale. The mission itself, rather, offers an opportunity for a broader revelation about the place of enmity in patriotic understandings. Thus one of the men, a Corporal Upham, assigned to assist Ryan's deliverance, grounds Spielberg's civic sermon. Thanks to Upham's role in the Ryan diversion, the war takes a curious turn. Nazi Germany, it soon becomes apparent, loses its place of privilege as America's principal enemy. The country must look inward to locate its greatest danger. The vilification of Upham—the strange power accorded the weak—energizes and stabilizes the remainder of the film. Thus Spielberg's extensive treatment of Upham furnishes insight into patriotism's logic. Reconstructing Upham's story reveals patriotism's necessary cruelty. If the audience resents Hadleyville in *High Noon*, it rages at Upham in

Saving Private Ryan. But with the numbing effect of Spielberg's spectacular set battle pieces, the contrapuntal details of Upham's odyssey, which run counter to the dominant story line, may pass unremarked.

Upham, cartographer and translator, works safely behind the lines at a desk in the least manly of military trades. Escorted ashore in France after the invasion, he is recruited by Miller for the Ryan mission, you learn, because Miller "needs" someone fluent in French and German. The introduction of Miller and Upham announces the trajectory of the film. Upham resists field assignment; his expertise lies elsewhere. Though he hasn't fired a gun since basic training, Miller doesn't care. Ordered to assemble his gear, Upham takes the command literally and tries to bring the tools of his trade, typewriter included. Miller holds up a pencil. Bring a helmet, Miller advises. Upham nervously grabs a German model. Miller flags the slip of the helmet. Marked for the audience, Upham makes the switch. You know he will betray Miller and thus America; you just don't know when or how high the cost. Alas, among the melting pot of American fighting men, Upham is an intellectual—cultured, effete, awkward, clumsy, effeminate, German-speaking—with a hint of a Bavarian accent, he boasts. Whereas Normandy negates speech, Upham represents speech's perverse perfection, articulate to the point of being verbose. While others fight and die, he writes a novel on a subject he cannot know or experience: the bonds of brotherhood formed at war. The world according to Upham is not just fiction; it is false, the product of thought and reflection. At their minimal best, words express truths found within. Upham imports his words; they are concocted, a lie.

Finding Ryan requires faith. In the meantime, Spielberg's apparently random collection of war incidents evinces a pattern. As Upham takes over the film, the tribute to the Second World War assumes ominous form. Miller and Company stumble across a reinforced German bunker. Miller orders it neutralized. They are still fighting the war, despite appearances. Reluctantly, unhappily, his men obey. Upham stays behind with the gear. As the assault unfolds, Upham spies the action through a sniper's scope. Once again, he lurks behind the lines at a safe remove. He risks nothing; Upham as voyeur.

The attack's success generates a friendly fatality and a German prisoner. Miller's men demand his summary execution—to balance the scales and sate their growing anger at Ryan. Miller balks. "Not yet," he says. He'll be questioned, put to work digging graves, then shot. Upham now comes to life, from cipher to moral censor. He converts simple wartime decision into moral quandary and would-be crisis. Self-righteously he pleads the prisoner's humanitarian case. Risk limited, he can endure the wrath of his fellows, though he cannot fight next to them. Miller orders him to help the POW bury the dead. Upham's identification with the enemy tightens.

When Upham is next seen with the German, they share a smoke and a friendly chat—in German. Fraternizing with the enemy, Upham seems more simpatico with the German than with his fellow Americans. Miller's men march to the burial site, murder in the air. The German begs for his life. No one is moved—except Upham. He again registers his protest. Surrendering soldiers cannot be executed, he intones. It violates the rules of war. Upham, now a man among men, challenges Miller. Miller relents— ignoring both the anger of his men and the danger of release. It is only a matter of time before this decision rebounds with deadly effects. We all know it. The scene's point: incite anger at Upham and prepare for the escalation to come. Though Miller makes the decision, responsibility has already been assigned to Upham.[32]

In Spielberg's hands, Upham resembles the townspeople of Hadleyville assembled at church. Speech, tantamount to perpetual postponement, negates action. In short, Upham alchemizes the battlefield into a debating society, rendering the obvious complex. Upham cannot appreciate that the country's ideals require defense and not interrogation during times of crisis, especially war. American identity and the values expressive of it enable action. Deeds that might appear to challenge them thus fail to register. Patriotic logic makes America's virtue unassailable (the war itself proves it). Upham's double offense: he levels a moral accusation where no moral issue exists.

Eventually Ryan appears, one of a handful of men defending a strategic bridge at "Ramelle." A German offensive imminent, they must hold it. Once informed of Miller's mission, Ryan refuses to leave and says his mother would understand his desire to remain and fight alongside the only brothers he has left. Ryan's refusal to leave nicely vindicates Marshall's decision to save him. Virtue inspires virtue and becomes its own patriotic reward.

At Ramelle Spielberg follows Rorty's patriotic storytelling advice and concocts a myth independent of the history that funds it. The bridge turns out to be critical; the war's outcome hinges on its retention. The road to victory follows a path from Normandy via Ramelle to Paris and Berlin. Only the loss of the bridge can stop the Allies. The war ends one way or another here, now. Not 1945. Thus saving Ryan pays unexpected dividends. By saving him they can save the war. It's as if an invisible patriotic hand were at work.

Rortyan fiction at its best, *Saving Private Ryan* may not be true, but it reveals truth nonetheless. Overmatched by the Germans, Miller devises a desperate, dangerous plan. The odds are overwhelming, but you take the chance you have. The juxtaposition of Ryan and Upham governs the film's conclusion. Ryan insisted on staying and refused to leave. Upham, hesitant from the start, resisted going. Yet Upham keys the defense plan. Excluded from the actual killing, he must supply ammunition to others— wherever and whenever needed. With a mobile defense, he must be the man on the spot. In contrast to Normandy's randomness, here success and failure can be reduced to a question of will. Patriotism makes heroes and cowards of everyone. Death and death alone defines you. Spielberg indulges what Fred Zinnemann refuses to do in *High Noon*: he makes reputed cowards fight.

Frightened though effective for much of the decisive battle, fear eventually overwhelms Upham. He fails to assist Mellish, who is locked in hand-to-hand combat. Upham, paralyzed, can hear the life-and-death struggle but does not move. Armed with a rifle, he cannot bring himself to use his weapon of war. Impotent, he totes it around like excess luggage. The camera lingers on him; and lingers; and lingers some more. He cannot even put finger to trigger. Upham's inaction galls the viewer, especially since helping Mellish involves no risk to himself. Though fearless when defending a German after battle, Upham panics when faced with saving an American in battle. Mellish fights on for what seems like an eternity. He is stabbed through the heart, the blade pornographically penetrating his breastbone. Upham lets the Jew perish. After Mellish's death (what amounts to an exquisitely staged murder, because of Upham's responsibility), the German exits, passing Upham on the stairs. Upham makes no move. The German knows his guilty secret. They too become allies. Upham removes his hand from the rifle and the German walks safely past. Spielberg's focus achieves sadistic proportions. If the Normandy invasion induces viewers to leave their seats and head for the exits, the sequence with Mellish induces viewers to leap from their seats and rush the screen. There is no quarter for patriotism's enemies. As David Brooks stated, patriots are revealed by what they hate. Spielberg makes it nearly impossible not to hate Upham. Insofar as Spielberg pursues Rorty's patriotic storytelling ethos, to tell the best of America, how does the film find itself here?

Since Upham cannot be killed, as the battle climaxes he cowers behind a dirt mound within arm's length of the enemy. At last the German POW whom Upham befriended and saved reappears. You watch him fire the kill shot into Captain Miller. Upham also sees what you see, though in the chaos of war both events amount to sheer nonsense. Nevertheless, the result perfects Upham's narrative abasement and stokes the viewer's outrage.[33] Having survived the contingency of Normandy, Miller deserved a fitting denouement, not the meaningless, gratuitous death attributable to Upham. War's brutal randomness has given way to identifiable responsibility. Ironically, the moral order that Normandy suspended has been restored at Ramelle, with Upham as the scapegoat.

America naturally survives Upham's repeated betrayals. Reinforcements arrive at the last possible saving moment. Finally, with the Germans repulsed, Upham springs to action. He "captures" a handful of retreating infantrymen all too willing to surrender. The POW recognizes Upham, who summarily executes him and releases the rest. With a craven act, a futile attempt at self-vindication, Upham violates the principles for which he had previously argued. There is no justice here, not even revenge. To displace his guilt, in a false show of fortitude, he murders the German. Such cowardice proves that America's Uphams have no place in war. The critical moral ideas that they painstakingly create about it, which might be turned against patriotism, become equally misplaced—not just irrelevant, but dangerous. Upham has much American blood on his ideals.

THE PATRIOTIC SHALL INHERIT AMERICA

Upham's fate is disconcerting. Why did Spielberg force Miller to bring him? He may have been a convenience, but a translator was unnecessary and Miller relied on his own map-reading skills. Why, then, force an Upham into such a context? In Spielberg's optic, war identifies the definitive setting for life. What you do in it uniquely marks you. Spielberg even has Upham agree. Early in the film, in a moment of pseudo-Nietzschean bravado, Upham decides that war experience will be good for him. Quoting Emerson, Upham intones that war educates the senses, perfects the body, and animates the will. Perhaps, but Spielberg places demands on Upham that he cannot meet. Nominally a soldier, suited for a place behind the lines nowhere near a weapon, Upham is set up for a fall by Spielberg, who then holds him accountable. Failure is treated as his and his alone. Upham emerges as Ryan's other. Ryan vindicates the efforts made on his behalf because he rejected them. Upham confirmed suspicions of him by being concerned above all with his own safety and survival. The war was not good for him nor was he good for it. Patriotism is another story.

Spielberg refuses to let story alone do his normative work. At film's end, patriotism's narcissism requires a summary voiceover to double the moral point. Thus with battle decided and Miller dead, General Marshall composes a Lincolnesque letter to Mrs. Ryan. Her son, the hero who chose to remain, is well and heading home. The words resound over a shot of Ryan, Miller, and Upham. As Marshall's reading proceeds, the frame squeezes Upham from it. He survived too, but Marshall's patriotic words do not cover him. To keep Upham in the frame with Ryan and Miller would demean and subvert them. The Republic has no gratitude for such men.

Given the nature of war, however, it is the Uphams of the world who require protection. They cannot protect themselves, especially in a battle between totalitarianism and democracy. Moreover, whatever separates Miller, the teacher, and Upham, the writer, cannot be attributed to them. Both read Emerson and know Edith Piaf. Each experiences bodily breakdown. Each succumbs to his emotions. But Miller, who breaks down after battle, wills himself into a soldier, or so the film would have you believe. Upham, of course, fails. Is the fiction of the will the difference that makes a patriotic difference? If so, Upham represents the other of American identity. He must be concocted for America to achieve its virtuous realization in Miller and Ryan. Though America's creation and responsibility, America disavows him. It both needs and disdains Upham. America must have it both ways. The good war, the moral war, turns out to be fully neither.

Perhaps, then, it's time to reconsider the self-conception of *Saving Private Ryan*. American ideals drive the mission to save Ryan. Marshall's decision seems to be an act of charity in a context that refuses it. Yet six men were knowingly sacrificed to keep Ryan alive. Can the toll be justified? With subordinates, Marshall pulls rank. Pressed to justify his decision, he cuts off conversation. He does not have to answer to them, or to anyone, for the mission. What would Marshall have to say to the mothers of those killed to save Ryan? Would they love their country? Marshall does both right and wrong. This is the moral ambiguity that Spielberg's patriotic tale cannot abide—whether in the mission or in the war.

The film closes where it began, at Miller's grave. John Schaar's conception of patriotism governs the discourse. Ryan reveals that not a day passes when he does not reflect on what Miller said to him as he lay dying. He has tried to live a good life, as Miller implored him to do, to earn the sacrifice others made for him. "I hope that at least in your eyes I've earned what all of you have done for me." Patriotism's logic, however, requires that Ryan himself be saluted. He served his country honorably and well, even refusing to return home early when ordered. Because he forms part of the greatest generation, he is part of the generation owed. How did he incur debt? Since he has served, Miller's dying injunction might be considered excessive, cruel even. Miller himself could not identify proper recompense for the debt allegedly incurred; does he understand the burden he has placed on Ryan? How could anyone possibly earn his life given the death of so many fine men? What if Ryan could not repay the debt imposed? Must he make payments in perpetuity? If so, what kind of debt demands payment without end? Such debt seems no longer the condition of possibility of life. It becomes a kind of indentured servitude, the antithesis of life.

High Noon and *Saving Private Ryan* tell tales to make America proud of itself. They belong in Richard Rorty's civic canon. Thanks to these films, the political moral of the cinematic story remains the same: patriotism, love of country, entails the ultimate sacrifice, life. The obligation to death, to kill and be killed, in turn reveals enmity's critical role in patriotic affections and attachments. Patriotism at its finest and patriotism at its worst commingle. The civic commitment that patriotism names secures and consolidates itself at the expense of those created specifically to bring it to life. Null without opposition, patriotism must have resistance, and enemies. In *High Noon* Will Kane needs Amy, the Millers, and Hadleyville. In *Saving Private Ryan* Steven Spielberg relies on Upham more than on the German army. I offer these reflections because America's remainders, Amy's faith, Hadleyville's democracy, Upham's dissent and decency disappear in the final accounting, mere byproducts of the country's inherent virtue. Patriotism's insistent self-regard makes it ignorant of its cost to what it purports to love. America might be less pure but better served if it were loved a little less.

Democracy has no monuments. It strikes no medals. It bears the head of no man on a coin.—JOHN ADAMS

And in any case, is it the truth or simply the falsehood of a society which one learns from its monuments?—ROBERT HARBISON

Indeed I tremble for my country when I reflect that God is just.
—THOMAS JEFFERSON, *Jefferson Memorial Inscription*

The American Memorial/Monument Complex I: The Architecture of Democratic Monuments

5 On the Washington Mall, the practice of commemoration disappoints. Informed and animated by an artless love of country, public memorial architecture specializes—with some exceptions—in the bland, the banal, and the big. Anchored in singular events of the past, commemoration's temporal aim tends to point elsewhere. To honor sacrifice, to mourn loss, to acknowledge achievement, to remember courage, to recall cost, to identify danger, to reiterate principle: these myriad architectural performances speak foremost to a time—to generations—to come. Accordingly, public political space lends itself to what is considered worthy of recognition and remembrance, and worthiness tends to be construed narrowly, jealously. In short, the practice of commemoration reveres and in so doing fabulates the past that it creates. Rorty's call for patriotic stories saluting the best of America finds consummate response on the Mall.

Commemorative reverence implies what may be the dominant assumption and priority informing the dynamics of memorialization at the nation's monumental core: settlement and finalization. To be carved or written in stone signals confidence, certainty, and the will to resolution. If, however, history, to say nothing of politics, renders dubious the project of settlement, then monuments not only describe and express, they fabricate as well—even if they routinely deny doing so. Consequently, with a pretense of settlement concealing a plethora of turbulence, the pretense tends toward exaggeration. Thus monuments prove troubling not only because they tend to offer a reduced, univocal account of a particular subject or theme, but also because they offer themselves as superior—because settled—renderings. Isn't this the condition of possibility of building or, on occasion, the impetus behind building? If so, monuments reflect forces and considerations other than the ostensible subject matter that precipitated them. Speaking to larger sets of concerns, they become as much occasions as causes. Truth here calls for an absence of doubt, hesitation, complication, ambiguity, or ambivalence. Matters commemorative, by nature hallowed, prefer to shun murkiness. The World War II Memorial may well represent the architectural apotheosis of this unthinking patriotic phenomenon. It is not so much, as James S. Russell suggests, the labyrinthine bureaucratic process of statutory advice and consent coupled with the need to reconcile and mollify powerful political factions that imprisons aesthetic and ethical possibilities on the Mall.[1] Rather what constricts architectural life on the Mall is the backdrop of patriotism—a thicket of presumptions, pressures, imperatives largely unexamined and uncontested.

Moreover, the practice of commemorating, however serious and solemn, can often be tantamount to self-celebration, mere glorifying and aggrandizement; in other words, narcissism. Glorification also tends to involve blindness, and at its worst bellicosity. This feature of commemoration may be obscured by its other components, but to ignore its presence raises ethical and political problems—for a democratic order in particular. Manifestations of pride, from an alternative angle of vision, may project arrogance, cruelty, and violence. Commemoration, I argue, can be a time not just for one-dimensional recognition and remembrance but also for reflection and examination. In the absence of one, the other may prove antithetical to democracy.

In short, because of the complicated investment inherent to commemoration, expressive peril lurks. Commemoration may be uniquely vulnerable to self-referential temptations precisely because the subject of remembrance often possesses legitimate title to spectacular, righteous, historical status; because celebration seems not only warranted but fitting and obligatory. Commemoration can all too easily become an opportunity to indulge the inclination or compulsion to see yourselves as you would like to be seen. Thus commemoration, as ordinarily practiced, tends to be insufficient. Selective and self-serving, it routinely insults and injures the democracy it would otherwise honor. Hence the dilemma that commemoration at its best faces: how to combine the high and low, commendable and atrocious, noble and base? For even great accomplishments entail that which subverts them. The recognition of painful truths does not compromise or undo commemoration. It can make it more impressive, as verisimilitude supplants wishful thinking. Thus civic space as a collective testament can flourish, by enacting what may be the most difficult, demanding value of a democracy: autocritique.

If successful, civic commemorative space, as it bestows recognition, can also engender disruption among the contending perspectives and diverse energies of a democratic political culture. Rather than privilege consensus—the lowest common denominator of commemorative politics—civic space can work to actualize democratic commitments.[2] Because of the agonism governing commemoration, a monument or memorial that fails to instigate multiple constituencies ought to be viewed with suspicion. It could even be considered an affront to democratic citizenship. Concerned with the state of commemoration in Washington, I explore the politics of the World War II Memorial and consider its narrative impact on the monumental core where, not surprisingly, it complements the Washington and the Lincoln. I plan to problematize this happy union. Taking the Memorial on its own terms, I subject it to critique and argue that it does not live up to its profession of values. I then offer suggestions for a reconstructed World War II Memorial more faithful to the democratic ethos that haunts it. The architectural thought experiments offered here may seem distant to the dominant sensibility governing the Mall, but I would argue otherwise in light of both the isolated instances of architectural candor on the Mall and developments in the nation's "heartland" where memorial experimentation finds freer rein.

MEMORIAL PENUMBRAS

The World War II Memorial enjoys—from every indication—enormous national approval. Because of the war's significance, it demands not just recognition but applause. At the Memorial's groundbreaking ceremony, Bob Dole, a prominent sponsor, articulated one of the ideas behind building a monument fifty-five years after the fighting concluded. The Second

World War generation finds itself fast disappearing. Over sixteen million served; close to six million remain alive, though dying at the rate of a thousand a day. As Dole observed: "In another 55 years there won't be anyone around to bear witness."[3] Monumental tribute to America's recently nicknamed Greatest Generation could wait no longer.

Dole's sentiments about the World War II Memorial resonate with Richard Rorty's recent political philosophizing on behalf of the American left. Rorty proposes self-conscious patriotic mythmaking. Since democratic citizenship is in such dismal condition, the mainsprings of political action require careful cultivation. He regards it as indispensable for American democracy that "inspiring stories about episodes . . . in the nation's past" be told and retold. In the twentieth century one event stands alone. During the Second World War the forces of democracy and dictatorship squared off in apocalyptic contest. What could be more appropriate than a monument to a war as epic as the cause itself was noble and just? A story told in stone forever: American power deployed for great purpose.[4] Though the Second World War exacted a terrible destructive cost and terrific sacrifices, American power ultimately proved to be creative in character. Not only did it save freedom at home, but it paved the way for miraculous rebirth in Germany and Japan as enemies were converted into friends. America's "moral identity" (Rorty's term) received perhaps its finest definition. The country saved the world when it could easily have turned away, as some isolationists advocated. America justified itself as Rorty's "vanguard of human history," deploying power godlike in nature. When the war concluded, America looked at what it had done and called it good. We pleased even ourselves. And this was just the beginning.[5]

For the Second World War, what kind of monument would be apt? According to Charles Krauthammer, no conceivable memorial could be excessive to its recipients. "They did, after all, save the world." If anything, architectural injustice posed the real danger. Krauthammer thus objected to the proposed site on the Mall. Compromises had to be made to ensure that the Memorial harmonized with its neighbors. Contra untold critics, this guaranteed its relative puniness. Krauthammer preferred a site on the eastern edge of Arlington National Cemetery because it could accommodate a fitting monument; in other words, there would be no spatial restrictions: "[It] could be the site of a triumphal arch or some other unapologetically bold architectural element."[6]

Trouble ensues, of course, with any effort to bring a monumental idea to life. The Memorial's design and location triggered criticism, protests, and lawsuits. The design, critics contended, was overbearing, exuding arrogance and resembling the imperial fascist style favored and perfected by the Nazi architect-in-chief Albert Speer.[7] How could America honor the Second World War by mimicking the tastes of its defeated enemy? The location would spoil the stunning vistas between the Lincoln and the Washington.[8] The possibility of an aesthetic offense began to haunt the Mall. The location, it was said, would compromise the Mall as a site of moral and political protest. What of marches and demonstrations once the Memorial opened? Why not select another site for the Memorial that could equally do it justice, as the American Battle Monuments Commission and the National Capital Planning Commission had both concluded? Many were determined to save the Mall from the menace of the World War II Memorial—to no avail.

Criticism of the Memorial floundered—in part—because objections to its grandiosity recommended it to supporters, who insisted that the Memorial would fit nicely with its Mall neighbors. Expressing mild surprise, they argued that "its vertical dimensions are modest in relation to the principal visual features of the Mall: the elms, the Lincoln Memorial, the Washington Monument, and the Mall itself."[9] The profession of modesty may have been disingenuous—the Memorial's twin arches stand forty-one feet tall and its fifty-six pillars seventeen feet tall—but the World War II Memorial did a fine impersonation of Ronald Reagan's Teflon presidency: no criticism stuck.

Consider Krauthammer again: "To memorialize what was not just America's finest hour but, in many ways, America's most important hour, an event whose revolutionary effect on American life and society, on everything from atomic science and aviation to race and gender roles, is acutely felt to this day."[10] The World War II Memorial both complements and completes the Washington and the Lincoln in that the Second World War represents the nation's third Founding. Behold the symbolic movement of the three memorials: the Washington signifies the birth of the country, the introduction of life. British rule overthrown, the freedom delivered entered the world imperfect, incomplete. Think of the Washington as ideal unrealized. The Lincoln announces rebirth. Hence the Gettysburg Address inscribed on one of the temple walls. Freedom extends across the land as the flaws of the founding recede. The World War II Memorial salutes the age of maturation and responsibility. Freedom reigns beyond America's borders with the defeat of unparalleled evil. The global mission that Hamilton declared in the *Federalist* comes to fruition as remote futurity arrives. According to America's genealogy, the World War II Memorial becomes the last piece of a tripartite architectural archipelago on the Mall.[11] To locate it elsewhere would be to defeat its monumental reason for being.[12]

Not coincidentally, the World War II Memorial affects more than the Washington and the Lincoln. Though the chronology of American military history in the twentieth century runs from the Second World War and Korea to Vietnam, symbolic incarnation on the Mall reverses this sequence. In effect, the World War II Memorial completes the response, architectural and political, to the Vietnam Wall that began with the Korean.[13] Ironically, what came first historically emerges last memorially, and by coming last recovers what came first memorially but last historically. The World War II Memorial's untimeliness becomes timely as it offers commemorative redemption. After all, America established its global hegemony after the Second World War and, energized by its newfound place of privilege, prosperity, and power, embarked on a forty-five-year cold war conflict, which included Korea and Vietnam. Self-styled patriots like Rorty treat the Asia wars as regional manifestations of this larger conflict. To deny these wars their due contextualization distorts them. Otherwise, even on Rorty's account, Vietnam, for example, amounts to senseless slaughter on a genocidal scale—not suitable material for the kind of narrative that Rorty sanctions.[14]

The World War II Memorial, as it induces awe, alters the architectural reception of its predecessors. The crowning achievement of a political and aesthetic triangle that incorporates the Korean and the Vietnam, it draws on the Washington and Lincoln for geopolitical support.[15] Consider its relation to the Korean. James S. Russell finds the Korean Memorial grossly inadequate, a sop to popular taste and pressure. Lacking subtlety and nuance, it is a dismal follow-up to the power and profundity of Maya Lin's Wall. Russell writes of the American soldiers on patrol at the Korean: "These mawkish images do not help visitors to unravel the ambiguities of this 'police action'; they help them to pity the inhabitants."[16] Russell's perceptiveness notwithstanding, the Korean Memorial works hard to elicit pity and tap into presumptive notions of American goodness. Thus what Russell identifies as one of the Memorial's definitive artistic weaknesses may also name one of its consumer or tourist strengths.[17] In the wake of World War II (the Memorial, that is), the Mall's hitherto strange commitment to and presentation of Korea achieves grandeur. Flush with power—but also fatigued—after a global conflict, America comes to the aid of a distant people in the name of freedom. America embraced global responsibility as the burden imposed by the Second World War and paid the price. The Rortyan narrative now finds expression on the Mall. No more Vietnams indeed.

The noble sensibility carries over to the Vietnam Memorial *complex*. Approached via the Korean, the Three Soldiers greet you. Young and naïve, they too traveled an enormous distance to an unknown land to assist a people in need. They have no idea what awaits them. The answer can be found at the Women's Memorial, where one of their comrades bleeds to death. It points toward the vertex of the Wall. America's global mission may have produced tragic results, but Vietnam's execution should not be confused with its intent. The 58,000 names of honored dead on the Wall live at the apex, if also the nadir, of the trajectory that commenced with victory in the Second World War. Vietnam fades as an aberration; it folds neatly into a larger context that the World War II Memorial resurrects and consolidates. The Dole generation, at least on the Mall, aspires to the last word on the Vietnam War, its war.

YET ANOTHER EFFORT, AMERICANS, IF YOU WOULD BE PATRIOTIC

The life and times of the World War II Memorial reveal, though unwittingly, the problematic aspects of a self-conscious patriotic icon. Nicolaus Mills has written a comprehensive narrative account of the memorial's conception, struggle for life, and emergence. The title chosen signals the saga related: *Their Last Battle: The Fight for the National World War II Memorial.* An all-American story of tribulation and triumph, Mills's tale is one that Rorty could well admire. And that is precisely the problem. Once again it seems that patriotism in its very unfolding exposes and defeats itself in ways to which it is blind. The story that Mills tells features an epic struggle between right and wrong, a set of enemies who refuse to acknowledge defeat, and the inevitable, yet scintillating victory of the greatest generation liberating the national Mall.

Mills's book consists of three parts: a tribute to the Second World War generation; a generous appraisal of the World War II Memorial; and a celebratory narrative with separate standing as a patriotic artifact. *Their Last Battle* provides a triple dose of patriotism's narcissism: a patriotic book about a patriotic object for a patriotic generation which ultimately becomes its own patriotic reason for being. With a "cast of characters," including Tom Hanks of *Saving Private Ryan*, whose campaigning and fundraising efforts were critical to the Memorial's success, Mills's book is also a script that mimics Spielberg's film. At home across genres, patriotism builds redundancy into the very structure of its operations.

Situated in the late 1980s, Mills's drama has a simple premise: the lack of a national memorial to the Second World War as scandal. With so many veterans dying annually, the need for correction is immediate. Perhaps Mills's favorite refrain is this: the World War II Memorial will take longer to get approval than it took American forces to win the war itself.[18] The country's homegrown enemies (lumped together under the term "opponents") include the usual suspects: liberals, progressives, academics, politicians, architecture critics, and lawyers. Through their opposition, they too produce casualties.[19] Responsibility for death aside, Mills dismisses the politics of the World War II Memorial. After all, the Mall's history includes contestation. The most popular memorial destinations all experienced great controversy. And since every memorial project ultimately built first generates controversy, controversy names a phase not to be taken seriously. Thus normalized, what Mills considers contemporary political correctness can be marginalized. Mills converts real opposition, in other words, into opposition for opposition's sake.[20]

Mills's story begins with the site. When the National Park Service first proposed a list of potential locations for the World War II Memorial, the Rainbow Pool, its ultimate location, did not register. With alternative sites eliminated one by one for political or patriotic reasons, the conclusory judgment formed that the Memorial required the Rainbow Pool. No other location could do it justice; the Second World War itself demanded privilege for the Memorial in relation to the Vietnam and the Korean.[21] If anything, the prior placements of these memorials dictated destination. The World War II Memorial's site was veritably forced upon it.[22]

Likewise, the memorial competition seemed designed to produce a specific outcome. Competition rules favored established powerhouses in the memorial business.[23] Design was secondary. The criteria were justified on the grounds that with such a huge project it was necessary for the applicants to prove in advance that they could deliver the goods on time. The immensity of the undertaking also required no repetition of the Vietnam Veterans Memorial. Maya Lins need not apply.[24]

Thus death too governed the competition. The Memorial, situated between the Father of the Country to the east and the Savior of the Country to the west, demanded unequivocal grandiosity. In view of Friedrich St. Florian's success, the alternative designs suffered from intrinsic flaws. Since they did not project American power, they effectively eliminated themselves.[25] More problematic still, they made the tragedy of war—its cost, its destructiveness, its ineffability—integral to their conceptions. One featured a statue of a grieving mother; another a glass star to mimic the stars that people hung in their windows during the war to signify loss; a third a combination of fire and water, producing a mist that suggested both war's violence and its hazy conclusion; and a fourth a bell colonnade to evoke a sound landscape of restraint and reverence.

Ironically, St. Florian's original memorial scheme flirted with a "tragic" sensibility.[26] Considering the final product, the details may be surprising: the capitals of the pillars that ring the Memorial in matching semicircles were despoiled, to signify the death that war brings; and the western edge housed a cenotaph to face the Lincoln Memorial. Behind the cenotaph, furthermore, St. Florian envisioned a cratered piece of basalt stone. War thus assumed explicit physical dimensions. These gestures to death, suffering, and destruction did not survive. The World War II Memorial's overseers refused to countenance what they perceived as contradiction.[27] Nevertheless, do not for a minute believe that Washington's architectural bureaucracies compromised St. Florian's design. Rather, his thinking evolved. St. Florian credits the influence of Benjamin Forgey, architecture critic for the *Washington Post*: "He said a memorial is not a school. It is a shrine. A memorial is not to teach. It is to inspire."[28] Governance of the affective experience would not admit ambiguity.

1. America's colonial possessions, World War II Memorial.
Photo courtesy of Bob G.

Mills's narrative trajectory leads to a predictable conclusion. Having conflated criticism of site selection and design specifics with opposition to a Memorial per se, having summarily dismissed every substantive criticism offered of the Memorial, having arrogated to himself patriotic credentials and reduced contestation to partisan self-interest, Mills would provide a public service and fix the Memorial with a single irresistible interpretation.[29] For example, he claims that the World War II Memorial embodies America's basic values. The fifty-six pillars express the unity of the nation fighting on behalf of a great cause, the world's cause, namely freedom.[30] Yet not all fifty-six entities are alike. Several territories were (and remain) colonial possessions and subject peoples: Hawai'i, the Philippines, Puerto Rico (fig. 1). What, then, does it mean to say that the Memorial's architecture expresses America's highest ideals and purposes? The very design of the Memorial gives voice to criticism of it.

Mills's hermeneutic insistence flows from a threefold memorial anxiety: (1) "How visitors in the future will come to judge the National World War II Memorial cannot be predicted." (2) "The truth is that memorials, especially those on the Mall, acquire an iconic and political life of their own that we cannot foresee." (3) "We do not, however, have to wait on

2. Freedom Wall, World War II Memorial. *Photo courtesy of Bob G.*

history before we make *any* judgments about the impact of the National World War II Memorial on American life."[31] Mills's "we" reads as part invitation, part command. Patriotic judgment must preempt interpretive uncertainty and provide rational direction. Mills would prefer that visitors to the World War II Memorial respond like visitors to the Lincoln: "stand in awe."[32] Rather than "a militarizing presence on the Mall," the Memorial makes genuflection possible. American citizens, unlike Vatican pilgrims, may not drop to bended knee, but the implication remains that they might be moved to prayer.[33] To prepare, if not induce, such a reaction, Mills provides instructions for the patriotic faithful, namely those who would join his affective community-in-the-making: "There is nothing Norman Rockwell-like about [it] . . . the National World War II Memorial upstages both the Vietnam Veterans Memorial and the Korean War Veterans Memorial . . . These are remarkable accomplishments for a memorial that has just been completed."[34] Indeed (fig. 2).

Mills's interpretation of the World War II Memorial discloses the problematic logic of debt critical to patriotism. President Truman's words inscribed in the Memorial's western wall sum it up: "Our debt . . . can never be repaid." Notably, veterans of the Second World War, once upon a time, eschewed the kind of memorialization that the nation would bestow upon them. Mills discusses the living memorials offered in tribute as well as the relative indifference of returning veterans to canonization.[35] It's not just that this generation preferred a living memorial (parks, schools, playgrounds, and stadiums elided the specter of death) to the common stock of monuments available. It's that this generation did not reflect relentlessly on itself. Nor did service call attention to itself and demand recognition and gratitude. True, veterans of the Second World War came to embrace, even insist upon, a national memorial, but their desire ironically sprang from an ethic of remembrance that came to dominate the country on whose behalf they unthinkingly acted.

Nevertheless, noting the iconic status that the Second World War enjoys in American popular culture, Mills (like Rorty and Schaar) still dwells on Vietnam. Saluting the Second World War tributes of Stephen Ambrose, Steven Spielberg, Tom Brokaw, and James Bradley, he writes, "Their aim is to honor that generation rather than put it under an historical microscope."[36] The will to honor makes instinctive good sense to Mills especially insofar as he recruits the World War II Memorial for America's September 11 crisis. Paying homage links "us" to the generation that knew how to wage war. By honoring veterans of the Second World War we force ourselves to live up to their example; or, better, the example we have them set. They won their war; we will win our war too. In Mills's hands, the Second World War generation has thus been made to serve us. The Memorial dedicated to them comes with a price after all: from a debt that can't be paid to a new line of credit self-extended. Patriotism reinvents narcissism with seemingly every instantiation.

DO WE MEAN WHAT WE SAY?

The World War II Memorial puzzles the visitor through its self-display. What compels the quintessential good war to resort to architectural ostentation? If undue revelation suggests a will to conceal, what might the Memorial, upon inspection, betray? Perhaps the values that the Memorial proclaims and embodies invite criticism that it cannot admit because of its role as commemorative architecture? Perhaps the Memorial suffers blindness to its own aporias and insistences?

Take these stirring words from the World War II Memorial's web site before construction: "The WWII Memorial will be the first national memorial dedicated to all who served in the armed forces and Merchant

Marine of the United States during the Second World War and acknowledging the commitment and achievement of the *entire* nation. All military veterans of the war, *the citizens on the home front, the nation at large*,
and the *high moral purpose and idealism* that motivated the nation's call
to arms will be honored ... It will *inspire future generations* of Americans,
deepening their appreciation of what the Second World War generation
accomplished in securing freedom and democracy. Above all, the memorial will *stand for all time* as an important *symbol of American national
unity*, a *timeless reminder* of the *moral strength* and *awesome power* that
can flow when a *free* people are *at once united and bonded together* in a
common and just cause."[37] Likewise, take the groundbreaking tribute of
Carolyn King, whose brother Thomas died at Anzio. The "great generation" of men who saved the world was great, she insisted, "because of what
they did, and *the way they did it*, and *how they* unified and *sacrificed in
every way*."[38]

Patriotism's fundamental tenets insist on matching word and deed; that
is the difference between authenticity and insincerity. In a strange twist
of fate, the World War II Memorial provides an opportunity not only to
recognize and celebrate the greatest generation's defining achievement
but also to put it to the test. Let's consider the Memorial's statement of
purpose, as well as Carolyn King's salute, and match them to certain actualities of the war.

The bombing of Hiroshima and Nagasaki, as well as the Japanese-
American internment camps, challenge the World War II Memorial's self-
conception. Here I do not wish to argue the merits of President Truman's
nuclear decision. I prefer to assume the military necessity, even justi-
fiability, of annihilating two Japanese cities. Thus I stipulate that Japan
would not have otherwise surrendered and that an invasion of the Japanese mainland would have followed. Thus I also stipulate that incinerat-
ing Hiroshima and Nagasaki saved upwards of a million American lives. I
still insist that the World War II Memorial fails to the extent that it fails to
commemorate Hiroshima and Nagasaki. After all, the Memorial's goal to
"inspire future generations" can take many forms. As the Memorial recognizes the sacrifices of American citizens to win the war, memorialization
represents symbolic payment of a debt (fig. 3). What, though, would it
mean to take the ethos of debt seriously? The answer: America, by virtue
of its own ethic, also owes a debt to the Japanese civilians whom it sacri-

3. Truman inscription, World War II Memorial. *Photo courtesy of Bob G.*

ficed so that it could win the war and save American lives. In short, they died so that we might live. Neither the war's opening salvo at Pearl Harbor nor its subsequent conduct—both seared into American memory— can alter the symbiotic relationship. The war's end calls into question our "high moral purpose and idealism." On Rorty's terms it can form no part of a patriotic story; it does not represent America at its best. Steven Spielberg's cinematic counterpart to the Memorial, *Saving Private Ryan*, likewise contributes to denial by "ending" the Second World War in 1944.

Hiroshima and Nagasaki also render problematic the very notion of love of country. What must love tell itself to account for nuclear death? Utilitarian logic may compel military assent, but love demands more than numerical abstraction. What does it mean to love that which commits horrific, if necessary, destruction? Here America's resort to nuclear weapons to win the war need not be construed as tantamount to confessing a crime. Acknowledging a terrible decision can also signal strength. Yet the monument does not address the war's end at all. Or if it does, it strangely celebrates the war's end. George Marshall's inscription, for example, insists that before the war concludes, the American flag must be recognized worldwide as the symbol of "overwhelming force." The words affirm, perhaps unwittingly, America's firebombing and nuclear attacks (fig. 4). Yet the World War II Memorial does not address the responsibility that accompanies the exercise of such violence.[39] Memorialization concerns only itself—our victory, our loss, our heroism, our sacrifice. America remains the Second World War's sole subject.[40] American exceptionalism equals American narcissism.[41]

The World War II Memorial enjoys no monopoly on self-regard.[42] Narrative creativity finds noteworthy expression with "The Japanese American Memorial to Patriotism during World War II." At once a war memorial to the Nisei troops who served with unrivaled distinction and a commemorative tribute to the Japanese-American citizens summarily rounded up and interned without cause in the winter of 1942, the Japanese American Memorial showcases devotion to America. Not only did Americans offer their lives to defend their country; they did so while their family, friends, and neighbors were imprisoned because of rank prejudice. Despite lives lost abroad and lives ruined at home, love of country nevertheless endured. A country that inspires such dedication must be remarkable indeed. Thus the Memorial neatly juxtaposes the best and worst of America, presented with a tension that combines pride with candor and criticism; if anything, the ambiguity enhances, consolidates, and reaffirms American greatness (fig. 5).

Nevertheless, geography belies the political significance that the memorial claims for itself. Located at the intersections of New Jersey and Louisiana Avenues and D Street NW, the memorial stands on a site that even residents of Washington would be hard-pressed to find. Although near Union Station and the Capitol, the memorial is on the outskirts of the Mall. Subject notwithstanding, moreover, it has no tangible connection to the World War II Memorial at the heart of the nation's symbolic sacred ground. It thus achieved at birth what other monuments take generations to accomplish: invisibility. It is situated on a piece of gently sloping land that doubles as a traffic island. Passersby are rare. Tour buses gesture at it. It is a memorial that you can visit solo—if you can locate or happen upon it. The irony of the memorial's "resounding bell" that calls people to gather and reflect is that it can succeed only with a prearranged crowd.

The Memorial's history further complicates matters. Unflagging love of country under extraordinary circumstances failed to bring the memorial to life. A tribute tailored to Japanese-American soldiers failed to secure official approval. The subject was seen as too parochial: something larger

WE ARE DETERMINED
THAT BEFORE THE SUN SETS ON THIS
TERRIBLE STRUGGLE OUR FLAG WILL BE RECOGNIZED
THROUGHOUT THE WORLD AS A SYMBOL OF FREEDOM
ON THE ONE HAND AND OF OVERWHELMING
FORCE ON THE OTHER

GENERAL GEORGE C. MARSHALL

4. Marshall inscription, World War II Memorial.

(below) 5. The Japanese American Memorial to Patriotism during World War II. *Both photos courtesy of Bob G.*

THE JAPANESE AMERICAN MEMORIAL TO PATRIOTISM DURING WORLD WAR II

had to be at stake. As for the internments, injustice alone would be un-thinkable grounds for a national memorial—unless, of course, America was understood to be the victim. Thus the memorial would never have been built if not for the Redress Bill of 1988, the legislation through which the United States formally apologized and provided token financial com-pensation to the Japanese-Americans whom it had wronged. Thus in a real sense there is no addressing of the past nor drawing of lessons from it, as the Memorial would have you believe. Instead the Memorial brings to life an apology itself tailored to make America look good.[43]

The Memorial, in short, perfects patriotism's narcissism. A dove with wings pinioned by barbed wire appears to be the Memorial's centerpiece. Appearances are deceiving. Opposite the dove, facing the stone panels naming the states that served as prisons, President Ronald Reagan speaks: "Here we admit a wrong. Here we affirm our commitment as a nation to equal justice under the law." The words impress and inspire. They impress because the United States publicly confesses gross injustice committed against (some of) its citizens. They inspire because the "We" that "apolo-gizes" makes possible and is joined (in the second sentence) by a We that includes the victims in the apology.

Nevertheless the Memorial's erstwhile lament calls itself into question. The so-called apology employs the passive voice, as if "we" can admit wrongdoing only grudgingly, under duress. What's more, the very lan-guage of the apology minimizes it. To speak of a "wrong," in other words, does not adequately capture the actions taken, their cross-generational consequences, and their legacy. The language also reveals a subtle re-fusal of responsibility: somehow, something happened. Apparently that's the most that can be said of the wrong admitted—here. The point of the apology seems to be the apology itself.[44] That is, the injustice done fades before the pleasing sight of a country congratulating itself for having the wherewithal to address its past. The foundation that built the memorial folded this very sensibility into the monumental purpose: "Reflect on the greatness of a nation which . . . would admit it had wronged Japanese Americans in World War II."[45]

FOR ARCHITECTURAL AMBIVALENCE

What if monuments and memorials were to manifest artistic elements that resonated with the intricacies of life and world? The change might turn otherwise homogeneous, redundant, sententious civic space—with a country's greatness already assumed, forever confirmed, and actively consolidated—into a harrowing, robust, democratic space with its values enacted rather than announced. Respect does not necessarily presuppose displays of deference, awe, fealty, and solemnity. Respect may entail refusing to blink.[46] More concretely, what if the World War II Memorial and the Vietnam Veterans Memorial complex invited the very objections and criticisms that they now seem designed to reject? What if their aporias also suggested the remedies to their shortcomings and failures?

How might the World War II Memorial be reconceived? In short, it could devote attention to the war's conclusion in the Asian theater. How can the end to this epic struggle not be marked? What other war concludes in such stunning and spectacular fashion? Truman himself conceded in a Congressional message in November 1945 that "the release of atomic energy constitutes a new force too revolutionary to consider in the framework of old ideas."[47] Why not take the president at his word and bring his cognitive insight to bear on traditional memorial architecture? Truman, if inadvertently, authorizes and encourages the World War II Memorial's refashioning.

First, split the oval-shaped pool that traverses the Memorial's center into two unequal parts. Disrupting the balance, flow, and symmetry of memorial space, it suggests a fissure or crack at the heart of things. This would represent the void of Hiroshima and Nagasaki. Visitors would gravitate to it amid the ubiquity of columns. Because atomic weapons are able to combust human beings, ground zero implies traces. Imagine the charred remains (or perhaps the vaporized outlines) of a Japanese family, blackened crumbs as it were, jutting an inch or two from the surface. Imagine similar remains scattered throughout the grounds. What if people had to walk on them to visit the site? The infinite and the infinitesimal thus combined, could you look down at the remnants? Do you have the stomach to face and affirm what American power did? These ghostly presences complicate George Marshall's inscription beneath the Atlantic arch (mentioned above): "We are determined that before the sun sets on this terrible struggle our flag will be recognized throughout the world as a symbol of . . . overwhelming force."[48]

Surrounding this impromptu open-air grave, inscribe a few words. Truman had this to say on August 6, 1945: "Sixteen hours ago an American airplane dropped one bomb on Hiroshima . . . The force from which the sun draws its power has been loosed against those who brought war to the Far East." J. Robert Oppenheimer wrote the following after the first successful atomic test on July 16, 1945: "We knew the world would not be the same. A few people laughed, a few people cried. Most people were silent. I remembered the line from the Hindu scripture, the Bhagavad Gita . . . 'I am become Death, the destroyer of worlds.' I suppose that we all thought that, one way or another." A Japanese housewife bore witness: "A mother, driven half-mad while looking for her child, was calling his name. At last she found him. His head looked like a boiled octopus. His eyes were half-closed, and his mouth was white, pursed, and swollen."[49] The matter-of-factness of Truman's words are chilling. He attributes to the Japanese responsibility not only for the war but for what he and the United States have just done militarily to them. American power finds no linguistic assertion here. A force has been loosed. Oppenheimer's words, on the other hand, resonate with a self-awareness and gravity appropriate to the occasion. "We knew" discloses a sense of responsibility that Truman's words lack. The Japanese housewife closes the circle. This is what the United States, what you, did. Can you own it, make it yours? How might the Memorial now be experienced? Might there be a moment when the very idea of a monument to a war, even the Second World War, feels dubious? Democracies may be forced to fight wars to defend themselves, but doesn't democracy also name a way of life that rejects violence, to say nothing of war? Can a democracy recognize war without simultaneously appreciating the paradoxical symbolic situations that it creates?

In the absence of the Hiroshima supplement, the World War II Memorial raises questions about its conception not easily answered. Recall Bob Dole's rationale for the monument (in another fifty-five years, no Second World War veteran will be alive to "bear witness"). The limited truth of his observation reveals its peculiarity. American political culture has immortalized the war in countless films, histories, memoirs, biographies, diaries, letters, and documentaries. Bearing witness suggests a need for retrieval, remembering, and recording. The Second World War, ironically, has no apparent need of the kind of memorialization that Dole would impose on it. Precisely because of the war's place in American history, politics, and life, the very idea of a memorial to it seems somewhat misplaced. The Memorial betrays an imperative that cannot be articulated without calling itself into question. Consider Krauthammer: "Does Washington need a World War II memorial? Yes. Its very absence is an oddity of the city's monumental architecture." He then notes the tributes paid to the Revolutionary, Civil, Korean, and Vietnam wars. How could the Second World War not also be honored? The answer: perhaps the Second World War has no need of traditional memorialization. It would be nothing if not redundant. But if St. Florian's blueprint expresses truths so deeply held in America that translating them to monumental form becomes gratuitous, what makes the formality a necessity? Why build a monument to obviousness? If all memorials ultimately reflect back on the culture that builds them, what does this monument reveal about America?

The memorial revisions that I propose run counter to the energies devoted to the Mall's homogenization. What if, however, repetition intimates vulnerability? Somewhat surprisingly, Washington enjoys memorial precedent for representing war's horror, even insanity. The Grant Memorial offers a fulsome lesson in narrative—and ethical—density. Perhaps the least appreciated site in Washington, it is worthy of what I take to be its internecine subject: civil war.[50] Impossibly located next to a traffic circle beyond the far edge of the Capitol's west lawn, the Grant defies discovery, let alone approach. Here is what I see.

General Grant sits tall on his horse, itself perched on a pedestal some fifty feet high. You strain to see him. The stress on one's neck recalls the Lincoln experience. Draped in formfitting raincoat, hat pulled down for protection, Grant looks old, weary, cold, grim, resigned, defeated. War has taken its toll. The horse is beaten too, tail between its legs. Sheer size notwithstanding, there is nothing apparently heroic here.

The Memorial's distinctiveness flows from the battle action to either side of Grant: two graphic scenes of war explode around him, even at him. While formally Grant presides over the war, the forces that he commands refuse control. To his left, pointing straight at him, a horse-drawn wagon pulling a cannon careers out of control. Three frightened men sit slumped on the bench as others try to bring the wagon under control. (It is not clear that they will succeed.) Two of the three look resigned to their inevitable demise. The horses resist the efforts to stop them. Two soldiers, out of desperation, have jumped onto the horses to get control of the reins. The horses threaten to stampede over the edge of the memorial.

6. The Grant Memorial. *Photo courtesy of Bob G.*

The scene betokens catastrophe. No amount of human exertion can prevent it.

Likewise, to Grant's right, a cavalry charge unfolds. The lead officer wields a sword. The men following him seem disconnected, uninterested in the assault. Though they gallop forward, they are hunkered down as if merely hoping to survive—somehow. They do not have weapons drawn. In the attack, they will not themselves attack. The self-consuming nature of the charge rivets the viewer's attention. To the immediate right of the lead horse, a soldier spills forward on the ground, horse collapsed both underneath and over him. He is also about to be trampled to death by the lead horse. You see it coming even though he cannot. But surely he can sense it. You stare death—his—in the face. This is a cavalry charge that is doomed from the get-go (fig. 6).

The Grant Memorial deromanticizes war. It also suggests war's self-defeating, suicidal character. Though Grant ostensibly represents the victors, the Memorial suggests that to speak of winning a war, especially a civil war, amounts to a denial of its actualities. War means death, destruction, devastation—self-inflicted. Unlike the Korean, which inspires our pity, Grant's stoicism scorns indulgence. We brought this war on ourselves, the culmination of our Founding legacy. The Memorial rebukes.[51] And now, in the direction of Grant's gaze, it rebukes the World War II Memorial with its sterile triumphalism.

The controversy over the World War II Memorial demonstrates the attention that the Mall can generate. American patriotic culture invests heavily in memorialization. Alas, the dispute was a more fitting tribute than the Memorial itself. The memorial supplements that I outlined above are meant to provoke. Nietzsche once remarked that a people can tolerate only those questions to which it has answers. So what happens when the world's leading democracy, engaged in the most noble of causes, commits acts of substantial evil in the course of doing good? Can the Second World War and the cold war accommodate a full accounting? Is not to presume otherwise to diminish the triumphs that they name? These are questions America cannot yet ask itself. Patriotism's narcissism precludes them.

The supplements considered here presume a more nuanced story: the problematic adventure of American democracy and empire. The very success of the Second World War sows the seeds of tragic failure; witness, for example, Vietnam twenty years later. Sanford Levinson has written of the dilemmas that emergent democracies face regarding the symbols gracing public space. What should be done with the monuments and memorials built to specification for communist regimes in the former Soviet satellites or the confederate southern states? Destruction? Storage? Relocation? Museums? Regardless of the answer, what exempts established democratic orders from similar architectural scrutiny?[52] With the World War II Memorial complete, the Mall can pause and reflect in the stillness. Perhaps it's time for a fourth founding. Here's one possibility. Insofar as the Washington Monument anchors America's sacred civic space, replace it with an artifact that addresses the ambiguities of the American founding. Or should I say American foundings, lest the inexorable expansion of the United States across the continent in the nineteenth century be forgotten? Why not accord America's manifest destiny the treatment it requires on the Mall? What about a Washington-Polk Monument? The traditional obelisk, symbol of life, misfires if one takes into account the death, destruction, and displacement brought about by a founding.[53] America needs a counter-Alamo memorial, if you will. Once the Washington has been reconfigured, the Lincoln, where slavery and secession seem present by virtue of their absence and erasure, might become anomalous: overblown, disingenuous, and self-serving. It could be the second in an avalanche of architectural dominoes toppled in the name of a democratic renaissance.

Since the closures in America's memorial imaginary work to conceal injuries and deny violences calling for engagement, efforts to open them to democratic reflection can be expected to foster resistance. Yet America's complexion keeps shifting and, as the experience of the former Soviet Union teaches, monuments do experience brutally interrupted life spans. While the behemoths on the Washington Mall need not fear Stalin's statuary fate, John Adams would insist that there is no democratic reason to accord them greater respect.

I am not sure but the day for conventional monuments, statues, memorials, &c, has pass'd away—and that they are henceforth superfluous and vulgar.—WALT WHITMAN

The profession of most monuments is to call forth a remembrance, or rivet the attention and give the feelings a pious direction because one assumes they somehow need it; and in this, their major profession, monuments always fail. . . . Well, doubtless this can be explained. Everything permanent loses its ability to impress. . . . In a word, monuments today should do what we all have to do, make more of an effort! Anybody can stand quietly by the side of the road and allow glances to be bestowed on him; these days we can demand more of monuments.—ROBERT MUSIL, "Monuments"

But this is good fortune—for men to end their lives with honor . . . and for you honorably to lament them: their life was set to a measure where death and happiness went hand in hand. I know that it is difficult to convince you of this.—THUCYDIDES,
The Peloponnesian War

The American
Memorial/Monument Complex II:
Political Not Patriotic

Late in the afternoon on July 3, 2000, in western Pennsylvania, authorities demolished the Gettysburg National Tower, a three-hundred-foot observation citadel on the civil war's decisive battlefield. While functional (it allowed visitors to view the entire field of conflict), it was also widely considered an aesthetic atrocity. A diverse movement determined to restore the battlefield, as much as possible, to its original condition in 1863 succeeded in eliminating the tower. The cost: $1 million. The secretary of the interior, Bruce Babbitt, presided over the destruction: "This is sacred ground. Americans come here to learn of their past, to understand how it was in those days when we remade ourselves as a new nation."[1] Also on July 3, the Washington Monument, again Babbitt presiding, was rededicated. Restoration work totaled three years and $10 million. Babbitt: "[This] is a sacred place. It's where Americans have come for generations to reflect on who we are and the extraordinary history that has converged to make our nation . . . We honor that experience and we honor this place by taking care of it."[2]

Secretary Babbitt's remarks at Gettysburg and the Mall seem fitting. The Washington Monument salutes the foundations of democracy. It speaks to America's "in the beginning." The obelisk stands for life. This constructed site has become "sacred" by virtue of its multiple political significations, and we as a people are responsible for its sanctification by making pilgrimage to it. As for Gettysburg, the battle bearing its name effectively sealed the Republic's future. The Civil War, moreover, recovered the nation's founding. In the American patriotic imagination this blood-drenched, grave-filled ground verges on the inherently holy. Death made rebirth possible. For what possible reasons, then, might Babbitt's declarations of sanctity be flagged?

Although a core part of the patriotism complex, the very idea of sacred space in a democracy seems problematic. To honor the eternal and unchanging, represent truth and right, command deference and devotion, commit to unity and consensus, elicit reverence and awe runs counter to a vibrant democratic ethos grounded in plurality and contestation, Babbitt's presumption notwithstanding. Sacred space may inspire debate— interpretive consensus seems notoriously elusive here—but differences tend to center on the content of the sacred. The sacred per se, however, elides theorization.[3]

How to explain democracy's piety? In a word: death. As George L. Mosse's seminal work suggests, death's importance to patriotism cannot be overstated. Yet where Mosse starts with a nation's need to conceal and obscure the horrors of war, I start with patriotism and investigate its deployment of death for its own self-aggrandizement. For Mosse, war and mass death pose problems for political orders to solve; I treat death, whatever its mode of production, as an indispensable tool in the arsenal of patriotism. Mosse starts with what he calls "the reality of the war experience," the horrors of which must not only be made palatable but also transformed into legitimating myth; for war's carnage, sacrifice, and loss threaten to unleash destructive forces capable of society-wide ruination. I start with patriotism's incessant demand for love, which takes death for granted and puts it to work. My suspicion is that patriotism cannot generate sufficient affective attachment and concrete commitment without the many horrors that it helped to bring about in the first place. For Mosse, war's meaning and purpose arrive posthumously, conferring retrospective meaning, inspiration, and value. For patriotism, simultaneity tends to prevail. That is, patriotism's power rests on death's prestige; death, in turn, undergoes social reincarnation through the nostrums of patriotism.[4]

The Washington Mall, sacred patriotic space in the nation's capital, specializes in death. Regal, even imperial in aspect, the Mall tends toward the static. With its civic mission well established, the Mall focuses on execution. Recognize, remember, revivify the nation's much-vaunted ideals, accomplishments, and sacrifices—especially the sacrifices. The controversy generated by the creation of the World War II Memorial shows the zeal with which the country guards and patrols its national patriotic space. Not even an unabashed tribute to the quintessential good war skirted scrutiny. Aesthetic objections were raised to the proposed location: it would mar the unobstructed view from one end of the Mall to the other, compromising the visual field between the Washington and Lincoln. Others argued that the design mimicked the architectural predilections of Nazi Germany. In response, proponents redoubled their efforts to vanquish opposition by whatever means available. Friedrich St. Florian insisted that his design transcended the mundane political world and its fleeting preoccupations, reaching into the past for inspiration and authority: "Our intention was to be timeless. It goes back to Jefferson and the founders of our nation."[5] St. Florian offered his declaration of intent (and self-assessment) as reassurance. While one must note the respectful spirit of his response, perhaps the formulaic, unthinking political disposition that it expresses ought to be a source of concern. Whence the will to timelessness? Whence the invocation of the founding and founders? What do such reflexive commemorative impulses indicate about the democratic order in which they not only circulate but govern public discourse?

Politics, we are told, fouls the question of monuments and memorials—from possibility to proposal, from conception to construction, from fundraising to finalization. Rather than embrace common American values, so-called partisan agendas seek influence and control. Assume this claim to be true for the sake of argument: should it necessarily be a source of concern, let alone rebuke? What if politics understood as contest were the norm, expected and embraced as commemoration proceeds, rather than something eschewed as inappropriate to public space, especially national public space? What if contest were folded into the very conception of monuments and memorials? What if it became constitutive of them and not just a lamentable byproduct? The choreography of contest, of course, might require careful tending to prevent a mere clash of competing dogmas. Nevertheless, if politics were welcomed into a reconfigured commemorative approach, the Mall in Washington, for example, might become a place of architectural distinction instead of a Disneyesque tourist destination.

Thus, I would like to put forward the thought of an architectural possibility, one that might shake and transform us. What if the legacy represented by the Washington and Lincoln, among others, might be better served—and the millions allocated to their upkeep better spent—by subjecting them to the wrecking ball? Ronald Reagan once mockingly challenged Mikhail Gorbachev to tear down the Berlin Wall, the cold war's quintessential symbol of repression. What if America's democracy aimed the deconstructive spirit of Reagan at itself, to demolish, intermittently, the monuments and memorials that it builds, recognizing the paradoxical character of architectural designs made for mass appeal and directed at remote futurity? What if standard practices of commemoration prove self-defeating, in that they ultimately disfigure and dishonor what they aspire to acknowledge and respect?

This is not meant to suggest that a democracy cannot recognize its history, appreciate its values, or respect its achievements. The counter-monument movement in Germany indicates otherwise. What if, however, the most appropriate, patriotic, of encomia were those that called themselves into question, those that once created, for example, dissolved by design? I believe that the Vietnam Veterans Memorial complex already embodies, however accidentally and immaturely, the ethos of a vibrant democratic polity at odds with itself. This may be one reason, unacknowledged, why it has become the most popular and emotive destination on the Mall. This may also account for the multifaceted efforts made—from the original criteria of the design competition to supplemental sculptures to subsequent memorials at the core—to integrate and harmonize the Vietnam Wall with its surroundings.[6] Even so, the Vietnam Veterans Memorial still works to expose the fabulous character of its larger home. Hence the tension that the site produces. What if the sensibility swirling through the Vietnam Memorial compound were extended? What might result?

Richard Rorty must love the Mall. Walter Berns positively oozes adoration.[7] The Washington Monument symbolizes the Founding of the nation. It aspires to timelessness. The obelisk, representing a ray of sun and by extension life itself, pays tribute to the birth of the republic, particularly Washington, the giver of republican life. It stands for that which made all things possible. Thus it ought to be imposing and godlike. Its phallic abstractness may seem cold, distancing, alienating; but these aspects also contribute to the power emanating from it.

Yet it is the Lincoln Memorial that transfixes the Mall. Framed by parallel lines of majestic trees, the self-styled temple housing a statue of Lincoln, the martyr who saved the union, inspires worship. If the Washington signifies the possibilities of newfound life, the Lincoln, despite the palpable aura of tragedy, signifies rebirth, a second Founding. Combining a slain figure draped in an American flag and unforgettable poetic formulations, the Lincoln pays homage not just to the nation's values and ideals, achievements and ambitions, past and future, but also to the costs of securing them. The Lincoln becomes the logical progeny of the Washington. The full realization of the republic required the timely intervention of successor generations positioned to perfect what the first generation initiated. The Founding had to be articulated and then overcome. Each exacted a price, the second even greater than the first. The movement from the Washington to the Lincoln recapitulates this monumental history.

Yet the Washington and Lincoln Memorials—as well as the patriotic memorial and monument complex that they oversee—give pause. While the idea of a polity attending to the cultivation of civic bonds of affection may barely register, the same cannot be said for the architectural forms responsible. On the Mall, commemorative efforts seem both problematic and perverse: problematic to a democratic pluralistic ethos, perverse to the values that they would embody. In that the Mall's classic structures represent the nation's dominant moral and political values, they confirm and intensify truths already known, believed, and felt. The scale of the Washington and Lincoln, for example, frame the experience of them. You struggle physically to look up to them. No matter how close you get, you remain at a certain distance. On approach, they induce a sense of instant veneration. Larger than life, they reduce the citizen to a passive, puny spectator. Since the monuments are not built to human scale, citizens go there to be fed, to imbibe from one common source. America's secular gods require worship at their altars.

Furthermore, the Washington obelisk belies the ambiguous character of founding. Slavery and ethnic cleansing notwithstanding, it mystifies and obscures the phenomena that it re-presents. What's more, the cruelties that bring a republic into being do not magically disappear after birth, a legacy that outstrips the Washington's capacity to signify. The Lincoln likewise embodies and conceals originary violence. Slavery and secession seem marginal, and Lincoln's second inaugural address suggests that even Civil War horrors pay tribute to America by being a fitting punishment dispensed by God.[8] The Lincoln seeks to transcend death by means of one ostensibly tragic figure at his sacrificial best. Since Abraham died for "our" sins, dying overcomes them and itself.[9] In the end, the Lincoln mimics the Washington's whitewashing. The storytelling ethos of the Mall dislikes moral ambiguity. As Robert Musil remarked, more can be demanded of monuments.

ARCHITECTURAL LEGERDEMAIN

From the founding of the republic to civil war, from cold war conflagrations in the mid-twentieth century to imperial annihilation toward its close, the United States has consistently practiced artistic evasion and denial: Washington, Lincoln, Korean, Vietnam. The World War II Memorial continues the amnesic tradition. First the so-called greatest generation saved the world; now the monument to it saves the Mall—not aesthetically but patriotically.

Ironically, Germany can teach its putatively democratic conqueror about public commemorative space and architecture. Unlike the United States, Germany admits to having a past.[10] And the German language, as Karen E. Till observes, harbors a complexity foreign to English when it comes to public architecture. In German there are two kinds of memorial that lend themselves to patriotism: *Denkmal* (celebration) and *Ehrenmal* (honoring). There is a third term for memorial, *Mahnmal*, which connotes admonishment—say for past crimes. Because it seems antithetical to patriotic sensibilities, English lacks an equivalent for Mahnmal.[11] As part of an effort to confront Nazism and the Holocaust, German architects have reconsidered the very nature and purpose of a monument. Hence counter-monuments, which James Young defines as "brazen, painfully self-conscious spaces conceived to challenge the very premises of their being."[12] Among other things, this means that the stories told by monuments and the experiences engendered by them do not assume, much less privilege, self-celebration. Taking to heart Musil's dictum that "everything permanent loses its ability to impress," counter-monuments rely on ephemerality to reconfigure civic space as democratic political space.[13]

At the invitation of city officials in Hamburg, Jochen and Esther Gerz conceived the Monument against Fascism. Designed to disappear where it stood, it would dissolve in the course of its actualization.[14] Why did the Gerzes refuse traditional monumental and memorial forms? Politically they objected to the authoritarian, quasi-fascist, character of art works that convert citizens into "passive spectators."[15] They argued that in traditional forms monuments tend to be self-defeating. They inhibit the formation of the ethic that they might otherwise induce. That is, monuments and memorials, because of their didactic permanence, do the civic work that only citizens themselves can do to lasting effect. To distinguish contemporary democratic Germany from its Nazi predecessor, the Gerzes developed alternative notions of public space and political architecture that would "embody" and enact a democratic sensibility. Unless citizens become effectively implicated in the complex act of commemoration, monuments and memorials seem fated to achieve invisibility, as Musil argued.

The Gerzes' architectural ethos not only runs counter to the patriotic aesthetic governing the Mall in Washington; it calls the latter's very reason for being into question. Consider several of the reversals that partially define the Gerzes' work. First, they refused to build the Monument against Fascism at a location specifically established for housing memorials. With pre-designated placement, citizens treat public space as a destination site. Memorials, on occasion, become antiseptic attractions;

citizens become patriotic consumer-tourists. Instead the Gerzes placed Monument against Fascism in the middle of a busy shopping mall. Thus people would be forced to encounter the monument. Dropped amid the rhythms of daily life, it could not be neatly avoided. The element of surprise would enable the monument to resist prior patriotic appropriation by those who knew they were going to see it. Second, while the Gerzes concocted an obelisk, theirs was an edifice with a twist. Unlike, say, the Washington Monument or the World War II Memorial, to complete its assigned task the Monument against Fascism would be dismantled where installed. A monument with mutable form, it was not meant to last. Yet perishing would be the prelude to a newfangled permanence. Third, the monument encouraged participation rather than mere consumption. Citizens were invited to sign their names on and become, so to speak, part of the monument. As the obelisk's panels were filled with signatures, they would be buried, one at a time, beneath the remaining panels. The obelisk, traditional symbol of life, would inexorably recede before the eyes of the public. The intent: the gradual dissolution of the monument would itself become a subject of civic discourse. Once each panel had been buried, a plaque would be inserted where the obelisk, now in pieces directly underneath, once stood. Even those who never actually saw the monument (but were confronted with its marker) might be induced to inquire about the provenance of the plaque. Either way, citizens would be doing the work heretofore performed by the monument. In short, the monument would be conjured through questions and answers, and citizens would thereby supplant it. The Monument against Fascism advertised both its own necessity and its insufficiency. Finally, the Gerzes assumed the dependence of their work on similar deconstructive-reconstructive efforts. Unable to succeed alone, counter-monuments presuppose and engender a web of public political art. With innovation perhaps the only prerequisite, they become the source of their own renewal. Predictability equals death.

On the Mall in Washington, Maya Lin's Vietnam Veterans Memorial possesses kindred architectural spirit. Innovation notwithstanding, the counter-monument movement also reveals the Wall's limitations and liabilities, shortcomings overlooked in the triumph of its well-known catharsis.[16] It's as if the success of the Wall—the number of visitors, the emotions provoked, the offerings left behind, the healing experienced—overcomes and erases the moral and political failures of the war. As a result, the Wall itself may elude a more thoroughgoing critical scrutiny. Informed by the Gerzes' work, which lends itself to a tragic sensibility about the limits to power, I would like to revisit and reconceive the Vietnam complex.

The very idea of a Vietnam Memorial was bound to incite. To minimize contention, organizers conducted a nationwide competition open to the public. Nearly fifteen hundred proposals were received. The winning design entry, submitted by Maya Lin, neither celebrated nor explicitly condemned the war. It embodied ambiguity. To opponents this was its crime. Tom Carhart, Vietnam Veteran and military historian, publicly rebuked the Wall, which he called a "black gash of shame."[17] To supporters of the monument, elusiveness would be its virtue.

If you approach the Wall from the East or South, the Memorial folds gently into the earth (many have observed that you stumble upon the Memorial). While carved into the ground, it nonetheless joins the landscape; it does not dominate it. In light of the war's sustained assaults on nature, this aspect of the Memorial rivets one's attention.

To traverse the Wall requires fortitude. Starting from either end, there is a gentle descent into the earth as a cascading flood of names—58,000 dead inscribed in polished black granite—inundates the eyes and overloads the emotions. What's more, the Wall's slope coincides with Washington's incremental disappearance. The city's proximate sights and sounds fade as the individual panels reach their apex at the memorial's nadir. The vertex isolates space. Death climaxes in a kind of vacuum. No color, no sound, no life—blackness, names, death.[18] The Vietnam Veterans Memorial feels like a sunken, open-ended mausoleum. As the names blur into one amorphous mass, there seems no exit.[19] Moreover, the Wall has reflective qualities, so to gaze at it is to look at oneself; this turns death back on the self and implicates the viewer. The Wall defies distance, both physical and emotional.

The Vietnam design competition required the Memorial to harmonize with its surroundings, natural and artificial. The architectural layout suggests that it represents a worthy addition to the nation's sacred patriotic ground. Standing at the Memorial's core, the Washington Monument hovers to the east, the Lincoln Memorial to the west. Sight lines precise, views sharp, the Wall forms part of a larger complex.[20] The atmospherics proclaim that the founding principles and national values expressed by the Washington and Lincoln extend to Vietnam. The Washington even reflects on the Wall. Integrated self-consciously into its surroundings, the Vietnam Memorial was to be made safe for civic space. Thanks to founding emanations, questions about the war can surface, if filtered, while potentially larger questions about America recede. Nevertheless, the Vietnam Wall resists official absorption and calls attention to its own foreignness. As for the three supplements also standing on Memorial grounds, they emphasize and exacerbate the anomalous, disruptive character of the Wall.

The Vietnam Memorial names one site with four parts to it: Maya Lin's Wall, Frederick Hart's Three Soldiers, Glenna Goodacre's Women's Memorial, and a small flagstone plaque near Hart's Soldiers.[21] While separate and distinct, these elements cannot be understood—or experienced—in isolation. The first led to the second, which in turn led to the third. And all three resulted in pressure for the fourth. Together they form an incongruous whole.[22] Not only is it difficult to visit the Wall without visiting the three other sites; each of the four memorials offers a contending interpretation of the War, the nation that fought it, and its proper place in American memory.

Because the Vietnam Memorial's four components are so close together, the Vietnam complex fosters self-interrogation.[23] Now in a war fought through architecture, how do the memorials interact? The short answer: in that the Vietnam supplements insist on their patriotism, they sabotage themselves; that is, they render obsessive the love that they would express and thereby discredit it.

The Three Soldiers monument stands directly between the Lincoln and the Wall and enjoys a spatial prominence with which the Women's Memorial cannot compete. Frederick Hart, angry competitor to Maya Lin, intended to detract and distract from the Wall: the soldiers as architectural agents of subversion in the name of restoration. Their mere presence aspires to rebuke. At the same time, Three Soldiers seems to stand guard between the Wall and the Lincoln, situated to protect the monumental integrity of the Mall's western end. Once again, the soldiers seem to be serving the country to perform a task of which they are kept in ignorance.

The Three Soldiers define youthfulness: macho, strong, vibrant, baby-faced, naïve, immortal. Unlike their Korean counterparts, these boys, innocents, stand at ease. There is no imminent prospect of combat. Placed under the sovereign protection of the American flag (which hovers in the background), they signal the unity of the military. By definition noble and heroic, they serve their country, fighting its war without complaint. They remind you that nations ask their citizens to fight wars for them, something that no nation wishes to do. This fact alone demands respect. Though Hart designed the figures to disclose something about the Vietnam experience, the character, conduct, and consequences of the war have been ignored.[24] For one thing, these three male bodies remain whole and intact.

Hart's intent further misfires. Though he conceived Three Soldiers to be looking for the enemy in the distance, directionality undermines aim. They gaze in the direction of the Wall (further linking the two memorials), as if catching a glimpse of the terrible fate that awaits them. They seem taken aback, perhaps confused by what they see, unsure of what it is. Perhaps they strain to read their own names on the Wall, where the endless number of inscriptions makes it possible to wonder if the Three Soldiers represent the innocence that led America to disaster and destruction. Notwithstanding Hart, maybe we have learned from Vietnam after all.

The Vietnam Women's Memorial likewise exceeds its design. It would honor the women who served in Vietnam with distinction equal to that of their male counterparts. While Three Soldiers responds to the Wall, the Women's Memorial contends with the Three Soldiers. Ironically, the Women's Memorial achieves definition not thanks to the three nurses tending a wounded soldier, but to the soldier himself. He is the center of the action. Singular; they are three. Prostrate; they are alert. Dying; they are full of life. A fallen hero worthy of the concern and anxiety that the women display, he may not survive. The woman standing appears to be waiting—perhaps hoping—for evacuation by helicopter. She looks skyward but does not point. The locus of action returns to the wounded soldier.

The Women's Memorial might have been titled American Suicide. It reduces America's military effort to one young man near death; life oozes from him, as the rag over his chest wound suggests. As the soldier lies limp and helpless, his fate may await one or all of Hart's Three Soldiers. His pain is America's pain; he was acting on our behalf. We sent him there. How could we have done this to him—and by extension to ourselves? War requires that you kill others; we were really killing ourselves. Yet in view of the imperial, technological terms of the war and the absence of Vietnamese on the grounds, the pain and suffering embodied at the Women's Memorial tends toward the self-indulgent and self-pitying.

While The Three Soldiers and the Women's Memorial pale before the brilliance of the Wall that redefines them, they could represent an important precedent regarding the elaboration of civic commemorative space in America. Or, better, the Wall started to breed the moment it won. It invited multiple, rival interpretations of the Vietnam War, some of which took monumental form. This quality distinguishes the Vietnam Memorial complex from the Mall's other structures. It is a memorial with four aspects. No single approach to the war could satisfy the war parties involved. Thus the memorial space is inherently dynamic, variable, at odds with itself. While the design competition mandated that the Vietnam Veterans Memorial "make no political statement about the war," the site has been political since its inception. The Wall aroused sufficient opposition—from Vietnam veterans, from Reagan's interior secretary, James Watt, from the financial contributor H. Ross Perot—that it required supplementation.[25] Jan Scruggs and the Vietnam Veterans Memorial Committee resigned themselves to compromise in order to realize Maya Lin's design.[26] Yet they might have interpreted controversy as a sign of memorial success. That no single structure sufficed for Vietnam (or anything else) does not suggest failure; rather it points to the need for memorial multiplicity, whether simultaneous or sequential. Here the Mall's presumption of a single treatment reveals itself to be conceptually flawed.[27]

Even the Wall turned out differently than planned. Parents, spouses, siblings, relatives, friends, vets, neighbors, and citizens routinely leave offerings at its base (medals, dog tags, flags, flowers, mementos, letters, poems, joints). The objects left behind not only implicate the visitor in the Memorial; they transform it. The Wall is constructed and reconstructed daily by means of this practice. The Memorial thus becomes participatory—and mutable—beyond what its designers initially imagined.[28] The combination renders the civic space itself democratic.

According to Scruggs, things started appearing at the "memorial" during construction.²⁹ By 1993 the number of items reached one quarter million. The practice of leaving items, known to be part of the experience of visiting the Wall, has generated much attention and worries some. The curators responsible for cataloguing and warehousing left items, for example, have raised the issue of authenticity. They do not wish to call attention to the practice, concerned that people may bring something precisely because they know that the curators save and itemize everything. They worry that people will not leave an offering for the Wall, the veterans, or the country but bring an object for inclusion in the permanent collection itself. The curators prefer objects left spontaneously, reflexively, without calculation and forethought. Purple Hearts, dog tags, and C Rations fall into this category. They scorn items left just to be gathered, put on display at the Smithsonian, or noticed by the news media. For the curators, intent governs choice and fixes a thing's identity. The taxonomy that they invoke distinguishes between real and artificial, genuine and fake, heartfelt and self-interested. While the distinction may bear truth, the quest for authenticity may miss a civic opportunity.

If memorials aspire to eternity, finitude haunts them. What keeps a monument alive, vital beyond the generation that built it? Regarding the Vietnam Wall, assume that the practice of leaving became common knowledge. Let people reflect with due deliberation about an offering. It could be a civic occasion to see what they create. The (alleged) importance of citizens' motivation would recede before the things themselves. Oftentimes floral arrangements from elementary schools appear at the Wall. That parents and teachers have to suggest the idea and assume logistical responsibility for the arrangements does not detract from the sincerity of the gesture or its visual impact. Besides, social norms and pressures could well operate to discourage frivolous or attention-getting gestures. Imagine a polity in which citizens felt an obligation to leave something, something fitting and appropriate, at the Wall. A pilgrimage to the Wall would be an opportunity for each generation of citizens to learn something about the war and its place in American history and culture. If I were to bring a gift to the Wall in 2007, for instance, it would be a miniature glass coffin with both POW/MIA and American flags laid to rest inside.³⁰

The politics of the gift that I suggest gesture toward the Vietnam Veterans Memorial's failure, contrary to self-promotional claims, to realize the criteria informing it.[31] Or if it does realize them, the cost complicates, perhaps vitiates, its success. Such an outcome is the stuff not of patriotic narrative but rather of tragedy. The Wall, designed to heal and provide catharsis, also inflames a number of old wounds. In providing relief to some it denies it to others; it includes and excludes, unites and divides, mends and rends. For example, with the establishment of criteria for inscription on the Wall, the Memorial rejected and diminished soldiers who lost their lives thanks to service in Vietnam but were not killed in action in the conventional, that is, heroic sense: in combat. Among those ineligible are those killed from the effects of Agent Orange, a new and insidious form of friendly fire, as well as those who committed suicide because of the war's traumas. Recognizing discrimination to be a serious problem, Congress ultimately passed legislation directing the Memorial to add a plaque recognizing the excluded—though not by name. Placed by Hart's Three Soldiers, one plaque honors all. With these soldiers thus acknowledged as a group, the Wall remains the prized and privileged place to be. The patriotic economy of death welcomes the lives of some veterans more than others. Jan Scruggs, though officially denying it, subtly signaled opposition to the plaque (fig. 7): "There are certain works of architecture in the world that should be allowed to make a statement *without additions. We must* get Congress to bring an *end* to *permanent new additions* to the Vietnam memorial . . . We are just concerned about *the next plaque. It's* just a matter of time."[32]

Thus Scruggs obscured and sought to monopolize the political character of the Wall. And he was right that it was just a matter of time before further permanent additions to the Vietnam grounds were proposed, for I would like to propose one here. The war was fought at home, not just abroad, and American citizens sacrificed their lives here as they tried to bring it to an end. According to John Schaar, patriotism's advocate, you can serve and support your country in opposition as well as obedience. And you need not leave the country to give or lose your life for it. The home front can prove lethal too. The students killed at Kent State and Jackson State, Vietnam veterans too, earned the right to be honored in Washington, on the Mall, on the Vietnam grounds, on the Wall itself.[33] To include antiwar opposition would recognize the national movement

7. Vietnam plaque.

(below) 8. Vietnam Veterans Memorial (wall) inscription.
Both photos courtesy of Bob G.

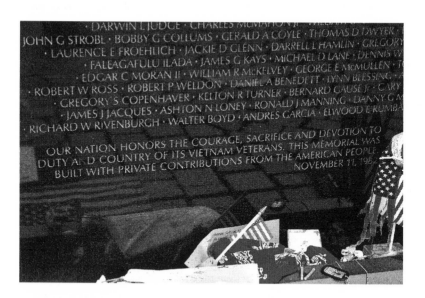

against the war and affirm that democratic citizenship expresses itself in a variety of ways. The American tradition supposedly admires and respects the defiance of state power. Soldiers do not own a monopoly on sacrifice or heroism (fig. 8).

Scruggs, I suspect, agrees. In *To Heal a Nation* he devotes a page to what he regards as the antiwar movement. "Back in late 1979, the VVMF learned that their *anticipated foe*—the antiwar movement—was awakening. Of all the thousands of letters the *Washington Post* received, the newspaper's editors had chosen to publish an *attack* on the notion of a veteran's memorial. 'The tens of thousands of young Americans who were forced—through the draft—to fight the immoral war certainly deserve better treatment today and recognition of their suffering,' it read. '[But] if this memorial is to serve any positive purpose, it must include all war resisters who were imprisoned for resisting the draft. This is the minimum, the very least that must be demanded.'"[34]

Scruggs's reading of the letter is disconcerting. Gratuitously resurrecting if not inventing a political adversary, it defines the so-called antiwar movement as the enemy, unless the movement remains silent or mimics the position of the Vietnam Veterans Memorial Fund. Though Scruggs misrepresents the letter as an attack—an attack, moreover, on the very idea of a veteran's memorial—the letter as quoted pursues a goal consistent with the healing and reconciliation championed by the Memorial: inclusion of those who sacrificed their freedom to oppose the war. Yet Scruggs equates the letter's expansion of the memorial idea with outright opposition to it. While the fund may have been unwilling to engage hardcore patriots who fought against the Wall and demanded Three Soldiers as reparations, it was ready to do imaginary battle with supposed remnants of the antiwar movement—despite Scruggs's claim that "the Memorial should have a healing effect for all Americans." Does healing therefore possess unwritten limits? Perhaps healing (of some) presupposes and engenders wounding (of others)? Or perhaps the will to reconciliation, converted to a mantra, fosters blindness to its logic? If anything, while Scruggs worried about the "next plaque," the Wall was attacked by other memorial developments: the Korean War Veterans Memorial (fig. 9) and the World War II Memorial.[35] Thanks to commemorative architecture, America continues to do battle with itself.

9. Korean War Veterans Memorial. *Photo courtesy of Bob G.*

Silence distinguishes the Vietnam Wall. The Lincoln and Korean feel chaotic by comparison. Everyone seems to agree: the churchlike atmosphere at the Wall is an authoritative sign of success. The Memorial offers a perennial regimen of ceremonies and tributes, especially on patriotic holidays. What happens at these solemn occasions? Does the Memorial's ethos, as captured by the design competition criteria, prevail?

At the Memorial Day ceremony in 2000, upwards of two thousand people gathered in front of the Wall. Thanks to General Barry McCaffrey, the keynote speaker, the commemorative space of the Vietnam Memorial morphed into an angry patriotic political space.[36] Remembrance of the dead remained privileged, but the ethos of healing vanished.[37] No one seemed to notice. Perhaps because of the Wall's reason for being, the Vietnam War continues. McCaffrey still fights what he takes to be the good fight. While some wounds may be healed by the memorial's therapeutic properties, to the extent that the Wall lends itself to contending interpretations of the war, it cannot heal as advertised; it necessarily exposes and reopens larger cultural and political wounds. And the goals of healing and reconciliation may be flawed in conception, compromised from the outset: flawed if the struggle over Vietnam represents a broader ongoing moral and political conflict over questions of American national identity and institutions; compromised if these questions, permanent and perpetual, befit a democratic polity. McCaffrey's strident offering may have jolted the peace and quiet of the site and the occasion, but under the narcissistic terms of patriotic self-assignment, manner and message combined to make eminent good sense.

According to McCaffrey, the (first) Gulf War offered the American military, at long last, an opportunity for redemption in the wake of Vietnam. Unconditional victory in the Persian Gulf demonstrated what could have been achieved in Southeast Asia had the military been similarly supported and set loose. McCaffrey's subjects of indictment included politicians and by implication the antiwar movement. Any other understanding of the Gulf War would set back Vietnam War revisionism.

McCaffrey's remarks, as they were delivered, transformed the Vietnam Veterans Memorial into a Vietnam War Memorial. To McCaffrey, the truth of things seemed clear. Vietnam represented "seven years of endless violence in an indecisive war" that "bloodied our generation of Americans."[38] As his thundering voice grew increasingly angry, the flood of names behind him buttressed the passions in play. The dead moved closer. He spoke to and for them. Borrowing their moral power, he became their voice. McCaffrey denounced the presence of so many names on the Wall. His antiwar speech harkened back to interwar Germany: there the political classes were said to have betrayed the nation's fighting men, hamstringing them at every turn and preventing them from fighting the war to win it. Similarly, young men served well in Vietnam; they were not well served by their political leaders. Nevertheless, their sacrifice—that they were sacrificed—made the later success of the Gulf War possible. This time the military enjoyed the tools it needed (including public support) to win and win decisively. Lightning triumph in the Gulf War meant that 58,000 men did not die in vain after all. Meaning replaced futility. Vietnam veterans were now truly, fully home. As for future Vietnams: Never again, McCaffrey intoned.

In the process of collapsing two wars, McCaffrey enacted Rorty's mythmaking patriotism. Victory in the Gulf War made vindication in Vietnam possible. The Gulf War's success miraculously reached back in time and became retrospective, retroactive proof of the military's prior victimization. It was as if the Vietnam War had been won and the nature of the war erased. McCaffrey thereby made the American military safe for the world today. Thus the fundamental issue becomes not what America did or did not do in Vietnam, but what America needlessly did to itself; hence the need to identify the real enemy, the one at home, the enemy within. Patriotism's virtuous circle turns vicious.

Thanks to McCaffrey, the Vietnam Memorial's architectural shortcoming emerges: the absence of the other. The Wall ducked the issue. Tactical evasion may have made emotional catharsis possible, but catharsis so arranged verges on narcissism. The emotions unleashed at the Wall—focused on America—seem retarded. The Wall itself stunts them. What of America's ethical condition? When will the country confront Vietnam in the round, what it did there not just to itself but to others? We stare at 58,000 American names. Forty walls would be needed to name the Vietnamese dead. You cannot fight a war alone.

Thus it seems timely to rethink the silence of the Vietnam Memorial. For silence can be read in many ways. At the Wall it encompasses respect, grief, mourning, and loss. It can also be symptomatic of silencing. Isn't it ironic that Vietnam, synonymous with passionate, pervasive moral and political upheaval, should yield a stilled civic memorial space? The Memorial, dominant practices and design criteria notwithstanding, provides a protected site where one understanding of the war reigns. Barry McCaffrey offers an example; Rolling Thunder Inc. offers another.[39] Thanks to it, the so-called POW/MIA cause thrives; yet championing the return of nonexistent POWs/MIAs, announced every Memorial Day in Washington through deafening—silencing—motorcycle engines, amounts to denying war's end. Rolling Thunder Inc.'s crusade converts the U.S. military into stabbed-in-the-back victim and allows the war's supporters to distract attention from the war itself. To perpetuate the MIA/POW myth shields the war (and thus the Wall) from reflection and potential criticism and holds out the promise that one day, the day of return, the war might be redeemed. In the interim, best to maintain a discreet silence while America remains at war. It is time to break the code of silence.

NARRATING THE VIETNAM MEMORIAL

The Vietnam Veterans Memorial resists a single interpretation. Nonetheless, Charles Griswold, like Nicolaus Mills with the World War II Memorial, tries to capture and fix its essence through an account of his visit to it. Griswold presents his narration of the memorial as reflective first-hand reportage. His essay also amounts to a political intervention, more specifically an instruction manual on how the Wall ought to be experienced and understood. He thus pursues what he calls "true objectivity" and "*the meaning of the* VVM."[40] Apparently Griswold would finish what Maya Lin began.

Griswold understands the Vietnam Memorial to be patriotic in aim and effect. It addresses the nation as a whole and seeks reconciliation by "rekindling love of country" as well as "a reaffirmation of the values for which [it] stands." For Griswold, patriotic politics must be distinguished from its sectarian counterparts. It transcends ideological or interest-driven intrusions into public affairs. Patriotism refuses the spirit of factions and the lure of particularity. Because the Memorial would "make no political statement about the war," it would not "exacerbate old wounds and reignite old passions."[41] Griswold assumes the impulses animating the Memorial to be noble.

Yet the Memorial's healing ambition depends in part on a prior interpretation of the War not subject to challenge. According to Griswold, "*the Vietnam War split* the American people into warring factions united only by their hate for each other."[42] Likewise Scruggs described the Memorial as "intended to help heal the divisions in the country *caused by the war.*"[43] And this interpretation dovetails with a normative vision of the American republic and its people. Oneness characterizes America at its best, located on the higher plane of founding norms, guiding principles, and defining values—in short, patriotism, which the Lincoln and Washington achieve and embody.[44] The Vietnam Memorial, according to Griswold, carries on the tradition.

Take Griswold's interpretation for granted. Does the Vietnam Memorial so conceived do a service to the republic? Supporters of the war can take pride in the sacrifices that veterans made on behalf of the country and the recognition they receive. Opponents can retain their objections to the war and nevertheless acknowledge and respect the soldiers who did what they were asked to do by their country. Warring sides can meet on the common ground of our "overarching values." On Griswold's reading, the patriotism that the Memorial invokes and celebrates privileges a conception of politics reduced to expressions of unity rooted in love of country. The domestic drama of the Vietnam War turned solidarity into a casualty. The Memorial thus helps restore America to its natural political condition.

Griswold presents the Memorial's dedication ceremony in 1982 as exemplary of patriotic politics, a Founding moment that defines and fixes the meaning of the site. According to Griswold, it was a day dominated by authentic patriotic sentiment. Expressions of love of country were open and abundant. The stirring sound of "God Bless America" reverberated through the air. American exceptionalism fully displayed itself. The country could once again feel good about itself and its place in the world. America resembled a ray of sun—America as life-giver. "In spite of everything," and no matter what, America is good.[45] Griswold thus meets Richard Rorty. Griswold privileges his brand of politics, patriotism, and refuses to grant to alternative conceptions any expressive possibility at the memorial. "On the other hand, the vvм has not—and again I believe will not—become a rallying place for unreflective and unrestrained exhibitions of a country's self-love."[46] Despite the prohibition against pro- and antiwar demonstrations on its premises, McCaffrey and Rolling Thunder Inc. belie Griswold's claim. Moreover, citing the patriotic dedication ceremony as a yardstick disqualifies forms of politics that a democracy routinely encounters while exempting itself from problematization. Once the Wall had extended such an open-ended interpretive invitation, Griswold's patriotic politics could be installed as a template only through the arbitrary prohibition of "other" forms.[47] What kind of democracy forbids rallies at the Memorial born of the very war made famous by moral and political protest?

Although Griswold does not acknowledge it, the Vietnam War can also be understood as revelatory in nature. Vietnam functions as code for an amalgam of moral and political divides that traverse the country. Vietnam can be understood, that is, more as occasion than cause. The end of the war could not end the conflicts that it came to symbolize. "Vietnam" can be displaced but not removed, and the language of reconciliation and healing suggests the latter ambition even if it does not quite insist upon it. Danger does not stem from exacerbating old wounds or reigniting old passions; it lies with repression.

William Hubbard, by contrast, considers the Vietnam Memorial a failure, a monumental failure, you might say.[48] Hubbard insists that while monuments speak, the Wall fails to talk. Allegedly an instance of a modern impulse that thinks of art not as creating something about the world but as something to be in the world, Hubbard considers the Wall inarticulate, mute.[49] This is not to say that Hubbard would prefer glorification of the Vietnam War along the lines of the Marine Corps Memorial. He concedes that to confuse and collapse the two wars would have been a lie.[50] Yet when it comes to commemoration, Hubbard privileges the will to glorify. He knows what he wants from his monuments. They reveal truths already operative in a polity. They tell us, in other words, what we supposedly already know. They answer, they resolve, they finalize. They confirm and thereby solidify. Thus when Hubbard writes that monuments ought to speak, he means that he wants to be instructed, informed, guided, told. Yes, monuments tell us things. They tell us, at their best, what to think. (Freedom is not free, for example.) They have messages that are "readily accessible to our ordinary understanding."[51]

Hubbard does not dismiss or deny the profound affective power of the Vietnam Veterans Memorial, but he insists that emotion alone does not and cannot suffice for public monuments in the absence of determinate advice on vexing human affairs. Insofar as Hubbard equates speaking with speaking one thing—such that nothing more needs to be said—he misses the other ways in which the Wall does speak and allows visitors to speak. As Griswold points out, the Wall is fundamentally interrogative. It prompts questions. While Griswold seeks a transcendent patriotic unity that can exorcise the specter of Vietnam from American culture and politics, Hubbard seeks an immanent consensus that provides final resolution to the conflicts the war supposedly produced.[52] Both Griswold and Hubbard seek denouements expressing certainty. Yet they each oppose politics. Not their own, of course, but the politics of others. They both presume America to be (naturally) one with itself, and if division and discord predominate, they blame the demon politics. Hubbard would resolve the war and heal the nation by demolishing the Wall. Griswold would resolve the war by domesticating the Wall through interpretation. Thus the Wall haunts each of them: Hubbard by its existence, Griswold by its elusiveness. What more could be asked of a monument?

TO DESTROY A MONUMENT IS TO SAVE IT

Perhaps suspicion fits a democracy that builds monuments of truth and memorials of fidelity to itself. What if instead, a democracy both committed itself to and ultimately betrayed its own affirmations as it pursued the commemorative enterprise? Imagine a democracy that could embrace and then release ad infinitum its own eternalizing impulses and imperatives. Imagine a democratic character enacted by a will to question and doubt, consummated by an ability to act on that doubt and let it take shape in the world.

A final thought. The Vietnam Syndrome exceeds American involvement in international affairs. In Washington, it includes a monumental aversion to innovation. The Mall's classic structures tend to starve and suffocate the public space that they govern and control. If anything, therefore, the World War II and Korean Memorials testify to the genius of Maya Lin's Wall. As James J. Kilpatrick remarked: "Viewing it, each of us may remember what he wishes to remember—the cause, the heroism, the blunders, the waste."[53] Kilpatrick's remembrance list, by no means exhaustive, reminds you that no reading can achieve final, privileged status here. Thanks to death, the Wall brings life—however faint—to a decrepit Mall. Perhaps America's democracy needs Vietnams—not patriotism—to be.

Antiquity had been a civilization of spectacle . . . With spectacle, there was a predominance of public life, the intensity of festivals, sensual proximity. In these rituals in which blood flowed, society found new vigour and formed for a moment a single great body. . . . We are much less Greeks than we believe. We are neither in the amphitheatre, nor on the stage.—MICHEL FOUCAULT, *Discipline and Punish*

I believe there is more to my films than their entertainment value. I have written and directed with the purpose of seeking out the truth as best I can . . . I pray for my country. I love it as much as any man. I served in its armed forces with some distinction, but that is not to say that I am a nationalist or a blind "patriot."—OLIVER STONE

We resolved a year ago to honor every last person lost. We owe them remembrance and we owe them more. We owe them, and their children, and our own, the most enduring monument we can build: a world of liberty and security made possible by . . . America.—GEORGE W. BUSH

Patriotism and Death:
Wounded Patriotic Attachments

Democracy, it is said, requires patriotism to be. If freedom promises life with distinction, patriotism makes life possible in the first place. This is a truth that the modern age has not only neglected but also forgotten—or so Richard Rorty, John Schaar, Charles Taylor, and others insist. Yet patriotism feeds on death. Death specifies patriotism's linchpin—moral, political, and affective. When it comes to love of country, democracies acknowledge many forms of service and signs of commitment; special honor, however, accompanies what is considered the ultimate sacrifice, namely that of life itself. Death seems unique in its ability to prove sincerity of commitment to country. Communities build shrines and cemeteries to the fallen;

fathers volunteer their sons for combat; mothers display their uniformed pictures on mantelpieces; citizens visit battle monuments and war memorials. Patriotic love, at its finest, discloses a willingness to die, and thus also to kill. Death furnishes the resources through which patriotism sustains itself. The benefits of death abound. Unity flows from it. Memories eternalize thanks to it. Meaning finds transcendence in it. Identity emerges in its wake.

In contrast to Foucault, I would argue that we are much more Greeks than we realize. Regarding death, even if the United States cannot make a strong case for its patriotic exceptionalism, it can at least argue for eminence. Consider the second half of the twentieth century: from John Kennedy's assassination to Vietnam, from the explosion of the spaceship *Challenger* to the bombing in Oklahoma City, from the attacks on the World Trade Center and the Pentagon to Ronald Reagan's funeral, America has mourned, memorialized, and brought itself to life in spectacular fashion—thanks to death. Whereas ritual patriotic acknowledgment formerly emerged from the inner logic of things, from willed contributions to commonly valued political achievement understood in advance to be such, patriotism has broadened its reach. Patriotism revels in postmortem identity politics. Patriotic ceremony and celebration attach themselves to lethal occasions as opportunities present themselves. And opportunities always seem to be presenting themselves. It's as if patriotism must seize on whatever mortality it can, whenever it can, to declare, demonstrate, and prove itself. Even too much death, it seems, is not enough.

Death's prominence raises questions, however. Can patriotism survive death's constitution of it? Can democracy afford patriotism's cost? Does democracy's alleged guarantor ensure its demise? What does it mean to theorize healthy forms of patriotism if all forms possess an umbilical link to death? What if the very success of patriotism's terms of discourse forces it to affirm that which it ostensibly opposes and abhors?

George Bush, for example, represents one of the latest instantiations of patriotism's addiction to death. After the mass slaughter in America in 2001, Bush turned the nation's military violence first on Afghanistan and then, inexplicably, on Iraq. The war on Iraq, I believe, involves something more than access to oil, regional military bases, familial revenge, or making the Middle East safe for Israel. America has debts to pay, legacies to fulfill, inheritances to expand, new obligations to impose. Simulating Pericles, Bush in classic Greek fashion goes to Iraq and creates his own living memorial to the victims of 9/11. With fresh contributions to Arlington secured, the cycle of patriotic death can repeat itself.

In short, patriotism and death tell stories both old and new. From Pericles to Oliver Stone, from Alexander Hamilton to George Bush, patriotism has married itself to death, and death, while faithful to patriotism until the utter, bitter end, has proved that undying loyalty kills what it purports to love.

DEATH TALKING

Enter Pericles, George Bush's ancient forebear. Patriotic performance art at its finest, Pericles's funeral oration to love of Athens standardizes civic eloquence, emotion, exhortation, and appeal. Given relatively minor modifications, it could travel with ease across political space and time. If the history of philosophy is a series of footnotes to Plato, then perhaps the history of patriotic discourse is a series of addenda to Pericles. Precisely because Pericles knows how to work a crowd of Athenian citizens, patriotism's problematic, self-subverting character can also be discerned. This doyen of death unwittingly announces the demise of patriotism at its rhetorical birth. Part history, part sermon, part eulogy, part polemic, part celebration, and part therapy, the speech strains under its own accumulated affective excess. Even as death inaugurates and sustains an order, it also seems poised to end it. Yet paradoxically, patriotism's tendency to self-destruct mirrors its ability to reconstitute itself and perdure in the world. Either as final accounting or perpetual postponement, for patriotism death keys the order.

Athens carefully orchestrated its public funerals, honoring its war dead annually. Burial grounds were located on the most prized land just beyond the city proper. Staging matters. Consider Pericles's oration. As if rising from the ashes, he walks from the tomb and ascends a stage that towers over the crowd, partly to facilitate communication.[1] After challenging the city's funereal traditions, Pericles salutes Athens's founding generation, whose multifarious virtues delivered a free city into the world. Remarkable though the first descendants were, Pericles claims that their own fathers deserve even greater praise, since they augmented the original bequest. Not content to preserve a legacy, they enhanced it. At considerable cost, they added an empire. This is what it means to pay a debt. You pay it with interest—without being asked. Neither nostalgia nor founding envy afflicts Pericles. While commemorating the past, he does not cravenly worship at its altar. He links present with past, but his is ultimately a forward-looking gaze. Athens, more specifically the free way of life that has made it great, anchors his concerns. "In this land of ours there has always been the same people living from generation to generation up till now . . . such that it is perfectly well able to look after itself both in peace and in war."[2]

Accordingly, Pericles launches into an account of Athenian exceptionalism, the purpose of which is to confirm publicly truths already held in common. Athens, like America three millennia hence, sets standards for other polities. It does not look elsewhere for yardsticks. Above all, Athens stands for democracy; the people reign. Equality before the law defines public life. In private, people are left alone to live their lives as they see fit. As freedom thus prevails throughout the city, Athens distinguishes itself from its neighbors, certainly from its enemies. Here Pericles has one target in mind. He fixes on—to emphasize—the differences between Athens and Sparta. Pericles celebrates Athens for the spontaneous affection and natural loyalty that it engenders in its citizens. Sparta, on the other hand, must artificially induce its people to serve the city. It relies on a relentless and repressive educational regime to manufacture its citizens' loyalty. Sparta must make a point of developing what flows freely in Athens. As a matter of course Athenians devote themselves both to city and to personal affairs.

Pericles's celebratory narration peaks with the judgment that Athens constitutes "an education to Greece."[3] Exemplary citizens made Athens great; Athens in turn made these citizens possible; hence a great democratic empire consisted of virtuoso citizens. Death links generations. With Pericles's narrative assistance, people can focus their imaginative powers and fall in love with their city. It is their duty to surrender to the emotions evoked. From recognition to reflection to lifelong commitment: like those who came before, the current generation must aspire to greatness. There is a model to emulate. Athenians must dedicate themselves to duplication. While Pericles acknowledges the difficulty of success, he does not so much rebuke the young in advance for shortcomings so much as invite them—dare them—to prove him wrong.[4] They too must be willing to sacrifice their lives—or have their lives sacrificed—for Athens.

Pericles's funeral oration is stirring. Yet its sheer brilliance calls attention to the patriotic logic at work. Pericles treats Athens as a condition of possibility; to be fulfilled, however, that possibility must be violated. At the founding, for example, Athens's creation presupposes destruction. Many lives are lost. Yet this death dynamic never ceases in the life of the city. Refoundings mean that death always returns; for a polity committed to its own glory, still more death looms ever on the horizon. Does death serve life or does life serve death? The greatness of Athens is the life that it makes possible through the sacrifice of its citizens. But the life is a life sacrificed for Athens. Life presupposes death which, to make life continue, must likewise continue. Death reigns.

Pericles attends to Athenian achievement, but the ceremonial occasion belies and obscures the city's simultaneous self-subversion. The city gives life and in so doing takes it. This is the tragedy the full force of which Pericles deflects. Service is natural; citizens accept risk; they give their lives; they willingly do battle; they die. Thus the reason why people love Athens also provides reason to hate it. The free way of life that depends on war, death, suffering, loss, and trauma cannot match the claims made on its behalf: "I declare that in my opinion each single one of our citizens, in all the manifold aspects of life, is able to show himself the rightful lord and owner of his own person."[5] Yet patriotism's lethal logic dictates disposable citizens at the city's behest.

Love therefore seems misplaced in politics, precisely because politics is intimately bound with death. The patriotic loyalty and affection demanded by Athens supposedly springs from the very nature of the city itself. It is said that Sparta cannot make this claim, for it must manufacture what it cannot evoke. Yet Pericles conducts a funeral ceremony, the elaborate details of which compromise claims to spontaneity. The ritual cultivates what it purports only to embody and express. Athens would not require elaborate communal rituals if its identity matched the claims made on its behalf. The very occasion that warrants the speech, war, reveals the challenge that death poses. Death's shadow might lead citizens to embrace something besides a life of absolute devotion to the city, since the city lives on without the dead, calling into question the city's paean to them. And dying for the city can be meaningful as an expression of freedom only with viable alternatives to it. Knowing this, Pericles insists that the man who does not involve himself in politics is not minding his own business; rather, *it is said*, he has no business at all in Athens.[6]

In *Émile* Rousseau famously turns to Sparta, Pericles's dreaded foe, as he describes the female citizen. "A Spartan woman had five sons in the army and was awaiting news of the battle. A Helot arrives; trembling, she asks him for news. 'Your five sons were killed.' 'Base slave, did I ask you that?' 'We won the victory.' The mother runs to the temple and gives thanks to the gods."[7] Similarly, Pericles offers comfort to survivors, to those who lost loved ones in battle. But he refuses to commiserate with them. Hence the oration that inspires also scorns expressions of sorrow or sympathy. Is this not the Spartan way? It's not that Athenians cannot or do not resent the sacrifices made for the city; they have "cares" like people everywhere that need to be addressed.[8] The city declines, however, to offer assistance for healing. Pericles tries to finesse the matter and render death unambiguous: "But this is good fortune—for men to end their lives with honor, as these have done, and for you honourably to lament them: their life was set to a measure where death and happiness went hand in hand. I know that it is difficult to convince you of this."[9] Pericles's rhetorical challenge faces an impossibility: Athenians must and yet cannot love the city. Because the city gives and takes life, makes life glorious and ugly, it also renders itself unworthy of the love it is said to engender but in fact demands unconditionally. Pericles succeeds in that he can "remind" people why they (must) love Athens and induce them to forget why they cannot love it. He must persuade without convincing, because parents, wives, and children do not equate the death of their children, husbands, or fathers with happiness. What kind of love resorts to death and its traumas to solicit it? Pericles thus enacts death's perfection and exhaustion. Death is not just necessary but constitutive, essential. Pericles figures an Athens slated to auto-destruct.[10]

Alas, we are Pericles's children. America, following ancient tradition, augments its patriotic legacy by reinventing goodness, a collective self-conception that binds the order as much as commitment to any political principle does. Thus in the second half of the twentieth century, America embraced the project of memorialization with a vengeance. Death provided indispensable occasion (and cover) to do political work that might otherwise have raised serious objections. While monumental proliferation may have been the ironic product of the Vietnam Veterans Memorial, I might trace America's memorial obsession with its own goodness to the success of another site that seemed unlikely to make a lasting name: John Kennedy's Grave.

In terms of memorialization, the Kennedy Memorial, Oklahoma City National Memorial, and George Bush's World Trade Center Memorial, among others, conjure a distinctive patriotic web.[11] Distinction derives in part from the events that inspired them. They are different: sudden, shocking, irruptive, inexplicable, unwarranted. Since the target is America qua America, land of intense love, the immediate victims become almost secondary. America suffers not just an attack but a hate crime, an identity assault. America suffers because of what it stands for, what it represents, thus for its very being. And because of America's unsuspecting role, the country's character uniquely announces itself. The attacks remind Americans of just how much they love their country, thereby enhancing it. In short, rather than pay tribute to the country for something achieved, these sites pay tribute to America in and of itself. Because traditional patriotic structures acknowledge, however imperfectly, sacrifice and suffering, they tie the processes of memorializing and monumentalizing to actual accomplishment—not to being. Here the route to revelation reverses common patterns. Thanks to others, America's true identity emerges— hence the repeated invocation of the nation's response to Oklahoma City and September 2001. That response proves—if proof were needed—that America was misjudged by its enemies. The sites of the attacks become deeply patriotic sites because they seem to transcend politics. The events brought out the best in the country. They disclosed character. They provided a test and the country excelled. In Rorty's terms, we know that we excelled. We congratulate ourselves on our performance. We pause, look around, and admire what we see: us. President Bush said of September 11: "After America was attacked, it was as if our entire country looked into a mirror, and saw our better selves."[12]

Paying homage to Periclean Athens, Bush's America forges a new road to "exceptionalism." After infamous events, the country attaches itself to wounds inflicted—to take possession of them, to make them its own. As Bush leads a National Prayer Service three days after the 2001 attacks, he acknowledges that wounds do not heal quickly. Yet Bush does not play the role of First Healer at this solemn occasion. Life must assert normalcy, but

America found its mission on September 11 and it must tend the sorrow and rage that gave birth to it. They can be generative, sources of energy on which to draw. American resolve for the long wars ahead must not falter. Death triggers life; life looks for death. Bush carries with him the police badge of George Howard, a daily reminder of the day's slaughter. The memorial gift of a mother in mourning, the death token gives a name and a face to murder. It concentrates and intensifies the unforgettable.

Like Pericles's funeral oration, America's memorial innovation forecasts danger. A community in mourning is one thing; a community aggrieved in perpetuity something else. Professions of innocence and victimization suggest a complex reality. Framing the world through wounds routinely opened and reopened reinforces a perspective prone to blindness and distortion. A reactive political optic also narrows the field of options unduly and converts one or two possibilities, retaliation dressed up as justice, say, into imperatives. A country that habitually builds memorial structures from and to a sense of its own victimization is a country to watch.

Accordingly, I revisit below the subjects of two patriotic narratives to ascertain whether patriotism's impossibility can be displayed and its magic spell broken. The first stars the myriad figurations of John Kennedy; the second the 9/11 memorial assemblage of George W. Bush.

INVENTING KENNEDY, INVENTING AMERICA

Philip Bigler's *In Honored Glory: Arlington National Cemetery: The Final Post* reads like Arlington's official biography.[13] The chapter devoted to John Kennedy provides critical information, against the author's intent, about the fabrication of not just the Kennedy mystique but also the manufacture of sacred patriotic space. Kennedy cannot be celebrated for his life and accomplishments, but only for his death. Death gave meaning to a life otherwise void of enduring political achievement. Kennedy's legacy is and must be his assassination. The mysteries surrounding the assassination offer abundant opportunity for political projection, and are a sign that this was no ordinary assassination, no ordinary victim.

Kennedy's killing stunned the country. After his spectacular murder Washington officialdom faced funeral quandaries. Though it was widely assumed that Kennedy would be buried with his children in Boston at the family gravesite, presidents require options. Sargent Shriver, Kennedy's brother-in-law, first contacted Arlington National Cemetery. When

Jackie Kennedy finally made her wishes known, she invoked the funeral of another murder victim, Abraham Lincoln, as a model. The decision to bury Kennedy in Virginia seems to have been driven by Secretary of Defense Robert McNamara and Robert Kennedy.[14] Of the several burial sites offered, Robert Kennedy selected the hill beneath the mansion once owned by Robert E. Lee. It provides a panoramic view of Washington and aligns beautifully with the Lincoln Memorial and the Washington Monument. It seemed as if Kennedy's place in history could be secured by grave-digging fiat. Mrs. Kennedy finished the plans by insisting the site include an eternal flame, an idea borrowed from France's tribute to the unknown soldiers of the First World War.

As Bigler notes, Kennedy's grave achieved instant success. While large crowds were expected immediately after the death and funeral, these expectations were exceeded. And no one anticipated the enduring popularity of the site.[15] In addition to offering architectural commentary on the design of the gravesite, Bigler ponders what has become the cult of Kennedy: "The eternal flame remains the focal point of the memorial grave and successfully symbolizes the continued legacy of the President's ideals." The ideals themselves do not require (mere) articulation. To state the obvious would be insulting. Besides, longing tinged with a double dose of frustrated anticipation seems to define the response to Kennedy's (un)timely death. Bigler leaves it to a Kennedy "friend" to synthesize: "the shame of the assassination is what might have been because today and tomorrow we shall miss him and we shall never know for sure how different this world might have been had fate" not intervened.[16] To read the assassination as a shame thus forges ample patriotic opportunity: Kennedy's truncated presidency becomes a blank slate ready for a suitable political script. Enter Oliver Stone.

Stone's cinematic monument to Kennedy, *JFK*, presents an answer to the "what if" speculation defining Kennedy. Stone conceives himself as no blind patriot; but love of country and clarity of vision do not ordinarily coexist, and Stone's cinematic paean is no exception. It constitutes one of the great patriotic works of art in the nation's cultural history. If anything, Stone raises Rorty's storytelling art to fairytale heights. Stone's world names a narrative paradise where believing something can make it come true. *JFK* thus offers additional cultural reportage on patriotism's narcissism.

JFK loves America. The specter haunting the film is not so much Kennedy's murder mystery as the Vietnam War—though these two signal events cannot ultimately be separated in Stone's optic. Each poses great challenges for patriotic appropriation. Though *JFK* addresses uncomfortable truths about America and refuses to flinch at the ugliness it discerns, it performs its own sleight of hand. America, according to Stone, suffers a tragic fall of Greek proportions, a downward spiral set in motion by Kennedy's brutal, calculated removal. Despite the demise, however, the country lives on unspoiled. America remains self-same, good and true to itself if people still believe in (the idea of) it. Hence *JFK* becomes a celluloid monument to an American leap of faith in itself.[17]

The film's posthumous task: to *make* Kennedy worthy of *his* assassination. Jim Garrison, district attorney of Orleans Parish, stars as the agent of transmogrification. He concocts an elaborate conspiracy theory animated by a complex web of geopolitical motivations that he seems to have discovered. Stone rejects as unthinkable, even unpatriotic the idea of a lone gunman acting on his own demented initiative to achieve fame. That idea de-romanticizes and de-politicizes Kennedy. Thus, the most ironic comment in the film may be Garrison's angry retort to Clay Shaw, reputed assassination ringleader, as he leaves Garrison's office after interrogation. Shaw indignantly asserts his patriotism in response to Garrison's accusations. Garrison replies: "Mr. Shaw . . . you're the first person I ever met who considered it an act of patriotism to kill his own president." Yet Stone's film likewise considers it an act of patriotism, if with a wrinkle. Stone fabricates JFK through his murder. The John Kennedy killed in Dallas in 1963, for all his fame, lived in American memory without sufficient legacy. Kennedy had to be re-killed and his legacy—preempted, stolen—magnified. Kennedy planned to remake America. That's why he was killed. Or, better, that's why Stone killed him. For Stone, Kennedy's death means that America can live. America's salvation depends on Kennedy's retrospective sacrifice. It's a question of storytelling.

STONE CONTRA REAGAN

Stone's American tragedy faces two serious narrative obstacles. First, assuming that Kennedy's assassination was the product of a conspiracy, why was he killed? Why did he have to be killed? Second, even with an explanation, how do you prove that which cannot be proven? How do you bring people to believe what they feel to be true but don't actually know?

Stone answers the first question in classic Greek fashion. Garrison's murder investigation climaxes when he travels to Washington to meet an unidentified source claiming to have critical information on Kennedy. Near the Lincoln Memorial, Garrison meets "X," a Pentagon intelligence officer with a long résumé. Critics of *JFK* complained that Garrison made no such trip to Washington; since Stone, they claimed, craves historical legitimation, many treated his cinematic license as a self-induced fatality. Admittedly, Stone inserts X into the narrative as a deus ex machina. As Stone's figment, X speaks the higher truth to which he aspires. Stone's patriotism generates him, for patriotism must have its truth.

X begins with a Rortyan history lesson in American covert operations. After the Second World War, the new Pax Americana treated the geopolitical universe as its plaything, arranging the fates of nations all in a day's work. The methods of choice were coups, assassinations, subversions, and installations. America, history's vanguard, would democratize the world in its own exceptional image. The Philippines, France, Italy, Guatemala, Iran, and Vietnam: X enumerates one American triumph succeeding another. "We were good, very good."

Not surprisingly, success fostered its own problem: hubris. America misjudged its talents and overreached. Cuba, for example, became an obsession resulting in the Bay of Pigs and the subsequent nuclear missile crisis. Kennedy, alas, inherited the mantle of geopolitical omnipotence. Rather than follow a dubious trajectory, he decided to reroute America's path. Possessing singular prescience, Kennedy understood Vietnam to be a nightmare waiting to scream. He ordered one thousand troops home in late 1963 and America's military presence terminated by the close of 1965. According to X, Kennedy thus branded himself a cold war turncoat. By November 1963 his term would expire. The country turned in on itself as the antidemocratic talents that America honed abroad came home.

In Stone's narrative possession, Kennedy understands that power's creative capacity flows not from wanton exercise but from self-imposed discipline. He thereby reinvents it. Kennedy's radicalism transcends Vietnam. He planned to dismantle the CIA, eviscerate Pentagon capitalism, and extinguish the cold war. Kennedy had to be killed because, in Garrison's words, "he wanted to change things." Stone's Kennedy intended to remake America and set an example for the world in a virtual second creation. Kennedy's America, as if inspired by George Washington, would cede what no nation of its level had ever voluntarily ceded: its own power. Peace would have become the ultimate sign of strength: godlike, America would have no actual need for its awesome power.

Stone presents the world according to X as irresistible truth. Garrison treats him as an oracular figure whose communiqués gain power through their brevity and opacity. The romanticizing of X, however, also betrays his narcissism. Evidently nostalgic, X longs for the heyday of an American Empire operating unchallenged but responsibly as a force for democratic good in the world. Not even imperial malfeasance made him aware of empire's inherently self-defeating character, namely that it destroys the democracy it allegedly serves. Thus X's narcissistic lament awes. He betrays no concern for the violence done to the world by America's exercise of its will to power. Only violence on America's homeland, specifically Kennedy's murder, becomes morally problematic for him. Still, X serves Stone's America well.

Stone's reinterpretation of Vietnam, through X, confirms truths of country already possessed. America's inherent goodness and innocence receive unprecedented respect. Stone's construal trumps the right's rendering of Vietnam as a noble endeavor, which rests on graves of denial about the war's prosecution. Stone posits a conspiracy behind Kennedy's murder. Powerful interests in and out of government demanded the Vietnam War. Lyndon Johnson, designated tool of these interests, delivered the war they wanted after Kennedy's elimination. Consider the upshot of X's claim: without Kennedy's murder, no Vietnam War.[18] Stone's revisionism suggests not just that Vietnam need not have happened. If not for the coup that took place in Dallas on November 22, 1963, it would not have happened. Thus American responsibility in and for Vietnam disappears. On Stone's fantastical account American democracy becomes the victim of the Vietnam War. It was hijacked by a secret cartel of self-serving vipers that would stop at nothing to secure its aims.[19]

If this is why Kennedy was killed, how do you prove it? *JFK* opens like a documentary. President Dwight D. Eisenhower, with resolution and solemnity, warns America of the new, unprecedented threat that democracy faces from what he names a military-industrial complex. Eisenhower's authority as the ultimate insider looms large: Supreme Allied Commander who orchestrated America's victory in the Second World War, general turned statesman who transcended party and served two terms as president. Like George Washington, Eisenhower in his farewell address alerts the republic to dangers ahead. His veritable last act is a gift to the country and its people. Eisenhower's introductory presence provides authoritative context for Stone's sweeping criminal indictment of American political life.[20] Stone's conspiracy makes real Eisenhower's patriotic admonition. Eisenhower, it seems, anticipated Kennedy's politically inspired murder. You may not want to believe Stone, but you trust Eisenhower.

JFK recounts the sacrificial odyssey of Garrison, the skeptic who must be convinced of the truth that he comes passionately to believe. Garrison dropped his first investigation into the murder when it exhausted itself for lack of evidence. He reopens the case three years later after a casual but provocative conversation with Senator Russell Long, which led to a close reading of the Warren Report. The document casts suspicion on itself. To read it is to read a lie. This is the ur-text that Garrison targets for destruction. As the evidence mounts, Garrison's anger soars. As the crime's cast expands, Garrison's fury converts to holy crusade. "I say let justice be done, though the heavens fall." Garrison's determination to complete his self-assigned task mimics Will Kane's.

Stone deploys character portrayals to communicate, if indirectly, important truths. As Garrison's obsession deepens, for example, Liz Garrison turns from skeptic to critic—at home anyway. She accuses her husband of persecuting Clay Shaw, the man ultimately indicted for Kennedy's murder, because he is gay. Garrison resents the accusation. What's more, he cannot live with opposition. Berating himself for years of civic somnambulance, he roars that life consists of more than front lawns and dinner parties. The character of the country matters too, and the Garrisons have a responsibility to bequeath their children a sound American polity. The marriage verges on collapse when death—in the form of additional assassinations—rescues it. With Martin Luther King and Robert F. Kennedy killed because of their opposition to the Vietnam War, Liz recants. Now Garrison's willingness to privilege the public at the expense of the familial testifies not just to his patriotic convictions but also to the truth of his endeavor. Once she stands by her man, our doubts are assuaged too.[21] Liz plays Amy to Garrison's Will Kane. Her truth must be his truth, the truth of patriots.

Once Garrison travels to Washington to meet X, he recognizes that he cannot prove the truth he has come to know and live. X refuses to go public. Speaking truth to power shortens one's lifespan. X's nonchalance, however, which matches his confidence, translates to authority. This is no crusader driven by personal motives. The ultimate insider, the keeper of secrets, he does not care whether Garrison believes him. Rather, he encourages Garrison to do his own investigative work and make up his own mind. X wishes Garrison luck and disappears into the Washington mist. You are persuaded in part because X did not try to convince. While Garrison keeps secret his conversation with X, Stone shares it with you. You watch Garrison continue undaunted yet unable to cite X and close the case. He knows he's right; you now know he's right. With such esoteric knowledge, you start to bear the burden of Garrison's investigation. You come to know the truth that no one believes, the truth that the conspiracy wishes to conceal.

The narcissism of *JFK* proves effective; it unfolds right in front of you. Critical characters—Eisenhower, Garrison, X, Liz—reflect and reinforce each other. *JFK* demands and enforces unanimity, oneness. Each character experiences and expresses Stone's patriotic metaphysic. Each must undergo conversion before reaching and speaking the truth, a sequence that enhances the authority with which each is endowed. Each character, in short, echoes Oliver Stone.

For Stone, truth's possession involves more than knowledge attained. The film's rapid-fire delivery inundates you with images, words, movements, sights, sounds, facts, figures, speculations, theories, and possibilities. The murder investigation implicates you in an infinite regress into the unknowable and irresolvable, whether it's Oswald's defection and repatriation, his arrest and interrogation, the notorious rifle and its bizarre purchase, the logistics of Kennedy's trip to Dallas, or the impossible shooting itself. What happens when mystery is piled upon oddity is piled upon coincidence is piled upon circumstance is piled upon enigma? As epistemological dizziness rises, moral outrage emerges, and Kennedy's status soars. There is no time to sort out the celluloid barrage that Stone throws at you, so you go with your gut. Garrison comes to feel the truth of the conspiracy he investigates. As in *High Noon*, anger authenticates the truth that *JFK* articulates. Anger illuminates what otherwise refuses to make sense. Anger becomes a sign of truth. Assent to Garrison's truth then becomes a test of faith in America. Deny the conspiracy, betray America.

After the pilgrimage to Washington, Garrison's determination doubles. Despite sabotage, a trial takes place as scheduled. Paradoxically, the lack of a credible case against Clay Shaw works to Garrison's advantage. Without pretense to the contrary, he proceeds for strategic reasons. He hopes to use Shaw's prosecution, a patriotic spectacle to spread the Word, to blow open the conspiracy he has come to know. Truth employs whatever means available to ensure its eventual triumph. The trial will fail to win conviction, but Garrison knowingly risks injury to reputation, career, and life to see justice done. Like Socrates at his trial, Garrison speaks the truth regardless of consequences, even if no one can hear it. He becomes the selfless agent of a greater cause. He sacrifices Shaw, but requires nothing of Shaw that he does not impose on himself. Both fulfill Kennedy's patriotic injunction to ask not what your country can do for you, but what you can do for your country. A single battle may be lost, but the war can still be won. Garrison looks into the camera—not at the jury—as he concludes his summation: "It's up to you."[22]

Stone likewise requires the public's indulgence. Garrison's trial speculation reaches its emotional peak with the Zapruder assassination film. Zeroing in on the kill shot, Garrison runs it repeatedly, describing the movement of Kennedy's head: back and to the left, back and to the left, back and to the left. The moment transfixes the viewer. As with Spielberg's Normandy, you watch it, if you can watch at all, in horror. Stone dares you to look away. If you don't, you conclude that death most foul must have a reason behind it. It must be made to make sense: hence *JFK*.

The memorial success of *JFK*, however, may obscure its principal effect. Stone's John Kennedy died for the good of America. His death proves America's goodness. America's love proves Kennedy's goodness. Kennedy's timely death secures him a place in history. He can be remembered for his promise, for what he might have done, for what America might have become, had he lived and served two full terms. The Kennedy "what if" fantasy then slides into what Kennedy and America would have done. Finally, it's as if he can be credited with accomplishments that do not exist. Save one. Because it was an assassination, Kennedy's death creates and becomes his legacy. It gives life to "America." A nation of necrophiliacs, we worship his deadness.

Richard Rorty would likely call Stone's patriotism nihilistic. Stone may intend to empower America's disenfranchised, but the conspiracy that he reveals defies hope. Rorty sees stories well told and images sharply drawn as critical to citizenship. Artisans must regularly devote some portion of their talents and energies to the storytelling art. For the United States to cultivate its perfectibility, a sense of possibility and even inevitability must be inculcated. Hope for a better future must endure. And hope for the future depends on creation of a halcyon past. Yet as Stone's *JFK* relates America's tragic fall, the great national success story—truth, progress, invention, freedom—stops. America effectively died with Kennedy. True, what has been done might be undone, but Stone's America suffers too many obstacles.

Though Rorty decries the lack of patriotic tales in circulation at the century's close, he exempts filmmakers from rebuke. America's novelistic best and brightest, he contends, betray no interest in contributing to the common project. They squander their gifts—much like Stone—on counter-narrations that engage in national "self-mockery" and "self-disgust."[23]

Rorty's *Achieving Our Country* performs the patriotic task that he assigns to others. He spins an inspiring narrative about the cold war struggle that engulfed the United States, the West, and perforce much of the world for close to fifty years. While the thousand-year Reich lasted barely twelve years, Soviet Russia would prove more resilient. Communism's wicked empire at times seemed immortal. With the advent of nuclear weapons, the world lived for decades on the brink of apocalypse. Thus the cold war would seem to offer ample opportunity for glorification. West versus East, democracy versus dictatorship, freedom versus fear, individuality versus sameness, life versus death: a Manichean conflict at its core. Because of the nuclear dimension, the United States and the Soviet Union could not square off like traditional enemies. Escalation to the nuclear level could not be chanced. Life on the planet might be extinguished. Mortal enemies, however, need an outlet. War required reinvention.

Cold war, then, raged behind the scenes. Conflict would be perpetual and invisible, waged not on battlefields but in society itself. Antagonists belong not to the military branches but to espionage services. And because of the unique vulnerability of democracy, where openness converts strength to weakness, democracies must respond creatively to an unprecedented enemy. Fought largely in secret, one day this war would become the subject of legend, thus of great stories. Encore Kennedy.

Don DeLillo's *Libra* is an indispensable guide to patriotism—in part because he does not conceive the Kennedy assassination, the novel's ostensible subject, through its terms.[24] DeLillo excavates America's heartland and locates a unique political culture beset by violence, conspiracy, obsession, fanaticism, amorality, and evil. Yet the America portrayed in *Libra* resonates. DeLillo's sordid tale of apparent murder madness tells a story of consummate political innovation, even genius. Patriotism, service to beloved country, flourishes in *Libra*. Ironically, DeLillo has already answered Rorty's call for compelling, inspirational patriotic prose.[25]

NORMALCY IN THE HEARTLAND OF THE REAL

Patriotism swirls through the pages of *Libra*.[26] It operates as both condition of possibility and consumer effect. Through its generative logic, John Kennedy emerges as the warrior-statesman who gives his life for country and cause and becomes who he is. As with Stone, Kennedy's death names his destiny. It is only through murder that he can live. The brutality of forced finitude renders him immortal. By reconstructing *Libra*, I therefore tell a counter-story that not only discloses what love of country permits and demands but also suggests that you cannot love your country; the logic that governs its routine conduct and defines its enduring character renders it criminal. Consider this the ironic culmination of William James's methodological advice to enter the position of another.

DeLillo's America resembles Stone's—minus the romanticizing. The United States finds itself at peace in early 1963. The Bay of Pigs fiasco and the nuclear face-off that threatened to rain annihilation on the planet recede from memory. A tense stability has been secured and a young, dynamic president augurs a protean future. Yet a country prosperous and confident suffers its own unique set of problems. Or so believes Win Everett, longtime CIA operative condemned to internal exile at a small women's college in Texas. Being made a scapegoat was Everett's reward for the failed Cuban invasion. What has been called "the American disease" troubles him.[27] America alternates periods of passionate commitment with equal ones of utter indifference. What do you do if the country refuses to confront a mortal peril? What if the problem lies with the nation itself, or at least with those charged with its welfare? What is a patriot to do?

Everett combines Socrates, Spielberg's George Marshall, and Will Kane. Possessed of truth, vision, and ruthlessness, Everett resembles a gifted student of Machiavelli. *The Discourses*, among other things, suggests that people have a tendency toward sloth and slumber. So how might citizens in a republic safeguard their freedom from the threats they must negotiate? Machiavelli recommends crisis artificially induced.[28] Patriots warn republics of freedom at risk, and politics makes for great theater. From the bowels of Texas, Everett composes an epic designed to shake and transform the country. Once his morality play encounters an unsuspecting public, Everett anticipates not catharsis but convection. To be roused from its sleepy state, America needs an opportunity to reaffirm its faith, focus its will, concentrate its energies, and employ its power to eradicate forces of geopolitical evil that threaten a new dark age.

Everett likes to imagine that his masterstroke will become legendary. "Someday this operation would be studied at the highest levels of intelligence in Langley and the Pentagon."[29] It would become a model of covert political action suited for a democracy under siege. Yet Everett has more than glory in mind. He aspires to make a "personal contribution to an informed public" and a transparent political order.[30] The truth of Everett's scheme may remain hidden from full public view, but its essence can be shared with the American people. The public requires civic instruction in the niceties of power politics in a benighted time. People must know what is done in their name. They must learn that to desire the end, you must will the means necessary to achieve it. Thanks to Win Everett, innocence has no future. "This was the major subtext and moral lesson of [his] plan."[31]

Everett epitomizes the cold war warrior. Though he mans a desk, he lives on the front lines of a distinctive war. Democracy has to adapt itself to wage it. Imagination forms Everett's principal tool. Given the resources at his disposal, mere thought can take shape in the world. Thinking something can eventually make it happen. So be careful what you think.

Everett's journey from privileged insider to disgraced failure to patriotic entrepreneur tells the tale of America reinventing politics. *Libra* also details the evolution of a patriot. You learn what Everett will do, will sacrifice, for his country. Since he does not sing his own praises, they must be sung for him. They must be shared with America's schoolchildren, as Walter Berns recommends. If you love your country, by implication you love Win Everett.

Libra unfolds during the heyday of the American imperial adventure. Yet disturbing signs have become manifest. Cuba, barely ninety miles offshore, taunts America. Castro can organize communist revolution region-wide from his island fortress. Something must be done to stop his menace. America's "former" island possession demands restoration. Democracy, alas, imposes requirements of decency. Empires cannot proceed heavy-handedly. Appearances count.

Everett is a man in the know. Well positioned in America's labyrinthine, clandestine bureaucracy, his role is to take general policy concerns that flow from above and interpret them. Those in positions of authority must be protected. "The White House was to be the summit of unknowing. It was as if an unsullied leader redeemed some ancient truth which the others were forced to admire only in the abstract, owing to their mission in the convoluted world."[32] Everett's expertise perfects President Kennedy's ignorance. It is imperative to protect the president from knowledge of the theatrical production in which he is to have the starring role.

Kennedy's determination to rid the world of Castro was no secret. Everyone knew what Kennedy wanted; he made sure they knew it, "but they weren't allowed to let on to him that his guilty yearning was the business they'd charged themselves to carry out."[33] Those in Everett's position have to assign themselves responsibility for the nation's dirty business regardless of its moral cost—even to themselves. They accept the sacrifice. Because the nation cannot acknowledge what it asks of its sentinels, the honor due them cannot be made public. Thanks must be silent, gratitude tacit.

Two years after the Bay of Pigs, Vietnam preoccupies American officialdom. Cuba has been bracketed and set aside. Forgetting takes such little effort. With things at a crossroads, Everett must force the matter. What, though, can stir a sleeping giant? People seem comfortable in their comfort. Here Everett reveals his authorial inspiration. The situation requires something stunning, shocking, and sickening. Everett drafts his script to the last detail to produce the necessary effect. Planning must be meticulous. Everett deems the time apt and the nation ready for a public spectacle to which no invitation will be issued but attendance at which is certain.

Everett plans to fake an assassination of the president. "We want a spectacular miss."[34] The evidence, artfully and ambiguously placed, will suggest Cuban intelligence. Because Cuban culpability might seem unbelievable, Everett will concoct additional evidence exposing CIA efforts to terminate Fidel. Truth names the beauty of the second move. Context can make the spectacle sensible and consumable. Every action produces a counterreaction: tit for tat. The American people will be appalled. They will demand a response. Work aborted two years earlier will be brought back to life. This time around nothing but a full-scale invasion will sate the nation's war fervor. Cuba will have its final resolution.[35] The American Republic will be safe in the world.

John Kennedy lends himself to Everett's creation. What must the president do? Everett's inspiration is that Kennedy need do nothing at all. He won't even know what is being done in his name. To include him in the planning would be to implicate and compromise him. Thus Kennedy need only conduct his presidency as before. Everett can handle the rest. Kennedy stars in a production of which he is technically ignorant. DeLillo's Everett will do for Kennedy what Stone's Garrison did: reduce and thus elevate him to martyred avatar of patriotism, the heroic centerpiece of twentieth-century America.

Everett's idea possesses Machiavellian beauty. Simple, economical, and surgical, it represents theatrical politics at its finest. Everett's plan is no mere whim. The risks are high, but the times call for daring. Besides, Everett knows himself to be a patriot.[36] He warrants dramatic license. Communist revolution menaces Latin America. Can the United States remain free with the rest of the world enslaved? As Everett articulates his brainchild, he experiences the truth that love of country entails, namely concordance between self and order. Once you fold yourself into a larger trajectory, epiphany follows. Truth established, faith affirmed, identity achieved—all at once: "Some things we wait for all our lives without knowing it. Then it happens and we recognize at once who we are and how we are meant to proceed. This is the idea I've always wanted. I believe you'll sense it is right . . . It is essentially right. I feel its rightness . . . This plan speaks to something deep inside me. It has a powerful logic. I've felt it unfolding for weeks, like a dream whose meaning slowly becomes apparent. This is the condition we've always wanted to reach. It's the life-insight, the life-secret."[37]

Everett enjoys Kennedy's prior script approval, no audition necessary. A commander in chief puts those under his command in harm's way. How can he exempt himself from the military ethos of sacrifice that he over-sees? If he found himself likewise situated, would he not lead by example? If the president's participation were required to accomplish a vital national objective, how could he refuse? He too assumed the risks of office. He cannot demur because something might go wrong. This is wartime, after all. He who wills the end also wills the means necessary to it. He thus wills that his own life be risked. At another level, Kennedy provided the moral example for Everett's exercise in politics. "The barrier is down . . . When Jack sent out word to get Castro, he put himself in a world of blood and pain. Nobody told him he had to live there. He made the choice . . . So it's Jack's own idea we're guided by. And once an idea hits."[38] Once it hits, it seeks refinement and realization. With eliminating Castro the goal, Kennedy naïvely presumed that targeting Fidel through assassination ex-hausted his options. Everett's patriotic inspiration—to remove Castro by going through Kennedy—becomes his original contribution to freedom's cause.

As Everett conceived it, there was to be no assassination. Death would be gratuitous. A near miss would suffice to galvanize the nation. One of Everett's associates, T. J. Mackey, discerned the inner logic of Everett's conception. Failed assassination possesses elegance, but actual killing possesses magic. Death alone gives birth to legends. Mackey thus took Everett's plot, which "lacked the full heat of feeling," and perfected it.[39] Everett knew that he could not control his plan once he set it loose on the world. Though it was susceptible of modification, reinterpretation, and expropriation, he nonetheless remained its patriot author.

Win Everett can make JFK a patriot too. Kennedy's assassination offers him redemption. Hatred of the president reverberated throughout the country, the Deep South in particular. In Georgia, one of Kennedy's hit men spotted a drive-in showing *PT 109*, the cinematic ode to young John's war mettle. Cliff Robertson might not have been a sufficient draw, so the theater's owner offered an additional reason to sit through the exercise in hagiographical excess: "*See how the Japs almost got Kennedy.*"[40] After Everett's bold stroke, fully realized by Mackey, angry sentiment would vanish from the land. Not because Kennedy had been killed at long last, but because his assassination would prove that he was the man for the job after all. Kennedy's life would be transmogrified by death. No longer the effete establishment liberal ready to surrender the country to communism, Kennedy, born posthumously, would be the consummate cold war combatant who gave his life for freedom. Those who loathed him would be refuted. Everett would assist Kennedy with what the president would want, with becoming who he is. Patriotism's logic reveals its own political truths. Death signifies the value of a cause. If communism must be defeated, if Cuba must be liberated, if war entails casualties, it must be worth killing Kennedy.

Everett's political morality tale exudes narrative virtue. Once executed, it invites retelling. A straightforward sequence of events climaxes in a historical conclusion: from assassination, shock, and outrage to calls for action, invasion, liberation, restoration, and at last redemption. Kennedy, with Everett's and Mackey's assistance, delivers a decisive blow in an apocalyptic struggle. In death, Kennedy's presidency experiences rebirth. As Everett's script writes Kennedy's future, it rewrites his past. Castro removed, Cuba free, communism reeling: this becomes his tripartite legacy. The world changed, Kennedy mystique, once the object of scorn, returns as pure potent fact. The boy king made worthy of Camelot. The President need only die. If *PT 109* reflects Hollywood fantasy, Dealey Plaza in Dallas reflects Langley legend. Death defines the difference between them.

The Kennedy family's desire to see a slain president buried at Arlington and Richard Rorty's call for a heroic patriotic universe may not have envisioned the worlds of Oliver Stone and Don DeLillo. Yet patriotism can engender matrices of thought, feeling, and conduct in which "murder" befits John Kennedy. Stone kills him to save America from Vietnam; DeLillo's Everett kills him to save America from Cuba and communism. Either way, Kennedy sacrifices his life or has his life sacrificed for country. Patriotism, dedicated to America and its goodness, necessarily feeds on death. If you love your country, you must be prepared to sanction anything and give up everything—including ethical objections to the patriotic logic requiring it.

John Kennedy's assassination provided fertile ground for American patriotism in the second half of the twentieth century. Death found new political life. The events of September 11 afford similar possibilities for American patriotism in the twenty-first century. It is time to turn from Jacqueline Kennedy, Oliver Stone, and Don DeLillo to George Bush, death's latest acolyte, and Alexander Hamilton, his muse.

Poetically speaking, George Bush is no Pericles. He's no Abraham Lincoln either. He can't inspire a people through eulogy or alter a nation with three paragraphs and 272 words, but he may be the most revolutionary president to date. In America it has become de rigueur to say that everything changed on September 11, 2001. What if, rather, the United States after the attacks, thanks to George Bush, took advantage of a lethal moment to reconstruct America, proselytize its way of life, and alter the planet? "From the day of our Founding, we have proclaimed that every man and woman on earth has rights, and dignity, and matchless value, because they bear the image of the Maker of Heaven and earth. Across the generations we have proclaimed the imperative of self-government ... Advancing these ideals is the mission that created our Nation. It is the honorable achievement of our fathers. Now it is the urgent ... calling of our time."[41]

At Gettysburg Lincoln seized on the North's (possible) triumph in the Civil War as the rhetorical occasion to reinvent America and realize more fully the inherent promise of 1776.[42] In Washington 150 years later, George Bush launches not words but wars to bring American ideals to the world, starting with the Middle East. Lincoln articulated American sin and sought a just peace; Bush locates evil abroad and plans to purge it from the face of the earth. Lincoln's ideals flowed from Jefferson and the Declaration of Independence, Bush's from Hamilton (and Thomas Hobbes). Placing himself squarely in the American patriotic tradition, Bush through his war on terrorism uses a political project to complete and finalize a Founding ambition of the United States. American patriotism comes to be in war's crucible.

For Bush Afghanistan could not sate America's need to reassert and reaffirm itself. Following Pericles, Bush vowed to erect monuments to the victims of September 11 across the globe by liberating peoples and nations heretofore consigned to tyranny. In the process, Arlington National Cemetery's ranks of the honored dead would multiply. When the memorial project falters in Iraq, Bush insists that America stay the course and thereby honor the (already) dead who have sacrificed their lives. Staying the course means more dead to come, which in turn makes staying the course more urgent. Thus, patriotism's death logic.[43]

Bush's affair with death exceeds Arlington. After the attacks of September 2001 he developed a new rhetorical tic. While reiterating the nation's resolve to bring justice to those responsible, he began to invoke America's founding. You might suspect that Bush turned to America's beginnings to bolster his authority, enhance his prestige, and generate cover for contestable policies and actions. Indeed Bush may be waging a late modern fundamentalist crusade to rid the world of evil and bring freedom to its every corner, but his political mission, especially the fear-laden war of choice in Iraq, makes for a worthy addition to American history. Bush, it turns out, knows the founding. With respect to American exceptionalism, including the will to remake the world in our image, Bush keeps august company—likewise with respect to theorizing an America under siege, beset by enemies abroad, aided by naïve, ignorant, or weak-willed enemies at home. In short, American patriotic culture enjoys a long-standing, intimate relationship with death. Patriotism could not be without it.

FEAR OF VIOLENT DEATH

America has implicated the world in its undertakings since its inception. In *Federalist* 1, Hamilton articulated the stakes of the constitutional controversy facing America: "It has been frequently remarked that it seems to have been reserved to the people of this country, by their conduct and example, to decide the important question, whether societies of men are really capable or not of establishing good government from reflection and choice, or whether they are forever destined to depend for their political constitutions on accident and force." [44] American conduct and example thus involve responsibilities that surpass territorial boundaries.[45] The United States aspires to more than distant admiration. The whole world watches America and waits anxiously: "If there be any truth in the remark, the crisis at which we are arrived may with propriety be regarded as the era in which [freedom's] decision is to be made; and a wrong decision of the part we shall act may, in this view, deserve to be considered as the general misfortune of mankind." [46] Despite America's success, Hamilton's question remains unanswered for many other "societies of men." Because of America's success, however, the nation has become politically authorized and morally obligated to answer "the important question" on behalf of those others—whenever necessary. This is America's calling, what Bush over two centuries later refers to as the calling of our time.[47]

To appreciate Bush's mortal pedigree and its deep roots in American political culture, what better place to start than America's ratification debate? The *Federalist Papers* enjoyed fame and influence at publication, but I propose an alternative appreciation: the *Federalist Papers* as national monument. Etymology offers instruction. Monument derives from the Latin *monumentum*. It is closely related to "memorial," from the Latin *monere*, which means to remind. It can also mean to warn. To what would the *Federalist Papers* be a monument? In a word: death. The *Federalist* insists that if we are to think properly about ratification, it must be properly framed. Fear of death provides it: death from imperial conquest; death from civil war; death from internal dissolution; death from the Indian Nations; death from institutional lethargy. Death wears many masks in the new United States. Because of the specters haunting America, Hamilton seeks to establish American political discourse officially as a discourse about power and put a patriotic stamp on it. The vision of power bringing order to a dangerous, disintegrative world defines patriotism.[48] Thanks to death, George Bush can become Hamilton's patriotic heir two centuries hence.

Hamilton commences the *Federalist Papers* with an act of aggression. Constitutions theoretically enable political life, but in America life also seems to be a product, ultimately, of death. Death menaces America's constitution controversy, more specifically the probability that America will perish in its infancy. Having won a war of liberation from England, America finds itself under siege. Hamilton's patriotic narrations not only reflect but foster the very fear that he decries. It is necessary, for example, to warn readers that America's natural geographic advantages could prove illusory. While the Atlantic Ocean seems to represent an insuperable divide, European powers have already established a beachhead on the continent. Spain and Britain, dictated by mutual interest, could well make common cause against America. In addition, the Indian Nations are to be regarded as Europe's natural allies and our natural enemies. With America they have fear (of expansion); with Europe they have hope (of survival). Europe lives in the American neighborhood, and America plans to return the favor and travel to Europe's. America's imperial project thus brings it into proximity with Europe. Danger doubled. Engagement becomes not just national but global. The enemy encircles us at home; we imagine its future encirclement abroad.[49] Encounter becomes total and the threat of war omnipresent. If ratification fails, the only question will be whether rape for a "naked and defenseless" America will precede conquest and exacerbate our humiliation.[50]

While Hamilton and John Jay promise discussion rooted in arguments and reasons, they abandon the conversational principle once it is articulated. At the close of the first essay, Hamilton turns to the evils that inevitably follow Constitutional rejection. The dialectic of dissolution is harrowing. To oppose ratification is to oppose the Union. To oppose the Union is to promote disunion. Since disunion amounts to death, to oppose ratification renders you America's mortal enemy. You wish America dead. Hamilton's presumption of patriotic monopoly rules out the possibility of legitimate opposition. This is the Hobbesian rhetoric that the authors of the *Federalist* wield in article after article—though Hamilton makes a point of denying that he plays on emotions. They convert possible dangers into certain threats and reject any challenge to their alchemy. Patrick Henry, however, refused their rejection. In the Virginia state ratifying convention he observed that the United States fought and won a war under the Articles of Confederation. He also disputed Hamilton's threat assessment. "On a fair investigation, we shall be found to be surrounded by no real dangers. . . . I know of no danger awaiting us. Public and private security are to be found here in the highest degree. Sir, it is the fortune of a free people, not to be intimidated by imaginary dangers."[51] As if anticipating Henry's exposé, the authors of the *Federalist* induce an experience that exceeds actuality. They seek to create rhetorically that which they claim merely to report. America has enemies. Many enemies: foreign, domestic, external, internal. Make no mistake, they wish us harm. To counter insouciant patriotism, the *Federalist* requires that America be threatened with death at its would-be birth. Patriotism must play the death card.

Thus the authors of the *Federalist* themselves give detailed voice, bordering on advice, to European imperial interest. Europe understands all too well the danger that America represents. England may have been defeated in the recent war, but it remains entrenched on the continent. And it is not the only imperial European power to reside here. France and Spain lurk. While the authors insist that an America split into separate and distinct sovereignties would invite European mischief, they recognize that a united America is an equally provocative prospect. England fought bitterly to retain its colonies. America was the most valued and valuable prize in England's imperial orbit. England may have been defeated in round one, but hopes of recapturing what it lost perdure. The stakes are too high simply to quit after surrender. Death hovers: America disunited solicits European meddling; America united invites it.[52]

The authors of the *Federalist* do more, of course, than argue for survival. They delineate the terms of America's entrance into the world arena. For America to compete with and ultimately supplant European states, the new constitution must be ratified; it alone can meet America's power needs. America represents the new order of things, an enlightened empire to replace old Europe, which has grown corrupt and decadent. America's privileged moral and political identity emerges through global comparison and contestation. Europe successfully brought its dominion to the world; the United States promises to bring the world freedom. American patriotism thus folds philanthropy into its basic structure.[53]

While American supremacy cannot be accomplished in a single generation, the founders bear sole responsibility for making it possible for America to rule the four parts of the world (Africa, Asia, America, and Europe). Britain's reign has ended. When it treated the world as a thing at its disposal, it made a grave mistake. America's mission thus becomes partly pedagogical: teach moderation to the British.[54] "Let Americans disdain to be the instruments of European greatness! Let the thirteen States, bound together in a strict and indissoluble Union, concur in erecting one great American system superior to the control of all transatlantic force and influence and able to dictate the terms of the connection between the old and the new world!"[55] Yet this mission is also suffused with greater purpose: "It belongs to us to vindicate the honor of the human race."[56]

In Hamilton's geopolitical imaginary, does a happy, secure, prosperous ending await the American colossus? Paradoxically, once America takes its rightful place in world politics as a commercial republic, peace fails to materialize. Hamilton's genealogy of republics discloses that commerce does not remove the motivations to go to war; rather it provides new ones. Commerce fuels the drive to acquire territory and dominion. Thus American prosperity leads not to permanent peace but to perpetual war. Hamilton's history lesson exacerbates an already tense analysis.[57] Those deluded by utopian speculation ("idle theories") might imagine a future with war purged from the globe, but nostalgia for a golden age that never was must be resisted. Hamilton invokes an "axiom of politics that vicinity, or nearness of situation, constitutes nations natural enemies."[58] America's global ambitions guarantee proximity—and enmity—with Europe as well as the rest of the world. Even after America terminates European presence on the mainland, hostilities continue. Displaced, conflict then proceeds on American terms.

In the optic of the *Federalist*, America rests on the edge of an abyss. If such a dire assessment seems remote or fantastical, if the menace posed by European juggernauts headquartered an ocean away seems overstated, the *Federalist* develops a homegrown version of foreign danger arriving. Should the United States devolve into contending sovereignties, European powers would take advantage of the resultant fratricidal struggles. That is, if the United States should split, its offspring would be subject to the same laws of politics that plague all states. As unity succumbs to self-interest, self-interest leads to war, and war begs foreign intervention. Foreign enemies and domestic opponents of ratification merge as identical apostles of death.

Hamiltonian reason of state peaks in paper 34, as he turns to "remote futurity." Contingencies cannot be predicted with specificity. Contingency per se, however, can be anticipated and preparations made. Since possibilities defy limitation, the power to respond must be unbounded. With arithmetic calculation unavailable, power need be open-ended, with a capacity to meet any eventuality. As Hamilton looks to Europe for a specific threat, his prophesies border on apocalypse. Danger can stem from ambition, the ordinary competition among states. Danger can stem from enmity, by those who would do America harm because it is America. Hamilton insinuates into the text the possibilities of political hate crimes without fully articulating them. His lack of precision contributes to the sense of menace.[59]

The presence of so many deadly possibilities provides sufficient warrant for America to erect Hobbes's veritable mortal god on earth, with the power to induce terror the world over. The Constitution, in short, aspires to generate power without known limit. In theory, it enables America to meet every exigency and survive indefinitely. Hobbes endeavored to build a commonwealth to overcome any internal disorder.[60] To the authors of the *Federalist*, however, Hobbes suffered from meager ambition. They would design a constitution that would not perish from "external violence" either. From the beginning Hamilton links American patriotism to American power; American power produces American greatness; American greatness means the ability to shape the world to conform to American will. The official terms of political patriotic discourse tolerate no other perspectives. Opposition must be effectively silenced because of the gravity of the evil that it represents. "No, my countrymen, shut your ears against this unhallowed language. Shut your hearts against the poison which it conveys."[61]

In a moment of perverse irony, Hamilton describes the dissolution that he simultaneously secures: "Safety from external danger is the most powerful director of national conduct. Even the ardent love of liberty will, after a time, give way to its dictates . . . the continual effort and alarm attendant on a state of continual danger, will compel nations the most attached to liberty to resort for repose and security to institutions which have a tendency to destroy their civil and political rights. To be more safe, they at length become willing to run the risk of being less free."[62] Hamilton's literary genius removes the temporal component of his grim forecast and incorporates it into the very design of American institutions, while ostensibly issuing a warning against precisely this outcome. Security trumps liberty at the moment of founding and conceals its triumph.

The Constitution as a monument to power also names an everlasting memorial to death. Patriotism, love of country, fealty to death entails power as panacea. Who knows what might happen in two centuries?

MEMORIALIZING PERICLES

We have become a September 11 country with a September 11 presidency, a September 11 Constitution, and a September 11 culture. Bush's September 11 address initiates what I am calling America's refounding. Absent for much of the day as Air Force One sought shelter, Bush finally emerges from refuge to speak to the nation. He begins by telling the American people what they already know. The United States has been attacked. He reminds them of the images that network and cable channels have been running ad nauseam: planes, buildings, crashes, fires. Bush then moves to the interpretive arts, for something must come out of what Michael Ignatieff coined apocalyptic nihilism.[63] Al-Qaeda's terrorism constitutes a compliment: it testifies to American greatness and becomes the occasion for self-celebration doubling as interpretive monopoly: "America was targeted for attack because we're the brightest beacon for freedom and opportunity in the world." Bush, like Lincoln at Gettysburg, capitalizes on the September attacks, essentially identity crimes. What Hamilton anticipated, Bush confirms: America's existence elicits violent reaction. Bush also speaks words of comfort and resolve. America cannot be terrorized. Buildings may collapse, but the country carries on. America always survives, just as it has against previous enemies. Bush asks for support, a veritable blank constitutional check to exercise nearly limitless military and police powers. One could say that Bush's patriotism perfects Hamilton's original intent. His gaze spans the globe as he extends an open hand: "America and our friends and allies join with all those who want peace and security in the world and we stand together to win the war against terrorism." America transcends self; American power serves not just national interest but world purpose. The cultivation of memory so critical to patriotism and its projects commences. "None of us will ever forget this day, yet we go forward to defend freedom and all that is good and just in our world."[64]

For Bush, the evil of September 11 had to be re-covered. The slaughter of thousands demanded redemption. Meaning must infuse it. Significance looks to the future. What can be done in the name of the dead? New York City can rebuild lower Manhattan, flush with memorial space where the towers once stood. And George Bush can launch his own international memorial tribute, starting in Iraq. Like Pericles, Bush privileges monuments that claim the earth as their rightful place. Building stone tributes in one's homeland pales by comparison to erecting symbolic monuments in foreign lands through force of liberating arms. Soldiers killed for freedom perform deeds that live in other peoples' hearts and minds. Where Daniel Libeskind's Freedom Tower, 1,776 feet tall, looks contrived, Bush's commemorative architecture feels corpuscular. The liberation of Iraq, so the story goes, amounts to a domino theory in reverse. Through America's professional military power, Hamilton's republican sine qua non, look for democracy after democracy to rise from the ashes of dictatorship, repression, and tyranny. Reconstruction of the globe bespeaks a fitting memorial to "9/11." Bush's democratic nation building emerges as the memorial project of choice. Though unannounced to the public, the war on Iraq began on September 11, 2001.[65] Bush, in epic fashion, converted a day of tragedy into a day of decision. Crisis erupted became opportunity seized. Death would beget life—through more death.[66]

Embracing the Hamiltonian tradition, Bush renews American patriotism through September 11. Freedom forms the altar at which Bush offers rhetorical payment. Power names the sermon delivered. When Bush spoke at the Washington National Cathedral three days after the attacks, he reassured those in mourning that they were not alone. This was no mere emotional gesture, the kind of rhetorical balm expected at state ceremonies from the one official, by virtue of office, who speaks for the nation. Those who lost someone on September 11 were not alone because a promise keeps them company and offers them comfort. History has placed a sacred responsibility on America. Evil must be eradicated. Mass murder requires it. The ambition may not express Christian sensibilities, but it reflects patriotic experiences. America's attack wasn't incidental. Synonymous with freedom, America was targeted because of its uniqueness. For America responsibility is nothing new. Prior generations have come to freedom's aid. Though the world has always known evildoers, peaceful coexistence can no longer be tolerated. The Founders promised freedom when they conceived America, and evil threatens freedom's reign. America's patriot Fathers fought and died for it. Not just for America but for posterity. And because the United States dedicates itself to moral and political propositions, to a set of principles, posterity includes all who would join America in common dedication to their advancement. The calling that speaks America's name speaks to the world.

Nine days after September 11 Bush addressed a special joint session of Congress. As he warns the military to be ready, he insists that America is not alone in the "war against terrorism." Since the attack on America was also an attack on the world, civilization finds itself threatened, with peoples everywhere implicated. Thus more than American freedom and security hangs in the balance. "This is the fight of all who believe in progress and pluralism, tolerance and freedom." Though Bush invites every nation to join America, since "an attack on one is an attack on all," the invitees do not need to respond, what with the injunctive terms of Bush's discourse.

The cause of freedom transcends diplomatic niceties. "Either you are with us or you are with the terrorists." [67] Bush notes that America did not ask for what happened on September 11, but the country's defining mission emerged nonetheless at this pregnant moment. September 11 represents the opportunity for which this generation had been unknowingly waiting. America welcomes the world's future depending on it. "Freedom and fear are at war," and there can be but one winner. As if tracing Will Kane's transcendent steps, Bush reduces the war's outcome to a question of will. More than mere macho posturing, Bush offers reassurance rooted in ontological certitude. The moral order that the United States would bring to the world matches the order that the world is ready to receive. The result is foreordained not because America possesses the power to define the times. The result is foreordained because God predisposed the world to its outcome. History moves in this direction. Hence America does not impose an alien vision on a resistant world. Rather, America aligns itself with Providence. God is not neutral on the question of good and evil. And because God is not neutral, no one on earth can be neutral either. Even refusal to acknowledge the choice to be made is to side with evil. Bush speaks with the authority of God's agent bent on avenging evil done and righting the world: "I will not forget the wound to our country and those who inflicted it. I will not yield, I will not rest, I will not relent in waging this struggle for freedom and security." [68]

Complicating Bush's task, America remains misunderstood throughout much of the world. Many identify America as crass and commercial, a land obsessed with wealth and material acquisition. America must show the world the values and ideals that it cherishes. Among those values: patriotism. America thus cares deeply about the fate of peoples around the globe, especially those strange to it. This has been true since America's birth. As John Schaar observed, humanitarian concern makes America uniquely valuable to the world. Echoing Schaar, Bush writes: "Our founders dedicated this country to the cause of human dignity, the rights of every person and the possibilities of every life. This conviction leads us into the world." [69] He takes it for granted that America must make its case to the world by going to the world and making it directly. Ironically, the peoples of the world have already legitimized America's initiation of the war. The foreigners who flock, generation after generation, to America's shores not only validate America's self-conception and sense of mission. They become predictive of America's success abroad. The truth that America confirms at home thanks to foreigners can be consolidated thanks to foreigners in their homes abroad. The United States can travel elsewhere when foreigners cannot come here. America's immediate ambition is a free Iraq. Since freedom is "God's gift to humanity," America's passion flows from God's will for human beings. America's godlike power makes it the right nation at the right time for the right job. "The Author of Liberty" has arranged it, a truth that Bush's America knows thanks to the trust that it places in the workings of Providence.[70]

Though Bush lauds America's founding generation, the country's more recent past can provide reassurance and inspiration, as well as an exciting challenge. The Second World War exemplifies American power, will, and principle. The "greatest generation" saved civilization as it defeated, simultaneously, Nazi Germany and Imperial Japan. And America's destructive power turned out to be intrinsically creative. Democracy was introduced to lands where it had no foothold. The transmogrification of former enemies into newfound friends was a veritable creation ex nihilo. Nonetheless, Bush, like Pericles, is not content to mimic predecessors, even honored ones. Patriotism revolves around legacies. Inheritance requires expansion. A people must make itself worthy of great gifts. The best way to honor a bequest is through augmentation and enhancement. Thus America's accomplishments in the Second World War were remarkable but limited. Europe and (parts of) Asia were liberated and reconstructed, but the West's ugly colonial legacy resumed. What's more, the struggle against totalitarianism shifted eastward. The cold war consumed America for much of the century and stalled freedom's forward march. Bush wants America to bring freedom to the world's remainder, starting with Afghanistan and the Middle East. Bush announced at West Point in the spring of 2002: "We have our best chance since the rise of the nation state in the 17th century to build a world where the great powers can compete in peace instead of prepare for war."[71] Bush trumps Hobbes and Hamilton in one sweeping architectural vision.

Nevertheless, since September 11 George Bush has been a president at war. America must understand that the country names a battlefield. War is here, at home, continual. The enemy could strike anywhere at any time. Everyone lives and works on the frontlines, from postal workers to the president. There are no safe spots. Bush's presentation of al-Qaeda is chilling. Composed of Islamic extremists, it has made America its favorite target for years. Al-Qaeda wages war against infidels: America, the West, Christians, Jews, and secular Arab regimes. It anchors a global network of terrorist organizations bent on jihad. No one will be spared its will to conquer and control. It seeks shelter from outlaw regimes. It hides in legitimate, law-abiding states. It is everywhere and nowhere.

Bush's alarms form masterpieces in Hamiltonian eloquence. Bush promises to deliver to America and the world a life of freedom, freedom from violence, freedom from fear. This is not the grand vision of Lincoln. This is a Hamiltonian—even Hobbesian—rendering of freedom according to which one can, on the state's terms, enjoy the rewards of a life lived in peace, quiet, safety, and security. This is the cause for which war is necessary. But to make the case for war, Bush invokes the events of September 11 and pronounces on its lessons. He reminds us—again and again—that we will all remember where we were and what we were doing on the fateful day when we learned the news. Such reminders make forgetting impossible. Moreover, Bush depicts al-Qaeda with increasing specificity and detail. By the State of the Union address in 2002, he has perfected the terror to be induced. The success in Afghanistan, he tells us, also proved sobering. America rightly suspected the worst. The enemy's hatred is insatiable, perverse. They laugh at the elimination of innocent life. The intensity of their hatred corresponds to the evil of their imaginations. Chemical attacks and assaults on nuclear plants form part of their mad arsenal of destruction. What's more, tens of thousands of terrorists have been trained and set loose on the world, ticking time bombs with detonations on call.[72] Fear thus governs American subjectivity and its new patriotic citizenship. Americans must be alert, vigilant, on guard. Treat the world as nasty, brutish, potentially short. The enemy may be among us already. A strike could occur anytime and the state cannot be everywhere. Citizens must align themselves with security imperatives. Terror warnings sound. Threat levels fluctuate. Subjects can make a contribution: keep your eyes open, ears attentive, report suspicious people and behavior. The state issues periodic reminders of dangers faced, lest they be forgotten, forgetful creatures that we tend to be. To live a life of freedom, freedom from fear, requires invocation of the very fear to be eliminated. George Bush's revolution in American thinking and experience mimics Hobbes. Or, in Hamilton's terms, he honors the Constitution as he wages war, the first war of the twenty-first century. Bush insists that America adheres to its core values as it engages the enemy. Far from engaging in bad faith, it is recapitulating founding principles in a world at war.

Thus America, thanks to September 11, creates a new generation of heroes to venerate. In his State of the Union Address in 2003, Bush vowed that the deaths of the September 11 victims would not be in vain. Amid smoldering ruins from New York to Virginia, the nation made a pledge that freedom would prevail over violence. Those killed were the first casualties in the war that Bush would start in their name eighteen months after their deaths. Jihadists stole their lives from them without warning. By making war on violence, Bush can restore their lives in retrospect. Otherwise the dead remain forever captive to murderers. A war for freedom can set them free. Rather than hapless victims of terror, they died for freedom, the first to give their lives for the greatest good.[73] Death provides the links that hold together the great chain of patriotic being. Bush depends on death as the cost that America assumes for freedom. Death vindicates his mission; it testifies to its rightness. As we are indebted to those who sacrificed for us, we pay the debt by sacrificing our own. In so doing, we secure the indebtedness of new generations, who in turn must recognize, honor, and repay it. Death leads to debt that leads to more death; more debt is thus incurred, with future death guaranteed. Death and debt form a virtuous circle that feeds relentlessly on itself. It is the stuff of patriotism.

THE PATRIOTIC WAY OF DEATH

Patriotism must have death, repeated death, to be. Death furnishes authenticity; death proves worth of cause or crusade. Death is to be pursued with cheerfulness. Death cannot be accidental; death requires deliberation. Civic faith decrees that death must disclose truth. Death provides not just the occasion but the very reason to love country. Patriotism lives with the guilty secret that it must procure more and more death to sustain itself and feed its habit: patriotism is death's pusher and consumer.

In *The Genealogy of Morals* Nietzsche mischievously imagines a political order possessed of such power and self-confidence that it can afford to ignore those who violate its basic norms, those who do it harm. What are parasites to me, such a polity asks? With identity secured, a self-possessed polity does not waste itself on even serious injuries, which become small and insignificant. Nietzsche has no illusions that an actually existing state might embrace his ethos of abundance, but as an aspiration it may have much to recommend it—both in politics and memorial practices.

For America, of course, Nietzsche's ethos names the unthinkable. George Bush, in the end, loves September 11. While conceding that no one would wish such violent horror on America, the country nevertheless responded as if blessed. Plaudits aside, Bush appears to be making the remarkable claim that in retrospect America would not refuse September 11. After all, September 11 proved revelatory and catalytic. As evil produced good, it disclosed America's true character. The country was reborn in the aftermath of violent death. Patriotism cannot let death be. Loving death, it brings September 11 to life.

September 11 has become Patriot Day. In George Bush's words declaring the occasion: "Those whom we lost last September 11 will forever hold a cherished place in our hearts and in the history of our nation. As we mark the first anniversary of that tragic day, we remember their sacrifice."[74] They died for a world to be made posthumously in their names—a world safe and secure, flowing in ordered beauty from God through nation, from president to reliable subjects. Like Hamilton's, Bush's constitution seeks to maximize American power. Power enables America to become Rorty's vanguard: "we've been called to a unique role in human events." America's privilege is to answer the call. When God speaks, it is not a request. It is a command. Freedom is found in service. Thus America does not impose its will on the world; it brings a gift to be welcomed by others. "No nation owns these aspirations and no nation is exempt from them."[75] Bush cautions potential critics not to judge America's efforts prematurely. The final outcome must be assessed. This too is the American patriotic way.

Nevertheless, perhaps an assessment can be made. The day the United States launched strikes against Afghanistan, Bush lectured the nation and shared a patriotic tale: "I recently received a touching letter that says a lot about the state of America in these difficult times, a letter from a fourth grade girl with a father in the military." Patriotism's truths are simple. "'As much as I don't want my dad to fight,' she wrote, 'I'm willing to give him to you.' This is a precious gift. The greatest gift she could give. This young girl knows what America is all about. Since September 11, an entire generation of young Americans has gained new understanding of the value of freedom and its cost and duty and its sacrifice."[76]

As if taken from the pages of *Émile*, the tale invites comparison with the Spartan mother who, according to Rousseau, defines patriotic female citizenship. Rewrite Bush's Rousseauvian story: A young American girl has a father in the army; every day she waits for war news. One day a pastor arrives; shaking, she asks him for the latest news. "Your father's been killed." "Foolish minister, did I ask you that?" Told Iraq has been liberated, she "runs to the temple and gives thanks to the gods."

According to Bush, America is one with itself. If so, it is also one with the Greek world of Pericles—recall that he refused to console Athenian mothers and fathers who had lost children to war. On behalf of the city that took them, Pericles exhorted parents to produce more children. The city needed its future dead.

Bush's moral to a fatherless nine-year-old insists that September 11 has been good for America.[77] People have reexamined their lives in its deadly wake—children included. With priorities newly reordered, patriotism, service to country, assumes its prized place. "Our great national opportunity is to preserve forever the good that has resulted. Through this tragedy we are renewing and reclaiming our strong American values."[78] Bush's patriotism suggests that America owes a debt of gratitude to those who damaged it. America had lost its way. Obsessed with the acquisition of wealth and goods, power and celebrity, it needed evildoers doing evil to put mundane concerns in perspective. Thanks to September 11, America re-found itself. As such, America's patriotic ethos inspires, even requires, lethal sacrifices from nine-year old girls and boys: Thank you for your parents. The death logic of patriotism means that the country you love refuses no gift. The power of patriotic love changes love's greatest attribute from giving to taking. It never occurs to George Bush to decline the gift that a nine-year-old makes of her beloved Dad. Patriotism disables its own self-discipline as it extols sacrifice. Hearing the tale, perhaps you love the little girl, but can you love your country?

The "real reason" for this war, which was never stated, was that after 9/11 America needed to hit someone in the Arab-Muslim world. Afghanistan wasn't enough . . . for American soldiers . . . to go into the heart of the Arab-Muslim world, house to house, and make clear that we are ready to kill, and to die, to prevent our open society from being undermined . . . Smashing Saudi Arabia or Syria would have been fine.—THOMAS L. FRIEDMAN, *New York Times*

At least what you are about to hear is new; and if you do not understand it, if you misunderstand the *singer*, what does it matter? That happens to be "the singer's curse."—FRIEDRICH NIETZSCHE, *The Gay Science*

But this does not happen without great ambiguity: sound invades us, impels us, drags us, transpierces us. It takes leave of the earth, as much in order to drop us into a black hole as to open us up to a cosmos.—DELEUZE AND GUATTARI, *A Thousand Plateaus*

First, there is the question of music, which, strangely, is never a question of music alone.—PHILIPPE LACOUE-LABARTHE, *Musica Ficta (Figures of Wagner)*

Bruce Springsteen and the Tragedy of the American Dream

In late summer of 2001 al-Qaeda attacked global corporate, military, and political targets in the United States as part of a campaign to remove it from Islamic holy lands in Saudi Arabia. In New York City, the World Trade Center towers collapsed; in northern Virginia, the Pentagon burned; in Pennsylvania fields, a Boeing 757 crashed. Close to three thousand people were murdered, most from the initial onslaught, some from rescue efforts. Consider two responses to the event that has come to dominate not just

American domestic politics but international affairs early in the twenty-first century. The first ought to be familiar; the second, initially, may seem out of place.

On September 11, 2001, George W. Bush addressed the nation and the world on network television. "Today . . . our way of life . . . came under attack in a series of deliberate and deadly terrorist acts . . . Thousands of lives were suddenly ended by evil, despicable acts of terror. The pictures of airplanes flying into buildings, fires burning, huge structures collapsing . . . Today, our nation saw evil . . . Our military is powerful, and it's prepared . . . The search is underway for those who are behind these evil acts . . . We will make no distinction between the terrorists who committed these acts and those who harbor them . . . We stand together to win the war against terrorism . . . America has stood down enemies before, and we will do so this time. None of us will ever forget this day, yet we go forward . . . in our world . . . God bless America."

On September 14 at the National Cathedral, Bush spoke at the nation's prayer service. "On Tuesday our country was attacked . . . We have seen the images of fire and ashes and bent steel . . . Just three days removed from these events, Americans do not yet have the distance of history, but our responsibility to history is already clear: to answer these attacks and rid the world of evil . . . This conflict was begun on the timing and terms of others; it will end in a way and at an hour of our choosing. God's signs are not always the ones we look for. . . . This world He created is of moral design. Grief and tragedy and hatred are only for a time . . . Our unity is a kinship of grief and a steadfast resolve to prevail against our enemies . . . we ask almighty God to watch over our nation. . . . And may He always guide our country."

On September 20 Bush addressed a joint session of Congress:

Tonight, we are a country awakened to danger and called to defend freedom . . . Whether we bring our enemies to justice or bring justice to our enemies, justice will be done . . . All of this was brought upon us in a single day, and night fell on a different world . . . There are thousands of these terrorists in more than 60 countries . . . We have seen their kind before. They're the heirs of all the murderous ideologies of the 20th century . . . And they will follow that path all the way to where it ends in history's unmarked grave of discarded lies . . . Americans should not expect one battle, but a lengthy campaign unlike any other we have ever seen . . . Every nation now has a decision to make: Either you are with us or you are with the terrorists . . . And tonight a few miles from the damaged Pentagon, I have a message for our military: Be ready. I have called the armed forces to alert, and there is a reason. The hour is coming when America will act . . . This is the world's fight. This is civilization's fight . . . I know there are struggles ahead and dangers to face. But this country will define our times, not be defined by them . . . Great harm has been done to us. We have suffered great loss. And in our grief and anger we have found our mission and our moment . . . I will not forget the wound to our country . . . The course of this conflict is not known, yet its outcome is certain . . . we know that God is not neutral.

On October 7 Bush announced war. "On my orders, the United States has begun strikes . . . Every nation has a choice to make. In this conflict there is no neutral ground . . . In the face of today's new threat, the only way to pursue peace is to pursue those who threaten it. We did not ask for this mission, but we will fulfill it . . . The battle is now joined on many fronts. We will not waiver, we will not tire, we will not falter, and we will not fail . . . May God continue to bless America."

On October 11 Bush spoke to the nation. "We are aggressively pursuing the agents of terror around the world . . . we must defeat the evil-doers . . . I am determined to stay the course. And we must do so. We must do so. We must rid the world of terrorists . . . It is essential. It is now our time to act . . . It is important that we stay the course . . . We learned a good lesson on September the 11th, that there is evil in this world . . . I think the American people do understand that after September 11, that we're facing a different world . . . I'm amazed. I'm amazed that there's such misunderstanding of what our country is about that people would hate us. I am—like most Americans, I just can't believe it because I know how good we are."

On 8 November Bush spoke publicly:

We . . . are learning to live in a world that seems very different than it was on September the 10th. . . . During the last two months we have shown the world America is a great nation . . . We wage a war to save civilization itself. We did not seek it. But we will fight it. And we will prevail . . . We are at the beginning of our efforts in Afghanistan. And Afghanistan is only the beginning of our efforts in the world ... We have refused to live in a state of panic or a state of denial. There is a great difference between being alert and being intimidated and this great nation will never be intimidated ... Since September the 11th many Americans ... ask, what can I do to help our fight? The answer is simple. All of us can become a September the 11th volunteer ... We will find ways to train and mobilize ... Too many have the wrong idea of Americans ... My fellow Americans, let's roll.

On January 30, 2002, Bush delivered his State of the Union address:

As we gather tonight, our nation is at war, our economy is in recession and the civilized world faces unprecedented dangers. Yet the state of our union has never been stronger. ... These enemies view the entire world as a battlefield, and we must pursue them wherever they are ... My hope is that all nations will heed our call, and eliminate the terrorist parasites ... If they do not act, America will ... History has called America ... to action ... to put our troops anywhere in the world quickly and safely ... Whatever it costs to defend our country, we will pay it ... America is no longer protected by vast oceans. We are protected from attack only by vigorous action abroad ... Now America is embracing a new ethic and a new creed: "Let's roll." ... America will lead by defending liberty and justice because they are right and true and unchanging for all people everywhere. No nation owns these aspirations and no nation is exempt from them. We have no intention of imposing our culture, but America will always stand firm for the non-negotiable demands ... Evil is real, and it must be opposed ... God is near ... we've been called to a unique role in human events ... May God bless America.

On June 1, 2002, Bush delivered the commencement address at West Point. "Some worry that it is somehow undiplomatic or impolite to speak the language of right and wrong. I disagree. Different circumstances require different methods, but not different moralities. Moral truth is the same in every culture, in every time, and in every place ... We are in a conflict between good and evil, and America will call evil by its name. ... We have our best chance since the rise of the nation state in the 17th century to build a world where the great powers compete in peace ... America has, and intends to keep, military strengths beyond challenge ... The 20th century ended with a single surviving model of human progress . . . there is no clash of civilizations. The requirements of freedom apply fully to Africa and Latin America and the entire Islamic world."

On Friday evening, September 21, 2001, Bruce Springsteen opened a nationally televised benefit concert to raise spirits and money after the attacks on New York and Washington. Performing live in New York, he introduced his song as a prayer for "our fallen brothers and sisters."

> There is a blood red circle
> On the cold dark ground
> And the rain is falling down
> The church door's thrown open
> I can hear the organ's song
> But the congregation's gone,
> My city of ruins
> My city of ruins
> Now the sweet bells of mercy
> Drift through the evening trees
> Young men on the corner
> Like scattered leaves,
> The boarded up windows,
> The empty streets
> While my brother's down on his knees
> My city of ruins
> My city of ruins
> Come on, rise up! Come on, rise up!
> Come on, rise up! Come on, rise up!
> Come on, rise up! Come on, rise up!
> Come on, rise up! Come on, rise up!
> Now there's tears on the pillow
> Darlin' where we slept
> And you took my heart when you left
> Without your sweet kiss
> My soul is lost, my friend
> Tell me how do I begin again?
> My city's in ruins

My city's in ruins
Now with these hands,
With these hands,
With these hands,
With these hands,
I pray Lord
With these hands,
With these hands,
I pray for the strength, Lord
With these hands,
With these hands,
I pray for the faith, Lord
With these hands,
With these hands,
I pray for your love, Lord
With these hands,
With these hands,
I pray for the strength, Lord
With these hands,
With these hands,
I pray for your love, Lord
With these hands,
With these hands,
I pray for your faith, Lord
With these hands,
With these hands,
I pray for the Strength, Lord
With these hands
With these hands
Come on, rise up
Come on, rise up

On July 30, 2002, Springsteen released *The Rising* and ABC's "Night-line" broadcast an interview with him.[1] About September 11, Springsteen said: "I was at the kitchen table . . . Someone came in and said plane's hit the World Trade Center. So I went into the living room and turned the television on right before the second plane hit. The rest of the day you were just sitting there with whoever came over and whoever was there. Just watching . . . Towards the end of the day . . . there's a bridge that you can see the World Trade Centers from. We're actually only about 10 or 15 miles from downtown New York here . . . You cross this little bridge and they always sat dead in the middle of it. And so towards the end of the day we got in the car and drove over it. And they were gone . . . It made it somehow realer than the TV images . . . It was a . . . day of gathering . . . people wondering what was to come."

About the origins of *The Rising*, Springsteen said:

We got asked to do the telethon . . . It was impossible to think about writing. It just seemed wrong . . . I had a song, "City of Ruins" . . . that seemed to fit the evening . . . I just went about my way writing other things and what I found out was that you're writing in a new world. You're simply writing in a new world. You're living in a new world. The world was very different. And what you were thinking and the way you were writing was contextualized by new experience and by the experiences that everyone had on that day . . . So songs just emotionally came out . . . If you go through everything on the record . . . even the [songs] that appear to be most directly about that day could be about just a loss, just someone's dreading mortality, unsure future . . . What I was trying to describe, the most powerful images of the 11th that I'd read in the paper . . . The emergency workers who were ascending and . . . that image, to me, was an image I felt left with after that particular day. The idea of those guys going up the stairs, up the stairs, ascending, ascending.

About the world after the attacks, Springsteen said: "We live in a very successful society . . . Maybe I'll just have to speak for myself . . . The things that really matter . . . The value system that's at the heart of what America's supposed to be about was, one of the things that happened was, an enormous light shone on those things. Just through the very sacrifices that were made on that day. People forget that people are brave. People are brave. It's invisible. It goes on every single day. People are brave at home, at work. And to me the things that . . . came forward on that day, I think, were the things that people like to think that the country is connected by and in some fashion felt, many people felt, had disappeared."

About music at its best, Springsteen said:

The point is to liberate ... The greatest pop music ... was music of liberation. Bob Marley, Bob Dylan, Elvis Presley, James Brown, Public Enemy, the Clash, the Sex Pistols ... Those were pop groups that liberated an enormous amount of people to be who they are, to suss through their identity, to begin to find a way of looking at the world, and to find a way to move through the world, and perhaps a way to impact upon the world. The best pop music reaches all the different parts of your life ... I wanted to address your family, I wanted to address your country, I wanted to address your Saturday night in the bar when you're dancing and having a good time, your relationships with the person that you love and the people that you love ... I found all of this inside pop music ... In the beauty of the singers' voices, in the way that the music made me feel, and also in what it made me feel that I could do.

In the figures of George Bush and Bruce Springsteen, then, we have the beginnings of a global crusade to do God's juridical work and a resolute yet humble mourning; a Manichean division of the world into us and them and an expression of human solidarity; a patriotic call to arms and a will to affirm life; a resort to apocalyptic military power and a leap of communal faith; ressentiment at a world beyond our control and musings about a world hard, opaque, and mysterious; a narcissistic insistence on American exceptionalism and a chastened worldliness. The one seeks to take advantage of a national horror to remake the world in his image of America while mobilizing the resources of patriotism traditionally understood; the other seeks to make some sense of overwhelming events that might also be an occasion for America's renewal and reinvention.[2]

PATRIOTIC INCANTATION

On September 11, the story goes, a new world exploded into being. The American media confirmed developments. *Time*: "Day of Infamy." *Newsweek*: "Our Worst Nightmare." *U.S. News & World Report*: "The Day the Sky Fell." The *New Republic*: "It Happened Here." The *Nation*: "A Hole in the World." The *St. Petersburg Times*: "A New Day of Infamy." The *New York Times*: "U.S. Attacked." The *New Yorker*: a funereal black cover obscuring the Trade Towers. Life would require adjustments, as things would never be the same. Commentaries from the obvious to the comforting to the predictably macho proliferated. The president of the United States finally appeared in New York City, at the site of the attacks, to boast that "the people who knocked down these buildings are going to hear all of us soon."[3] No matter what, something had to be said. The United States, once geographically secure from the world's political and religious violence, could no longer presume itself protected by two oceans.

Incomprehension accompanied news coverage both mind-numbing and affect-deadening. In a void created by excess, a mantra took hold: 9/11; September the 11th; nine-one-one. Mantras do work.[4] Derrida argues: "we repeat this, *we must* repeat it, and it is all the more necessary to repeat it insofar as we do not really know what is being named in this way."[5] The mantra allows us both to "conjure away, as if by magic, the 'thing itself,' the fear or the terror it inspires . . . and . . . to deny . . . our powerlessness to name in an appropriate fashion, to characterize, to think the thing in question . . . something terrible took place on September 11, and in the end we don't know what."[6]

Patriotism abhors a narrative vacuum. While *Le Monde* empathized, its headline reading "Nous Sommes Tous Américains," the United States decided to reverse the sentiment and make America coextensive with the world. In its response to al-Qaeda, assisted by the 9/11 mantra, America rejected historical continuity: the world before September 11 was gone. Though the Bush administration already preferred, in Habermas's words, "the self-centered course of a callous superpower," the preference intensified after what America deemed the historical discontinuity created by September 11. Habermas, while discussing its religious fundamentalism, conceded that al-Qaeda does not mimic traditional terrorists: "they do not pursue a program that goes beyond the engineering of destruction and insecurity."[7] If actions speak louder than words, al-Qaeda has successfully frightened the United States into frightening itself.

Yet consider the implications of Habermas's description. Al-Qaeda's moral and political bankruptcy positions the United States to master its attacks and reverse its incendiary purpose. As we saw earlier, Nietzsche mischievously theorized a self-assured polity capable of transcending the provocations of its enemies. Strength truly possessed feels no need to display itself.[8] Enemies as such become unrecognizable. Since Nietzsche's vision seems unthinkable for American patriotic culture, what would have to be true for the United States to respond to the attacks of September 2001 with creativity aforethought, that is, to respond without reflexively treating the world as the mere object of whatever action (military, of course) the United States, and it alone, judges requisite? I raise this possibility not to deny or downplay the carnage inflicted in 2001, but to challenge the patriotic presumption of death's necessity in politics.

President Bush's insistence notwithstanding, al-Qaeda poses no substantive threat to America's political way of life. A distinction must be made between violence committed against America and the response to that violence. Even if the threat posed by Islamic fundamentalist extremists sets the terms of American self-destruction, in the end we are the only ones who can destroy the principles and ideals associated with the best of America.[9] The attacks of September 2001 do not self-evidently entail a Manichean metaphysic. Bush's fundamentalism posits an interpretation of events conducive to war, in which adversaries translate to evildoers to be dealt with by military means until eradicated from the face of the earth. There is a corresponding militarization and moralization of potentially every aspect of existence. This is the world described and created by "9/11."

Return to Springsteen and the benefit concert of September 21. Dressed in trademark black, equipped with acoustic guitar and harmonica, accompanied by a chorus of seven, candles everywhere, he dedicated his offering to "our fallen brothers and sisters." "My City of Ruins," part dirge, part appeal, part plea, part prayer, seemed penned for the occasion. Though Springsteen composed the song (for Asbury Park, New Jersey) before the attacks, the context of its performance transmogrified it. The lyrics speak of desolation, emptiness, misery, loss. Yet it is the refrain that haunts us. It haunts because of Springsteen's palpable emotion. Through the art of performance he channels passion and anger to give them fitting voice; but he fights to control them as well. The act of singing the song, this song, in public, on this occasion, requires and promotes discipline. For Springsteen, for America, overcoming can begin.

Springsteen deploys the song to call on people, urging them to respond. Even Springsteen's invocation of the Lord fades before what becomes the song's challenge. "Come on, rise up! Come on, rise up!" Thanks to Springsteen's voice, the refrain's invitation combines command and dare, challenge and insistence. It seems as if he will sing the demand until you comply. Springsteen himself leads the way. Thus the singing of the song itself answers its own question: "My soul is lost, my friend/Tell me how do I begin again?"

Notably, Springsteen's call is not a call for vengeance. It does not press the case for violence. We are to rise up precisely because we have been struck, knocked to the ground. But we rise up—to rise up. In Springsteen's hands the song lacks bitterness, ressentiment. An act of self-restoration, it is complete unto itself. It is not the prelude to retaliation. Rising names a self-generating motion. By song's end, you may feel that Springsteen's call has been answered. Thus he can stop singing—for now. Springsteen's performance resisted the boundless fear that Derrida identified as the legacy of the September attacks. Springsteen conducted a self-contained exorcism.

Springsteen and Bush love America. Both think themselves patriots. Both were enraged by the attacks. Yet Bush, unlike Springsteen, would make war on the world and render the Constitution one of its casualties. What might account for the discrepancy between their understandings of September 2001? Springsteen's career, the culmination of a thematic odyssey launched some thirty years prior, enabled him to sing to and for New York and America, and beyond. His long-standing encounter with America has been marked by an examination of its contradictions, including the violence that has constituted and compromised it. Springsteen does not suffer from illusions or naïveté about the country he adores—even if he embraces some of its dominant fictions. If anything, his distinctive brand of patriotism, through the details of its narrative unfolding, unknowingly suggests its very impossibility. Thus unlike Bush, Springsteen is not predisposed to war.

THE REBIRTH OF TRAGEDY

In late summer 1975, Columbia Records released Bruce Springsteen's third album, *Born to Run*. Two months later, Springsteen, relatively unknown except on the east coast, appeared simultaneously on the covers of *Time* and *Newsweek*. One declared, "Rock's New Sensation"; the other, the "Making of a Rock Star." Each missed the opportunity for a more apt story line: the rebirth of tragedy. I treat Springsteen's music as if tragedy were thinking and articulating itself. That is, I treat Springsteen's work as if it formed a series of responses to an underlying tragic condition chameleonic in character.[10] While it might be possible, from *Born to Run* to *The Rising*, to trace a line of development along which tragedy shows signs of emergence, struggles to find expression, matures, and ultimately defines itself, I believe that a tragic ethos has been present since the beginning of Springsteen's recordings.

Tragedy from Aristotle to Shakespeare, Pascal to Nietzsche, Rousseau to Springsteen, though subject to repeated theorizing, resists a single definition. Nevertheless tragedy, I argue, names not just a condition with recurring outcomes but also a dense web of convictions, dispositions, imaginings, moods, and possibilities. As an article of faith, tragedy presumes a world indifferent to human schemes, projects, and exertions. Tragedy conceives life to be animated by myriad forces engendering irreconcilable conflicts, terrible necessities, paradoxical demands, unavoidable dangers, and frustrating limits. A tragic perspective recognizes and embraces, if tentatively, the world's mysterious, sometimes cruel dimensions and the parameters that they insinuate. Tragedy thus deflates the will to power as a will to control to which humans are susceptible. It resists the temptation to seek vengeance for life's contingencies or to launch a war for every problem identified (poverty, drugs, terrorism). At the same time, tragedy eschews a posture of withdrawal; rather it suggests that we live and act in a world not ours or anyone else's. Tragedy, if anything, prompts a daily struggle to live and live well, with any success by definition virtual given the costs that success exacts (from oneself, others, and the world). Tragedy at its best suggests an ethos in which resolve morphs into defiant creative energy. It counsels comportment toward being marked by modesty, good cheer, wonder, and generosity rather than, say, aggression, resignation, or ressentiment. Thanks to our very best efforts, the human condition combines the ambiguities of simultaneous accomplishment and defeat, triumph and dissolution, realization and subversion, joy and pain. Tragedy's summation: achievement combines intention secured and damnable byproduct acquired.

Springsteen, though not a tragedian, subjects America to perpetual narrative theorization—set to music. America inspires and haunts him: America as ideal, America as way of life, America as the land of dreams, America as a site of freedom and opportunity. Springsteen's America thus generates its own questions. Does America's self-conception correspond to the actualities of American life? If not, what accounts for the discrepancy? If not, what can be done to bring about agreement? If not, how do you live with the tensions, the contradictions? If not, how best to express both the love and the fury that home elicits?[11]

Springsteen's America demands possibilities. The American Dream not only presumes faith but inculcates a will to believe.[12] Springsteen celebrates his craft in that "great rock . . . makes the dream seem possible."[13] Springsteen's art of appearances seeks not to deceive but to offer hope to those who have lost faith. The Dream exceeds the reach of too many. Because things can be different, faith requires sustenance until the Dream can be democratized. The gap between America's inherent promise and the country's historic performance demands closure. For Springsteen's America, the task defines the work of a lifetime, of generations. If the gap remains, the country, Springsteen's America, dedicates itself to the work still to be done.

Yet, what if Springsteen's songs, contrary to design, reflect the experience that life invariably refuses what you would have it become? What if life, at its best, necessarily produces casualties, victims, and walking wounded? What if life takes them for granted? Here tragedy implies an ontological appreciation of life as a structural combination of fulfillment and failure. Contrary to Springsteen, the gap between ideal and reality defies closure. What's more, the discrepancy to which Springsteen objects is what makes the American Dream possible—indispensable—in the first place. At the same time, tragedy contains a curious twist, namely the recognition that life's core dynamic, at once creative and destructive, leaves a remainder with which to work. To the extent that tragedy is always about what comes next, it fosters life-affirming energies.

Tragedy's productivity may seem counterintuitive, especially if you (mistakenly) reduce it to this or that horrible event. Yet tragedy can prove surprisingly seductive. You know its logic, at once beautiful and relentless, as well as the outcomes that it engenders. The world's mysteries and challenges seemingly invite you to engage them, to best them, and in the process to prove yourself. Tragedy tempts you. Armed with sufficient knowledge and worldly experience, you may think that you can resist, postpone, cheat, or even temporarily defeat it—against the odds. Illusion springs the trap that tragedy sets for hubris. Eventually tragedy prevails and exacts payment. In the meantime, life's parameters remain unspecified and uncertain. You can move in numerous directions; you can experiment with various possibilities; you can push new developments; you can accomplish great things; you can pave the way for future achievements. Tragedy possesses a self-perpetuating irony that enables every settlement, combining payoff and payment, to forge a space for initiative.

Springsteen seems well suited to illuminate patriotism. A recent foray into partisan politics notwithstanding, Springsteen can't be reduced to party or interest.[14] If anything, his politics constitute a critical patriotism. Nevertheless Springsteen's music ultimately helps make possible a politics that he himself does not articulate, the result of a creative tension between Springsteen's nuanced affirmation of the American Dream and the narrative details of his compositions subverting the idea of the Dream itself. In short, I find much in Springsteen's response to the world exemplary and worthy of endorsement, but I would also like to extend the logic of his work. He can thus be of assistance in articulating a tragic conception of life uniquely appropriate to democracy.

Thus Springsteen can be the occasion for an ethical thought experiment. What do you do when you realize that love is misplaced when it comes to country or homeland? What do you do when you realize that America, the object of your love, does not and could not deserve it? That patriotism cannot justify itself? That patriotism is dangerous and potentially deadly to what it claims to serve in light of its love affairs with enmity and death? Unlike Springsteen, I argue that America cannot withstand the gaze fixed on it. Springsteen's engagement with America, accordingly, takes an unexpected turn. Love of country can prove clarifying. While blindness ordinarily accompanies love, love's concentrated focus can also reveal not only blemishes but impossibilities. You might, of course, redouble your efforts to bring promise and performance into alignment. Or, rather than bring the world into line with prior conviction, you might let go of what you now experience as infatuation and projection. Love can overcome and suspend itself when it comes to politics and patriotism, to the betterment of democracy.

NO PLACE LIKE HOME

Born to Run is a paean to liberation, to possibility, to youth. Released in the twin specters of Vietnam and Watergate, Springsteen's rock anthem makes a plea for patriotism as untimely as John Schaar's prose poem. Springsteen's characters ooze discontent with things as they are; to them, the world invites challenge and rejection. At the same time, new worlds can be made or discovered just around the next corner. The characters never doubt escape—should they choose it—to be a sure thing.

Necessity is at work in these songs. The idea of a promised land out there, somewhere, animates and informs the imperative to run. Springsteen sings of America as the land of new beginnings, of second and third chances. There is little concern for actual destination. "Someday girl I don't know when / we're gonna get to that place / Where we really want to go / and we'll walk in the sun." Despite the quotidian grind governing life, the idea that there may be no exit from this hell refuses to be considered seriously. Springsteen, moreover, issues a warning. Do not pray for rescue by a would-be savior who comes out of nowhere. The world issues an invitation to join it every day. There is no reason, save the inertia of generations bound by passivity, fear, and hesitation, not to accept. Meant to encourage and inspire, *Born to Run* shifts between light and grandiose. Guitars race, saxophones erupt, drums explode, pianos dance.

Yet Springsteen's work carries a subterranean flow. Even if America affords people abundant chances, it is no cornucopia. A suspicion grows that time is short, with possibilities fleeting, perhaps momentary. "We got one last chance to make it real." Opportunities do not make themselves available whenever you decide you are ready to take advantage of them. Because of the experiences that create the desire to flee ("Baby this town rips the bones from your back / It's a death trap, it's a suicide rap / We gotta get out while we're young"), the realization that an eternal return of the same lies on the horizon seems inescapable. You may escape the prison that your home has become, but what ultimately makes the next stop down the road any different? The world teems with people whose homes are veritable prisons.

Though *Born to Run* may initiate what Schaar termed a lover's quarrel with America, its romantic, effusive sensibility dominates the record. Ronald Reagan may have immortalized morning in America, but Springsteen sang it first. Thus the quarrel's intensification will have to wait. The spirit of liberation that marks *Born to Run* may also, however, be its greatest limitation. Too much of a good thing can feel like denial. Further, the knowledge that you can always seize the day can also mean that you never reach for it at all.

Springsteen unleashed *Darkness on the Edge of Town* three years later.

Tribute paid to the American Dream engenders a test of its authenticity, which in turn engenders an appreciation of the country's complexities, including the flaws that accompany its beauties. Like *Born to Run*, *Darkness* springs from a specific set of circumstances. The stories told feel rooted in the viscera of the world, whether streets, factories, or fantasy life.[15] Since *Born to Run*, life has acquired gravity and weight. *Darkness* rages at the world. Circumstances reveal and teach certain "facts" about life, facts with which you best become acquainted. America feels different—the American Dream too. Facts, some spoken, others not, haunt the lives portrayed. Those who build a society from the ground up do not necessarily share in its success. Those who labor at the menial jobs which make society run can't always make their own lives work with the money they earn. Those who readily fight the country's wars may do so only to be abandoned later. Life in the modern industrialized world seems a pitiless cycle of service and exploitation, labor and destruction.

Springsteen's angry critique quickly transforms itself into a democratic jeremiad. Love leads to denunciation, if implicit. "The Promised Land" narrates a man made impotent through hard work. He insists that *if* he "could take one moment into [his] hands," the world would turn. But his insistence reveals the hollowness of the claim. More facts: doing the right thing every day, living and playing by the rules, leads slowly nowhere; it certainly provides no reward in itself. People find themselves excluded from the rewards to which they, by virtue of their contribution, are entitled. Societies make conditional promises to their members, but there are no guarantees that the promises can be kept even if the conditions are met. If anything, American society routinely makes promises that it knows cannot be kept. Yet the promises must be made; they will always be made. This combination is inherently unstable. Sooner or later, as the rage builds, something has to give.[16]

Nevertheless, as "The Promised Land" tells the story of quotidian struggle, it also suggests acts of perpetual postponement: "Working all day in my daddy's garage / Driving all night chasing some mirage / Pretty soon little girl I'm gonna take charge." Despite the recognition of a battle lost before it even began, the protagonist can insist on his intention to act because he still believes in a promised land. An article of faith thus inspires a leap of faith. By the song's conclusion, however, nothing but belief in belief remains. The protagonist has to insist on the action that he recommends precisely to the extent that he has no intention of taking it—ever. To act would be futile and thus unbearable.

In Springsteen's *stories* America "fails" not because of the aporia between promise and delivery (Springsteen's musical conviction). America can't be what it pretends since the success of the American dream for some presupposes its denial to others. If anything, the very positing of the American dream means that not everyone can realize it. The story of succeeding by one's own (heroic) efforts depends for its power on a backdrop of failure. If just anyone, anytime could succeed, what would make the dream distinctive and attractive? Springsteen's faith, however, may not allow him to sing such truths to America.

PATRIOTIC LOVE TRIANGLE

In light of Springsteen's self-conscious meditation on America's core mythos, what becomes of the love of country that his songs would express? Can love survive its own enactment? Does Schaar's lover's quarrel, transformed into adversarial contestation as it unfolds, lead not to sweet reunion but to distance, alienation, perhaps affective divorce?[17]

"Born in the U.S.A.," an account of the American experience, offers insight. Springsteen wrote and recorded the song for *Nebraska*. Dominated by a slightly menacing acoustic guitar, the original, stripped-down version subverts the ambiguity of its electric cousin. The song tells the tale of a man whose life was written at birth. America advertises itself as the land of possibility and mobility, where limits consist of nothing but the difficulties that you put in your own way. But the song exposes this as self-serving mythology, with self-creation and self-control sheer fantasies. "Born down in a dead man's town / The first kick I took was when I hit the ground." Faced with the choice of prison or army, the song's protagonist opts for Vietnam. The war may be pointless violence at best, racist aggression at worst, but it remains preferable to jail. Service becomes just another episode in life, more or less like any other. Disposable men sacrificed in Vietnam. No thanks given; no debt acknowledged. What's worse, America lost the war, its first such loss. Upon returning home, the veteran is greeted with unemployment and scorn. Haunted by memories, he finds himself trapped in limbo. The past pains him; the present excludes him; the future laughs at him. Life has been nothing but a series of hard blows. In the song's final verse, the refinery and the penitentiary sit side by side.

With no essential difference between them, his life could unfold in either place. For all the downtrodden narrative of "Born in the U.S.A.," it is the song's chorus that resonates. By converting "Born in the U.S.A." into a mantra, the song slowly leeches the privilege of the words, to say nothing of their triumphal connotation. With Springsteen's hollowed-out vocal, "Born in the U.S.A." states mere geographical fact. His subject remains America, but the status accorded to it changes. Country lies beyond love and hate. Your place of birth could have been elsewhere. Thus America possesses no inherent meaning or significance. Country names mere contingency, one of many governing our lives.[18]

Springsteen did not include "Born in the U.S.A." on *Nebraska*. The decision did not spare the song great controversy. Recorded later with The E Street Band, it was transmogrified into an anthem. Springsteen brought the tension that he likes to cultivate in his songs to the brink of perfection. He thereby became the site of a battle for the political and patriotic "rights" to his music. Conservatives latched onto one dimension of the song's complexity and embraced it. George F. Will, for example, converted Springsteen and his band into national assets who stood for traditional American values, some of which Will endorsed, some of which (cars and girls) he did not.[19] Will's concert experience alerted the Reagan campaign to Springsteen's political possibilities. This Dave Marsh could not abide, despite his admission that "People were invited to read as much into *Born in the U.S.A.* as they cared—or dared—*and so they did*."[20] Marsh concluded: "Will was not the first conservative to attend Springsteen's shows and become confused about *the* message."[21] Divining that Will listened neither to Springsteen's lyrics nor to his spoken introductions to the songs, Marsh claimed that Springsteen's music "was not the optimistic, hard-working patriotism [he] wanted to purvey, so the columnist simply ignored it (presuming he was still there to hear it)." Finally, he derided Will (and thus Reagan) because he "never held a job in which his hands were more than metaphorically dirtied and was proud of it. The notion of his lecturing on the joys and rewards of labor to steel-workers who risked their lives in filthy, unsafe mills every day was such a perversion of what Springsteen was trying to communicate that it constituted an obscenity." But the underlying problem was larger than George Will. With the record released "in a time of chauvinism masquerading as patriotism," both liberals and conservatives seized on it for their own patriotic purposes.[22]

Eric Alterman likewise abused Will, accusing him of "ignorance" and "chutzpah."[23] Marsh and Alterman excoriate Will, of course, to exonerate Springsteen.

Yet the protestation, especially that of Marsh, cannot be sustained. Springsteen believes that an author cannot—should not—determine the fate of his art once presented to the world, especially when it treats patriotic themes.[24] Springsteen thus keeps a distance between himself and his audience, to let it ponder his material on its own.[25] This is an ethical and musical position. What's more, George Will to some extent perceived the ambiguous core of Springsteen's work and responded to it. In other words, the music's visceral power (Will called it a "sensory blitzkrieg") touched him. Consider the following quote (which Marsh overlooks): "I have not got a clue about Springsteen's politics, if any, but flags get waved at his concerts while he sings songs about hard times. He is no whiner, and the recitation of closed factories and other problems always seems punctuated by a grand, cheerful affirmation: 'Born in the U.S.A.!'" Though Will seems uncertain if Springsteen wages class warfare, he notes the irony of "Born in the U.S.A." as "its anthem—its Internationale."[26]

True, Springsteen himself contested Reagan's appropriation of his work. Reagan understood the profound connection that people feel to their country. They want and need to feel good about it.[27] Springsteen shares the impulse. Yet to Springsteen, Reagan's vision of America operated in a mythical realm flowing from nostalgia for a world that Reagan thought tragically lost.[28] If anything, the impossibility of Reagan's world—that it never existed, that it could never exist—lent seductive power to this vision. It could always be dreamed, thus never defeated, as an ideal. This also rendered it politically problematic. Reagan presumed the American dream susceptible of realization, failure the responsibility of those "denied" its fruits. This is not Springsteen's starting point. Speaking of Reagan: "I think there's a large group of people in this country whose dreams don't mean that much to him, that just get indiscriminately swept aside."[29] Springsteen fought Reagan over the politics of the American Dream.

Alterman, like Will and Reagan, would monopolize Springsteen. Regarding right-wing appropriation of "Born in the U.S.A." for feel-good patriotism, Alterman writes, "It is a complicated and ultimately unanswerable question as to just how much of the responsibility for these interpretations can be attributed to Springsteen himself."[30] And, "Did

Springsteen accidentally empower Reaganism . . . as he simultaneously denounced it?"[31] Determined to acquit Springsteen of lending aid and comfort to the political enemy, Alterman bemoans the phenomenon of cultural significations obliterating artistic essence: "Unfortunately, millions of people heard the band version with exactly the opposite message of what Springsteen intended. For many, the music's visceral power made the lyrics seem beside the point. And when Springsteen unfurled an enormous American flag as he sang the song in concert, the anger of the lyrics became further obscured by the patriotic symbolism that surrounded it."[32] Given Alterman's own description, how he speaks of Springsteen's intent—or insists that intent trumps presentation and reception—is mystifying. There seem to be a number of possible intentions at work, some at odds with each other. Thus George Will himself can respond to Springsteen's music. It struck him. He appreciated its hard-edged qualities. Will did use Springsteen for his own purposes, which I believe testifies to Springsteen's impact, since George Will takes politics seriously. Yet rather than push Will where Springsteen touched him, and perhaps risk their own reassuring political readings of Springsteen, Alterman and Marsh focus on his so-called usurpation. If anything, Springsteen's music itself is the enemy they share. While left and right fought a war of interpretive maneuver, the music made selective appropriation impossible. Both invoked Springsteen for their cause; the music rebuffed each. There was an opening, created by the force of Springsteen's tension-filled art, on which they failed to capitalize. In short, that George Will wrote about Springsteen in the first place provided the real story. Springsteen penetrated Will's considerable personal and political defenses, even though he came equipped with the equivalent of full-body armor: "a bow tie and double-breasted blazer is not the dress code."[33] I suspect that Will sensed Springsteen's musical dangerousness to dominant political fictions; hence the serious effort to co-opt him to a traditional patriotic agenda. George Will, if he misread or misheard Springsteen, did it deliberately—for the American Dream.

YOU CAN'T LOVE YOUR COUNTRY

Springsteen's danger to patriotisms left and right emerges as he bores into the bowels of American life. The stories that result, over the course of a career, do not feel like a love affair with America. Or if it is an affair, it's an affair gone wrong. One or two stories running against the grain of the American Dream might function as exceptions to prove the rule. What if "Born in the U.S.A." turns out to be representative? Springsteen's music, after all, accords violence a prominent place in it. Neither episodic nor incidental, violence seems to characterize, even constitute American life. In "Badlands," "The Promised Land," or "Factory" from *Darkness on the Edge of Town*, "Point Blank," "The River," "Independence Day," or "The Price You Pay" from *The River*, "Atlantic City," "Mansion on the Hill," "Johnny 99," or "Reason to Believe" from *Nebraska*, or "Downbound Train," "Cover Me," "No Surrender," or "My Hometown" from *Born in the U.S.A.*, life ends and feels done long before it's officially over. This is not supposed to happen in America. Springsteen's narrations possess the power to wither self-conceptions. They live in minutiae. Indictments of the American Dream, they accumulate evidence the sheer weight of which threatens to crush everything in their vicinity. It's not just that they decisively disclose the gap between promise and actuality; the very idea of the dream starts to feel cruel. Springsteen's music is no patriot.[34]

"Youngstown" exemplifies the American Dream's death as it peels back the layers of violence undergirding the American way of life. Springsteen writes of the Ohio steel mills and their disposable workers. Once upon a time, these industrial giants forged the United States into a global economic, military, and political superpower. The men who worked the mills, and the sons who followed in their paths, sacrificed their lives for America. They sacrificed them at home through a day's labor; they sacrificed them abroad on foreign battlefields. They would die working at one; they would die fighting on the other; either way, they would die. Yet the very accomplishments that these men made possible and embody also resulted in their marginalization and eventual irrelevancy. In America's rustbelt, "The story's always the same / Seven hundred tons of metal a day / Now sir you tell me the world's changed / Once I made you rich enough / Rich enough to forget my name." Creation presupposes and fosters destruction and the destruction does not give pause. It is the law of life; it passes unnoticed, unlamented, and unremarked.

Well my daddy come on the Ohio works
When he come home from World War Two
Now the yard's just scrap and rubble

He said: "Them big boys did what Hitler couldn't do"
These mills they built the tanks and bombs
That won this country's wars
We sent our sons to Korea and Vietnam
Now we're wondering what they were dyin' for

Here the vaunted American Century crumbles beneath the burdens of its success. From victory in the Second World War to cold war stalemate in Korea and to calamity in Vietnam, American life exacts a heavy death toll without death benefits. The most serious threat to the American way of life and the greatest generation turns out to be domestic not foreign. The country expects service, but has no corresponding sense of obligation or reciprocity to those who serve. Such truths can be intimated but not articulated. America, the country you are supposed to love and to have loved, names your enemy. Patriotism's impossibility thus emerges.[35]

Springsteen's meditations on violence transcend class. They encompass race as well. America's race problem is the founding gift that lives in perpetuity. It also names a founding gift that patriotism disowns. "American Skin (41 Shots)" bears a strong family resemblance to Woody Guthrie's "This Land Is Your Land." Whereas "This Land" would claim a citizen's rightful inheritance, "American Skin," an alternate take on the American Dream, speaks to its denial, its theft. Springsteen started performing the song toward the end of his 1999–2000 tour. It provoked a torrent of criticism, including hysterical denunciations from New York City police officials who had not listened to it.[36] New York City provoked the song, but America produced it. Here Springsteen carries out Guthrie's injunction to write and sing what you see.

"American Skin" details the killing of a boy—felled by forty-one shots fired by the police. In the first verse, Springsteen jerks the narrative back in time and you relive the lethal moment from the vantage point of the trigger: "Is it a gun, is it a knife / Is it a wallet, this is your life." The ugly reality of race in America has taken another life. Denials and protestations to the contrary, everyone knows that "You can get killed just for living in your American skin."[37]

As if the brutal opening were insufficient to what America must face, Springsteen makes you relive the shooting. The second verse enters the home of Charles, the victim, before events unfold. Death has been undone and life restored—for now. A mother prepares her son for school. She reminds him of what he already knows, what she has told him countless times before. Rules govern urban America, rules according to race. The police interpret and enforce these rules as they see fit. The advice is haunting because it is both prescient and futile. One of the rules governing American cities: even if mothers teach their sons well, they can't protect them. Another is that the rules cannot be rewritten.

In the live DVD version of "American Skin," Springsteen, having sung two verses nearly motionless, steps away from the microphone as he rips into his guitar, as if the rage that has been building through the first two verses can no longer be contained. Chords wail in grief—though no release can be adequate to the need for it. Yet death's ubiquity requires acknowledgment. The steady chorus of forty-one shots renews the pain with each articulation. Finally Springsteen can do nothing but scream the lyrics, turning away from the crowd as he unloads. For "American Skin" death does not give meaning to life. Death represents its gratuitous negation. Charles doesn't die to teach America a valuable lesson that it would not otherwise learn. America can't redeem his life and thus itself by retroactively drafting him for moral or political purposes.

According to Springsteen, we are all implicated in the deaths that surround and define us. "It ain't no secret / It ain't no secret / No secret my friend." Sung gently, the lyrics seek official recognition of a known truth. Sung fiercely, the lyrics turn to accusation and denunciation. Race in America refuses remedy. Crimes committed in its name expose an aspect of America's identity that traces to the country's origins. Some things never change. You can't love this kind of country, can you? Here, once again, the details of Springsteen's songs subvert the America they would otherwise salute. The tragedy of American life cannot be captured by its failure to deliver what it advertises. It's not supposed to deliver what it advertises. The tragedy of American life results from its exclusive success, the singular joy of which relies on a context of limitation. The American Dream, in short, rests on a bedrock of failure, including death and dying, which Springsteen's songs describe without admitting.

FROM PATRIOTISM TO TRAGEDY

What are the prospects for American life in the new millennium? What obligations would Springsteen's songs impose on America? Assuming that life cannot be lived without cost, without producing remainders, the tragic dynamic does not remove the need to minimize or eliminate pain. Life understood through a tragic lens spurs action, that is, politics. Even if we are not to blame for tragic outcomes, we are still implicated. Accountability takes the form of responding to a situation both inherited and made. The assumption of commitment in specific circumstances can lend nobility to democracy. There is a tragic condition as well as a response to it. You might respond with resignation; you might indulge ressentiment; or you might seize upon the tragedy to do something new. Tragic outcomes do not necessarily have to be accepted. Indeed Springsteen's songs leave listeners, whether individually or in concert, with work to do. No song or album will do the work itself. Thus Alterman is right that Springsteen presents no solutions—which may be his point. There is a key moment in "Badlands" that deserves notice. The frustration, anger, and pent-up rage of the opening verse deploy the first person singular ("I'm caught in a cross fire," "I don't give a damn," "I want control right now"). The defiant reaction of the chorus, however, invokes the second person and then moves to the first person plural—part command, part invitation:

Badlands, you gotta live it everyday
Let the broken hearts stand
As the price you've gotta pay
We'll keep pushin' till it's understood
And these badlands start treating us good.

In a world not predisposed in our favor, life's tragedies may spur the formation of a "we" that can address them. Springsteen's chorus suggests the permanence and perpetuity of conflict and struggle ("We'll keep pushin'"). This is the space of politics, which has no prior guarantees. Notably, Springsteen's characters do not respond to violence with violence. In the wake of tragic encounters, modesty folds itself into their ways of being in the world. If limitation can be accepted, if it can be affirmed, you resist the urge to bend the world to will. A sense of limitation also means that there is always more to be done about life's cruelties, if not now then perhaps at a more opportune moment.

To understand more precisely tragedy as spur to life, reconsider the narrative of "Youngstown." Wars fought by a democracy in the name of principle succeed by sacrificing at least one of them. War, that is, cannot be won except by deliberately sending to slaughter the lives of your own. Spielberg's Normandy invasion in *Saving Private Ryan* testifies to this truth. More generally, societies cannot be built and provide the good lives they promise to people without sacrificing the health, well-being, and very existence of those who build them: witness coal mines and steel mills. Life's tragedies thus produce debts to life. These debts, strictly speaking, cannot be repaid. Rather than trumpet debt's impossibility (which exacerbates the sense of indebtedness), you seek to become worthy of it, knowing in advance that you cannot be. Because of life's aftermaths, there is much to be done. Tragedy: as creation presupposes destruction, it can bring about a new commitment to life. With patriotism, on the other hand, life privileges death, which imposes debt, which leads to the romanticizing of all three as holy trinity.

REFUSING FEAR

With tragedy in mind, I now return to late summer 2001.

Springsteen's stories of the American Dream, its costs and consequences, can illuminate the country's standing as a global commercial and military republic. In short, the tragedies of the American Dream may inadvertently create the conditions for 9/11. How might such a discomfiting situation unfold? Consider two possible scenarios. First, the American Dream exceeds the will to prosperity and happiness. It names a drive to fend off the poverty, insecurity, and death bedeviling life. The logic of the American Dream thus contributes to extremism in its pursuit. On the Dream's terms, life itself hinges on its success. Thus at the Dream's core lurks a nightmarish possibility that cannot be shaken, namely spiritual and physical extinction. And when the American Dream suffers endemic failure at home, it lays the groundwork for the generation of endless enemies abroad, specifically those who do not believe in its self-evident rightness and object to American global policies in pursuit of its realization. America's sundry efforts in the world thus produce predictable counter-reactions.[38] Second, the September attacks announce the culmination of the American Dream. As we have seen, the Bush administration has converted the attacks into unabashed triumph. We are hated, Bush insists, for who we are, for how we live. Enraged by America's success, jealous of America's achievements, "the terrorists" would rather kill us than see us prosper. Thus Al-Qaeda's slaughter vindicates America and renders its Dream alive and well. In return, the Dream's preferred terms of political discourse—power, control, self-assertion—sponsor reassuring narratives with comforting conclusions. The result is the rhetorical field in which a complex event (al-Qaeda's attacks) becomes a mantra (9/11) and the mantra makes necessary a war to confirm the truths that it radiates—for Bush, that is, not Springsteen.

Springsteen released *The Rising* in July 2002, less than a year after the previous September's attacks. If anything, the album may embody, with a twist, the ethos that Richard Rorty defines as the narrative heart of American patriotism. Tell stories of America at its best. Springsteen offers *The Rising* as a civic gift to a country in mourning.

Even if an impressive publicity and promotion campaign featuring Springsteen himself had not accompanied the recording, *The Rising* would have sparked controversy. Does rock and roll, a popular form of entertainment devoted to pleasure and diversion, have the same gravitas as poetry to contend with horror? Does Springsteen's effort to sell records amount to exploitation of a national tragedy? If the dead can speak on the subject, the answers are a confident yes and a resounding no. Springsteen's music played a prominent role in the lives of many of those murdered in September, as coverage by the *New York Times* of their funerals disclosed. Moreover, as Eric Alterman observed, why should serious subjects be reserved to the likes of Steven Spielberg? If Hollywood addresses the Second World War without censure, why should rock not address September 2001?[39] Besides, Springsteen himself prefers that art itself be allowed to speak. Do not assess it in advance. Give it a hearing.[40]

The Rising conceives an America to be imagined and enacted after the September 11 attacks. The disc cannot be understood without the trauma, nor can it be reduced to it. Exactly what kind of background do the stories presume? Al-Qaeda executed with breathtaking daring and simplicity a series of brutal strikes aimed at American symbols of global power. Even if the plan failed to fulfill its original intent, the authors have no grounds for complaint. The United States quite understandably reacted with shock, awe, and horror. Its military response in Afghanistan notwithstanding, the United States cannot undo or reverse the day's carnage or the damage done to the country's self-conception. Bin Laden and his associates triumphed. The attacks revealed that a determined foe, with ample resources, can inflict great physical harm on the United States and that there may be nothing the nation, much vaunted military power or not, can do to stop it. Furthermore, despite funerals held, memorials built, speeches given, ceremonies conducted, rituals implemented, and wars launched, nothing can give meaning to an "event" that seeks—as Habermas noted—destruction and fear for their own sakes. Fundamentalist religious violence operates in a solipsistic universe—others are irrelevant, save as occasional props in self-dramatizing gestures of will.

The Rising prompts America to ask questions. How is the country to assess terrible events? How is America to conduct itself in the context of horror? With calls for strength a given, what does or should strength mean? Might this be a unique occasion for America to redefine or reinvent itself? Contrary to Rorty's and Bush's preferred modes of national self-assertion, Springsteen's America characterizes itself not just by what it does but by what it declines to do.

For Springsteen, life—not death—proves remedial. "Into the Fire" runs counter to patriotic appropriations of the day. As buildings collapse, a spouse sings of her beloved responding to an alarm. Love and duty enable people to perform remarkable acts under impossible circumstances. Yet love of city, commitment to the job, and a sense of care for other people informed the initial responses. The attacks were at first a mystery. To view the day's events through a patriotic lens distorts them for political purposes. Fire and police workers, people not patriots, rushed to lower Manhattan. They were there to serve life—not contribute to patriotism's death-driven agenda. The spouse whom one of them left behind imagines her beloved ascending the stairs to do the work of rescue no matter the consequences: dust, smoke, fire, death, ashes, burial. The violin-driven music possesses an equanimity that allows death's inevitability to be approached with some measure of calm. Bravery inspires ("May your strength give us strength / May your faith give us faith / May your hope give us hope / May your love give us love"). Rescue workers become exemplary precisely because they did not seek the role of civic models. Springsteen's incantation invokes extraordinary deeds and suggests that those who died continue to give, if only you will let them. They performed, and performed generously, on behalf of life.

Springsteen sings of emptiness and loss. In "You're Missing," absences function as signs of death: from the gargantuan buildings that no longer define New York's skyline to the partner who no longer takes his familiar place in bed. To be reminded of loss is to feel the desire for revenge. The desire could become overwhelming because the reminders seem perpetual, threatening permanence. Clothes unused hang in closets; shoes unworn litter hallways; coffee cups lurk empty in kitchens; and newspapers unread lie on doorsteps. Signs of life become indicators of death, death that cannot be, for everywhere there are signs of life. The evidence, of course, proves unreliable. Cherished pictures can turn cruel. "You're missing." Rather than act precipitously, however, Springsteen lets the loss be loss. There are some things in life that have to be absorbed. You do not strike back randomly. Strength lies elsewhere.

Springsteen closes *The Rising* with "My City of Ruins." In light of the American nation's reaction to the attacks, the title alone makes it notable. Springsteen does not sing of country or nation or people, but of city, his city. By singing of his city he personalizes the attack but also depoliticizes it. The city names a site of variety, foreignness. New York welcomes, and feeds on, immigrants, strangers, and others, those new and different. This is what makes New York a city of possibility, energy, openness, wonder, and wildness. New York belongs to America but surpasses it too. It forms part of a wider world of culture, art, music, commerce, enlightenment, wonder, awe. The multifarious composition of New York makes its geography boundless. The French declared not only "We are all Americans" but "We are all New Yorkers."

New York is not the only metropolis to suffer violent attack, even if the scale differs. The names Paris, Athens, Tel Aviv, Moscow, Jerusalem, Rome, Istanbul, Berlin, London, Madrid, Bogotá, and Buenos Aires contribute to the list. They are just some of the cities that have been targeted. New York enjoys good company. The song, a kind of international, is a reminder that America's devastation bespeaks experience that is ordinary not exceptional, temporary not permanent. Springsteen sings of his city; others sing of theirs. New York provides an opportunity to cultivate new attachments to new places—not marching in lockstep with a larger patriotic community according to prearranged national scripts, but in a manner consistent with the rhythms of daily global life, and the cross-border connections and solidarities that emerge from life lived both in and beyond a certain place. New York stands for life's fragility—and resistance.

What if *The Rising* were treated as a public gift? Consider its affinities with the counter-memorial tradition. Though born of horror, the music cannot be reduced to it. The songs possess such amorphousness that with time September associations can fade or morph. While Springsteen understands the felt need to remember and acknowledge, he allows for commemorative work to be done by others as much as he performs it himself. *The Rising* largely requires others to finish the work that it starts. "Mary's Place" and "My City of Ruins" take tentative steps to restore life after death, but to map them with specificity would be to monopolize or colonize an idiosyncratic experience. Springsteen refuses to offer a single interpretation of an event around which the country and the world can gravitate. He refuses, among other things, Bush's Manichean optic. Rather than become Bush's ally, let alone his patriotic foot soldier, in America's war against the world, Springsteen composes contrapuntal music. At the dawn of a new century, Springsteen turns to an immanent transcendence, a faith anchored in the material realities of family, friends, work, love, neighborhood, and community, rather than indulge the impulse for retribution rooted in something intangible or abstract.[41]

Thus *The Rising* refuses to elevate September 2001 to place of privilege in the national consciousness; rather, it puts trauma in perspective and accords it corresponding treatment. Bush, on the other hand, wages a war in Iraq as a memorial tribute; and when the war engenders opposition, Bush dismisses criticism by insisting that "we" stay the course to honor the dead already fallen. Without acknowledging it, Bush accelerates the vicious circle of patriotic death. More Americans must die to honor those previously killed—themselves sacrificed for those who died first.

America has great plans for what it calls ground zero. Imagine, though, if the United States were to refuse a *national* memorial to the attacks of September 2001, whether in New York City, Arlington, rural Pennsylvania, or Iraq. Entertain the following narration inspired by Springsteen and Rorty. Al-Qaeda launched devastating strikes. Roughly three thousand people were murdered unthinkingly as the banality of fundamentalist evil expressed itself. September 2001 combined enormity of attack with smallness of perpetrator. America's core values cannot be implicated, since the country's enemies, undeniably real, lack substance. They pose security threats, but they offer no challenge to American ideals, principles, or identity at their best. They stand for nothing—apocalyptic vision or no. September's attacks, however spectacular, however stunning, however catastrophic, amount to mere slaughter. As Bush once remarked, bin Laden is a parasite unworthy of thought. Might not America's billion-dollar memorial immortalize his perfidy? Might not a national monument simultaneously, perhaps predominantly, pay tribute to his evil genius?

Since September 11 there have been numerous anniversaries commemorating the attack: one-month, two-month, three-month, six-month, one-year, two-year, five-year. Since the attacks America has experienced the first Veterans' Day, the first Thanksgiving, the first Christmas, the first New Year's, the first Super Bowl, the first Easter, the first Memorial Day, the first Fourth of July, and later, the first Congressional elections, the first national political conventions, and the first presidential election. The macabre repetition suggests that America has become unduly attached to its wounds. With September 11 having become an axis, the danger is to prioritize resentment at life's injuries and authorize whatever treatment may be deemed necessary to salve them—with possibly catastrophic consequences to democracy. To refuse national memorializing could be considered a test of democratic strength. Strength here brings to the surface the paradox of actively remembering to forget what happened on September 11, "forgetting" by refusing to inscribe a memory of it in national public space created for that very purpose. Let the services and ceremonies already conducted, the temporary memorials, suffice. Listen to Bruce Springsteen. [42] Forgetting, even if it's a conceit, might be the ethical thing to do. America would thus define itself for the ages. September 11 was not tragedy but slaughter; tragedy can come only if America uses the 11th, in the name of freedom, or freedom from fear, to destroy democracy. Patriotism can live with America ruined; America can't.

HERE'S TO LIFE

Patriotism tends toward a paradox: to conduct an extended critique of it implicates you willy-nilly in a world that you might otherwise refuse. Who but a patriot would spend a book challenging its very possibility? Still, I argue that patriotism presumes and promotes a mortal logic of enmity, sacrifice, and death; minus these, you don't properly belong in patriotism's mental or affective universe. I prefer the tragic political world of democracy—because it serves life. It would better serve life without patriotism.

A commitment to life has informed the tragic alternative I have juxtaposed to patriotism. Springsteen, for example, employs his concerts to adopt the pose of a traveling preacher. On the DVD *Live in New York City*, he addresses the faithful at Madison Square Garden. In a confessional moment he distinguishes himself from what he calls his ministerial adversaries, his "competitors." Springsteen can promise much, he says, but he refuses to "promise life everlasting." Instead he promises "life right now."[43]

What might it mean for Springsteen to promise life? His musical compositions treat the world as replete with joy and loss, exhilaration and despair, love and cruelty, creation and death, community and isolation, opportunity and foreclosure, faith and injustice. These experiences are symbiotic; one implicates the other. Life's fundamental dynamic, tragic at its core, invariably consists in fighting the good fight that one did not initiate. It entails, that is, a commitment to respond affirmatively and imaginatively to life's polymorphous, productive energies. Patriotism calls us to a love, but a love of country enacted by a passionate attachment to enmity and death, perfected in mortal sacrifice undertaken on behalf of the nation. Yet life presents sufficient challenge (hard choices, moral dilemmas, irreconcilable conflicts, perverse trajectories, tragic necessities) without embracing death, without insisting that death and death alone uniquely imbues life with meaning, worth, and validation. Patriotism's reliance on death as its lifeblood renders it anathema to democracy.

Springsteen's devotion to life, which requires America to account for itself, recovers the best of Socrates, effectively resuscitating his ethos of provocation. Springsteen is to America and America to Springsteen what Socrates is to Athens and Athens to Socrates. In concert Springsteen forges a turbulent public space of reflective and affective possibility. He takes ideas and loves seriously, and requires an audience to articulate them. He sings to anyone and everyone. In conversation Socrates interrogates anyone in proximity who is willing, citizen or stranger. He chides Athenians for wasting their lives on shallow pursuits. People care for the wrong things and neglect the most precious. Springsteen endeavors to disturb and disrupt people from their daily routines. He will bring performances to a halt and silence crowds to maximize his effect. As Springsteen holds a mirror to America to measure official promise against performance, the reflection displays people denied the lives they seek, the lives they have earned. Socrates compares Athens to its reputation for greatness and finds it wanting. America cannot survive, dream alive, Springsteen's stories. Athens cannot survive, image intact, the scrutiny to which Socrates subjects it. Springsteen lives to sing another day, hopeful that he might engender a response. He carries his message across national borders. Socrates, like Springsteen in Spain, where European audiences know the lyrics better than American audiences, might have taken his performance on the road—with Crito as his manager. Crito, recall, had conversations lined up with eager listeners. Socrates, rather than dare Athens to death, could have taught the city from a distance, reinvented his art, and expanded his audience. Springsteen insists that his music must serve life; Socrates, by taking a walk, could have refused patriotism's demand that death is the only true test of commitment to one's principles, and kept on talking until he died of natural causes.

Thus Socrates might have inspired Will Kane, the Socratic gunslinger who prefers silence to loquaciousness. Revisit the conclusion of *High Noon*; then rewind to the scene in which Kane and Amy first leave Hadleyville. Kane angers himself into thinking that he must return. Imagine, instead, that Will heeds Amy's pleas and keeps driving. The decision would respect and reinforce the democratic judgment of Hadleyville that he walk away from a needless confrontation with death and affirm his new life with its unknown possibilities. Kane made his founding mark on Hadleyville; transferring responsibility for his legacy to the next generation—for good or ill—would reinforce it. Kane would in effect break the sword and disclose enmity's constructed character. Communities insist that commitment to a way of life proves itself in crisis and danger, including the potential sacrifice of life. The sequence from community to crisis to commitment to sincerity to death presents itself as necessary, the product of reason itself. The natural course of events merely discloses it. Without death's anchor, life's possibility ultimately unravels because of a boomerang effect. If Kane walks away, however, he reveals not just the links in the chain that intimately connect community to death *but their artificial character as well*. If Kane leaves and never looks back, he walks into screen history by erasing himself, as it were, by refusing the immortality that Socratic death promises as life's validation. No one dies; Hadleyville flourishes.

If Kane overcomes himself he joins the likes of Robert Gould Shaw, William James's literary experiment who did right independent of patri-

10. Vietnam Veterans Memorial wall (from the North).
Photo courtesy of Bob G.

otic economies of glory, heroism, and death. James's contrary dedication
speech for the Shaw Memorial is a more apt monument than the architecture itself. It resonates with Shaw's own life. If anything, James's reflections illuminate an aspect of Maya Lin's Vietnam Veterans Memorial,
the sublime design of which deflects patriotic verities. That is, should a
country not wonder about itself and its norms when so many young are
sent—and so many go—to their deaths for a dubious war? James argues
that countries never lack for young who will thrust themselves headlong
into battle—no matter the cause—as long as there are thousands to accompany them. Patriotism works to ensure a steady supply of volunteers.
Steven Spielberg's James Ryan offers one example. *Saving Private Ryan*
closes at Normandy's American Cemetery. Ryan refused to leave France
as ordered to guarantee that his mother would not lose all her sons to
one war, however just. Ryan's love for country, channeled into loyalty to
his brothers in arms, made leaving impossible, a fate worse than death
(à la Will Kane and Socrates). As a result, John Miller, the Army captain
charged with retrieving him, loses his life. A needless death, and James
Ryan bears responsibility for it: he could have left when he received the
news of his brothers' deaths. Ryan's departure, ironically, would have re-

quired patriotism's assistance: a country to be loved would be a country that makes impossible an unthinking commitment to death on its behalf. There is no such country; which neatly captures patriotism's impossibility.

It's time for patriotism to face the phenomenon of death that it presumes and inspires. On the Mall in Washington, the Vietnam Veterans Memorial created a national sensation by eschewing traditional martial form. Nevertheless, George Bush's conquest of Iraq suggests that one purpose informing the Memorial has failed: America still wages illegitimate, pointless wars, which invocations of patriotism help to make possible. Perhaps the greatest tribute to Lin's design would be to extend one of its motifs. Let the earth fully claim it, testimony to the new intuition that you can't love your country. What if, starting in 2009, the fiftieth anniversary of the American War's first American casualty, we erased each name on every slab, roughly ten a day, and then, as with Hamburg's Monument against Fascism, buried the panels underneath the ground on which they previously stood (fig. 10)? At ten a day, it would take the same number of years, sixteen, to erase what the war took to kill. This would restore them to what they were before they were made patriots by the war, the Wall, and the Vietnam complex. The country would disavow its lethal addiction and let death be. Consider it a gesture not only to new architectural life on the Mall but to life itself.

Notes

1. "WITHOUT EXTERNAL PICTURESQUENESS"

1 For its partisans patriotism works best loosely defined, its meaning treated as obvious. Based on traditional manifestations, however, I suggest the following provisional characterization. Patriotism means love of country, an affective comportment as strong as any other attachment or affiliation in life. Rooted in the faith that your country is special, even unique, and the resultant conviction that love obligates you—and others—to certain norms of feeling and conduct, patriotism necessitates a willingness to sacrifice life given the omnipresence of enemies in a dangerous world.

2 Schaar, "The Case for Patriotism," 285–87.

3 Brooks, "The Osama Litmus Test."

4 Brooks, "The C.I.A. versus Bush," *New York Times*, November 13, 2004, § A, 15.

5 Nietzsche, *The Birth of Tragedy and The Genealogy of Morals*, 221–22.

6 Douglass, "The Right to Criticize American Institutions," *Selected Speeches and Writings*, 77.

7 Douglass, "The Meaning of July Fourth for the Negro," *Selected Writings*, 192.

8 The revolutionary generation of blacks might disagree with Douglass's assessment of the founders. While blacks fought willingly for the colonies when afforded the opportunity to do so, slaves "defected" en masse to the British. See for example Nash, *The Forgotten Fifth*.

9 Douglass, "The Meaning of July Fourth for the Negro," 189.

10 Ibid., 196–97.

11 Ibid., 197.

12 Ibid., 194, 195.

13 Douglass denounces the long war of American slavery on blacks. To narrate it with candor is also to wonder how America can love itself, for patriotism is ultimately about self-love. The past, of course, can always be colonized for political purposes. Douglass himself cannot claim exemption from this narrative phenomenon. His July 4th speech, giving voice to one American atrocity coeval with founding, offers no words on the subject of America's mass slaughter and dispossession of native peoples, the original destruction fostered by creation. The luminaries whom Douglass salutes conducted a war of ethnic cleansing while fighting—and at the time, losing—a war of national liberation to the British. See Anderson and Cayton, *The Dominion of War*, chapter 4, "Washington's Mission: The Making of an Imperial Republic."

14 Douglass, "The Meaning of July Fourth for the Negro," 189.

15 Ibid., 193.

16 Even where Douglass turns to supplements, America manages to remain self-sufficient. As he anticipates slavery's defeat by the cosmopolitan world then emerging (oceans and armaments can protect and repel every invasion save one: truth), Douglass welcomes English assistance to eradicate slavery. After all, the English seek its abolition in the name of values borrowed from us. Ibid., 205; Douglass, "The Right to Criticize American Institutions," 79.

17 Douglass, "The Meaning of July Fourth for the Negro," 204.

18 Schaar, "The Case for Patriotism," 287.

19 Ibid.

20 Douglass, "Why Should a Colored Man Enlist?," 528, *Selected Speeches*.

21 Ibid., 531.

22 Ibid.

23 Ibid.; "Address for the Promotion of Colored Enlistments," *Selected Speeches*, 535–36.

24 Douglass, "The Commander-in-Chief and his Black Soldiers," *Selected Speeches*, 541.

25 Douglass, "Why Should a Colored Man Enlist?," 529–30.

26 Schaar, "The Case for Patriotism," 288.

27 Thanks to Menand, *The Metaphysical Club*, 147.

28 James, "Robert Gould Shaw," 65.

29 Ibid., 67.

30 Likewise, for all this rhetoric of country that Douglass asserts, the

colored soldier, if anyone, can make the claim that he fights for principle and not passion, which suggests an ethical stance prior to and independent of patriotic politics. Doing right reigns decisive.

31 Dedication speeches by Booker T. Washington and Henry Lee Higginson treat Shaw as a martyred, Christ-like figure who died for the nation's sins. For them his death defines his life.

32 James, "Robert Gould Shaw," 66.

33 Ibid.

34 Ibid., 67.

35 Ibid., 74.

36 Ibid.

37 Ibid., 73.

38 George Kateb pursues a similar line of thought when he writes: "One does and sometimes should love persons 'beyond good and evil,' so to speak; but to love a country, an abstract entity capable of so much harm . . . that is an unacceptable idea." Ultimately Kateb wonders if love of country is love properly speaking at all. For Kateb's riveting indictment of patriotism see "Is Patriotism a Mistake?"

39 James, "The Moral Equivalent of War," 1.

40 Ibid., 1–2.

41 Ibid., 4.

42 Ibid., 5.

43 Ibid., 5–6.

44 Steiner, " 'Tragedy,' Reconsidered," 2.

45 Ibid., 3.

46 Ibid., 5.

47 The term may be Heidegger's but the use is mine.

2. THIS PATRIOTISM WHICH IS NOT ONE

1 Charles Taylor, "Why Democracy Needs Patriotism," *For Love of Country*, ed. Nussbaum, 119; Rorty, *Achieving Our Country*, 3; Viroli, *For Love of Country*, 169; Ben Barber, "Constitutional Faith," *For Love of Country*, ed. Nussbaum, 31; Hilary Putnam, "Must We Choose between Patriotism and Universal Reason?," *For Love of Country*, ed. Nussbaum, 97; Robert Pinsky, "Eros against Esperanto," *For Love of Country*, ed. Nussbaum, 88; Dietz, "Patriotism," 191; MacIntyre, "Is Patriotism a Virtue?," 276; Wendy Brown, "Political Idealization and Its Discontents," *Edgework*, 36; Schaar, "The Case for Patriotism," 286.

2 Perhaps patriotism theorists privilege its salutary dimensions precisely because they seem to appreciate its contingent ambiguities—as if conceding

that patriotism *can* turn ugly constitutes sufficient preemptive response to criticism. Hence Taylor's contention that patriotism flourishes in the United States *given* the reactions to Watergate and Iran-contra. While Taylor concedes that patriotism may inadvertently encourage ("in its darker forms") the likes of Richard Nixon and Oliver North, the outraged reaction to them proves "essential" and "irresistible." He does not seem to consider that patriotism may render the crimes of Watergate and Iran-contra equally essential and irresistible. Taylor, "Cross-Purposes," 173–75.

3 Ibid., 165, 171.

4 MacIntyre, "Is Patriotism a Virtue?," 279.

5 MacIntyre's discussion of Adam Von Trott, who conspired to assassinate Hitler, seems pertinent here. According to MacIntyre's patriotism, opposing Hitler meant protecting and preserving "the Germany brought to birth in 1871" even if it also meant aiding and abetting "the cause of the Nazis." Supporting the project of the nation thus involved denying its responsibility for the Nazis, for acceptance of responsibility would entail rejection of the very order that enabled the cause in the first place. MacIntyre accepts that patriotism could involve strengthening the Nazi cause, even as an "unavoidable consequence." Ibid., 278; see also 282.

6 Taylor wonders whether "our patriotism [can] survive the marginalization of participatory self-rule." Let us upend Taylor's question and ask whether the presence of patriotism on today's theoretical agenda makes sense *absent* the marginalization of political self-rule. Does patriotism become imperative precisely because a robust republican conception of freedom is no longer viable? The stress on all manner of political education, then, would amount not so much to pre-political preparation as to a usurpation of politics itself. This would allow the mandatory celebration that Taylor identifies as critical to patriotism.

7 Taylor, "Why Democracy Needs Patriotism," 121.

8 Consider this injunction from Proverbs 27:1–2 (King James): "Boast not thyself of to morrow; for thou knowest not what a day may bring forth. Let another man praise thee, and not thine own mouth; a stranger, and not thine own lips."

9 Rorty, *Achieving Our Country*, 14, 11.

10 Ibid., 54, 83, 85–86, 60.

11 Ibid., 87.

12 The means: agreement on a People's Charter. Rorty's left is to be defined in economic rather than cultural terms. Class issues have the ability to unite disparate constituencies, whereas things cultural, rooted in questions of difference and demands for recognition, tend to fragment.

13 Rorty, *Achieving Our Country*, 50–51.

14 Ibid., 43–44.

15 Ibid., 21.

16 Ibid., 22.

17 Ibid., 16; emphasis added.

18 Ibid., 22, 23, 29.

19 Ibid., 25.

20 Ibid., 18.

21 Ibid., 31, 35.

22 Ibid., 28.

23 What is the provenance of Rorty's religious impulse? Impulse suggests a natural force that churns deep within the fiber of our being, one to which we would be well advised to attend and respond. But why does Rorty not pursue the possibility that he might be producing the excitation upon which he merely wants to draw? What would happen to the status and standing of his patriotic project if it were shorn of divine intimations?

24 Rorty, *Achieving Our Country*, 22; emphasis added. Rorty's mythical vision enjoys cinematic confirmation. *The Patriot* tells the Job-like story of Benjamin Martin, who initially opposes war as the means to America's independence. Martin must make amends not just for his opposition, not just for predicting the war's horrors, but for losing political faith: two sons killed; property burned; the remainder of his family endangered. Eventually Martin joins the war despite his doubts. His entrance signals America's reversal of fortune and ultimate victory. At the film's close Martin finds himself duly rewarded for having reaffirmed his patriotism. The new American nation, standing in for God, delivers the goods. An impending marriage to his first wife's sister (with newborn) not only replaces his marriage and lost first son; it holds out the promise of additional offspring. His commanding officer has named his newborn son after Martin's second lost child, nominally replacing him. When Martin returns home to South Carolina he sees friends and neighbors, racially united, rebuilding his home in the new world that his sacrifices made possible. All that Martin lost has been restored—and more. In short, if you love your country, you find meaning and purpose in the death that the country required. It gives you precisely the life you want and know to be right. Love of country also re-covers the crimes that achieved victory. It forgives and forgets that you turned two of your prepubescent sons into killers; that you forced them to witness their father's unquenchable desire for revenge. With America's role as the vanguard of human being established, patriotism can afford to revel in a civic virtue that obscures its violence.

25 America may continually create and recreate itself in Rorty's self-styled utopian vision, but it seems to move, however haltingly, toward a pre-existent goal. Rorty's chosen terms of redescription bear teleological residue: essence,

soul, realization, creation, fulfillment, expression, promise, harmony, resolution. While Rorty overtly rejects a notion of progress or evolution toward "something specifiable in advance," clearly he has some end in mind as specific problems are solved in the name of justice.

26 Rorty, *Achieving Our Country*, 11.

27 Ibid., 32–33, 37–38, 43, 45–46, 52, 54–56.

28 Ibid., 14, 15; emphasis added: "The academic Left has no projects to propose to America, no vision of a country to be achieved by building a consensus on the need for specific reforms."

29 And yet, once upon time in America, another generation of citizens, what we call the founding generation, rejected the possibility of working within the system and replaced it with another. Rorty's arbitrary litmus test suggests that his call to unity falls short of the ideal it allegedly embodies, for Rorty has initiated a struggle within the left based on the possession of proper credentials, that is, on patriotic identity.

30 Rorty, *Achieving Our Country*, 32.

31 The racial character of the crimes that Rorty remembers seems to have escaped him. And even where he considers a possible objection to his ringing defense of national pride, he jettisons the linguistic conceit of the first person plural in favor of the third person singular. Thus "one might protest" to his project of national pride but none of *us* would. Elsewhere Rorty rebukes much of the Left for becoming passive spectators rather than active agents in politics. Yet Rortyan remembrance does not call for, even as a moral gesture, any specific act of repentance. Nor is there any mention of forgiveness, which would depend on the goodwill and generosity of others rather than our own self-making abilities. Rorty, *Achieving Our Country*.

32 Ibid., 18.

33 Ibid., 23.

34 Rorty, "Fighting Terrorism with Democracy," *Nation*, October 21, 2002.

35 Rorty, *Achieving Our Country*, 21.

36 Ibid., 33.

37 Here Emerson is invoked: "the only sin is limitation." Ibid., 34.

38 Galston, *Liberal Purposes*, 242–44.

39 Callan, *Creating Citizens*, 111.

40 Ibid., 118.

41 Ibid., 121.

42 James Madison, *Notes on the Debates in the Federal Convention of 1787 Reported by James Madison* (New York: W. W. Norton, 1987), 77.

43 See Morgan, *American Slavery/American Freedom*. Slave labor, for example, produced the commodities that procured assistance from France and others.

44 Berns, *Making Patriots*.

45 Berns shares Rorty's penchant for enemies. Thus Marxists, postmodernists, liberals, intellectuals, and all manner of academics worshiping at the altar of moral and cultural relativism thwart his advice. Ibid., 79–86, 111, 135, 142.

46 Ibid., 9.

47 Ibid., 3, 5, 32.

48 Ibid., 112.

49 Berns tends to treat the founders, for narrative purposes, as a single unified entity. Here I tend to mimic him.

50 Ibid., 105–6, 111–12.

51 Ibid., 104.

52 Ibid., 106, 124, 127.

53 Ibid., 118–19, 128.

54 Schaar, "The Case for Patriotism," 287.

55 Schaar seems to forget the uncanniness of the home (inscribed in the unheimlich) and all the exclusions, hierarchies, and bellicosities with respect to intrusions into the home.

56 Schaar, "The Case for Patriotism," 287.

57 Ibid., 291.

58 Ibid., 293.

59 Maurizio Viroli offers similar reflections on patriotic discourse: "we have a moral obligation toward our country because we are indebted to it. We owe our country our life, our education, our language, and, in the most fortunate cases, our liberty." *For Love of Country*, 9.

60 Schaar, "The Case for Patriotism," 288.

61 Schaar's brief historical recapitulation of patriotism proves evocative. It's as if he wants to fashion the experiences he assumes intrinsic to us. When he narrates America, his use of the first person plural "we" can be read as part invitation to join the patriotic community, part injunction to do the right thing and recognize who we are and what we owe. Schaar thus mildly rebukes as he (re)educates. Ibid., 286.

62 Ibid., 297.

63 Ibid., 292.

64 Ibid., 288.

65 Ibid., 297.

66 Ibid., 294.

67 Ibid., 300.

68 Ibid., 290.

69 Ibid., 295.

70 Ibid., 286.

71 Ibid., 295–96; emphasis added.

72 Gitlin, "Varieties of Patriotic Experience."

73 Ibid., 107.

74 Ibid., 128, 125, 136, 126, 134.

75 Ibid., 109, 110.

76 Ibid., 119.

77 Ibid., 121.

78 Ibid., 120.

79 Ibid., 114, 116, 123–25.

80 Ibid., 109.

81 Ibid., 124, 125, 131.

82 Ibid., 134–35, 137.

83 The same can be said of Gitlin's insistence that Flight 93 was downed by patriots, a claim he repeats over and over.

84 Gitlin, "Varieties of Patriotic Experience," 123–24.

85 Ibid., 124.

86 Ibid., 120.

87 Ibid., 119.

88 Even Rorty recognizes, if grudgingly, the genocidal character of the Vietnam War.

89 Gitlin, "Varieties of Patriotic Experience," 111.

90 Ibid., 124–25, 134–35.

91 Ibid., 116.

92 Ibid., 112.

93 Ibid., 129–30.

94 Ibid., 131–32.

95 Ibid., 124, 131.

96 Ibid., 138.

97 Podhoretz, *My Love Affair with America*, 183.

98 Ibid., 95–96.

99 Ibid., 96.

100 Ibid., 179–80.

101 Ibid., 97.

102 Ibid., 98.

103 Ibid., 101.

104 Ibid., 105.

105 Ibid., 106.

106 Ibid., 187.

107 Ibid., 177.

108 Ibid., 174.

109 Ibid., 222, 228.

110 Ibid., 173.

111 Ibid., 174; emphasis added.

112 Ibid., 172.

113 The attacks of September 2001 enabled Podhoretz, again, to revisit the Vietnam War. While he insists repeatedly that he is telling "the story" of America since September 11, for him American history continues to revolve around Vietnam. September 11 affords America the opportunity to rid itself of Vietnam's deleterious legacy. In fact, September 11 already achieved a miraculous retrospective victory. One-time opponents of the Vietnam War were now proud to display the very American flag previously suitable for burning. They had been cured of thinking ill of America, that is, of indulging a self-hating "America the ugly" ethos. For Podhoretz the Vietnam War was first and last about America, about how we felt toward our country. The actual fighting was a sideshow, the Vietnamese themselves invisible. Podhoretz likewise launches a jeremiad to counter America's domestic September 11 enemy, known collectively as "the new antiwar movement." It includes television; America's universities and its tenured guerrilla professors; Michael Moore; the literary community; the media; intellectuals; and the Democratic Party. See his essays in *Commentary* listed in the bibliography. Note: I believe the flag story to be a reference to Todd Gitlin.

114 Podhoretz, *My Love Affair with America*, 171.

115 Viroli, *For Love of Country*, 8, 2. Viroli accordingly emphasizes the importance of politics to his conception of patriotism, which can only be political patriotism. In pluralist, multicultural societies, it alone can transcend the very real differences that obtain between and among people. This means not only that patriotism must be political in content, as Lincoln imagined, but that it can be practiced only through a participatory democratic ethic. Like Taylor's, Viroli's solution—or its absence—names the problem.

116 Ibid., 179–81.

117 Ibid., 13.

118 Rorty is silent on the question of war reparations to Vietnam, for example. Apparently he cannot match Germany's record toward its victims after the Second World War.

119 Simon Stow argues that the critique offered here presupposes a romantic notion of love and that a critical patriotism need draw on other forms. Perhaps, but Rorty is the one who proceeds as if the patriotic love extolled were romantic, meaning that his version entails jealousy, exclusiveness, tempestuousness, intolerance. Perhaps this should come as no surprise: for Rorty patriotism names the love that makes life itself possible. Rorty's love leads to various forms of blindness, including a performative myopia enabling him to justify and eventually erase the crimes that countries rou-

tinely commit—and to attack those who criticize those countries for those crimes. To argue that the future to which we aspire can function as a goal we never reach may thus serve to excuse a present that never changes. And we live in the present. How much history does Rorty need to see this? See Stow's "Land of Hope and Dreams (41 Shots): Bruce Springsteen, Richard Rorty, and the Possibility of a Critical Patriotism," Western Political Science Association meeting, Albuquerque, 2006, for a powerful and persuasive articulation of the position that I critique here.

120 I emphasize patriotic love. As Jane Bennett argues in *The Enchantment of Modern Life*, love as enchantment, characterized by a sense of wonder about the world, can be a source of ethical and political energies impressive in its ability to enact. This love is not tied internally to love of country.

121 Viroli feels compelled to cite, even quote, Schaar's account, which he takes to be true. *For Love of Country*, 15.

122 Schaar, "The Case for Patriotism," 287.

123 Ibid., 291, 293.

124 Ibid., 293.

125 Ibid., 302.

126 Ibid., 287; emphasis added.

127 Schaar can be read to subvert his own patriotic plea when he concedes that citizens would have no need for it. Precisely, I would argue. The problem is a lack of citizenship; thus the problem is politics, or its lack, not patriotism and its lack. This can be seen in Taylor's argument. He sees the outraged reaction to Watergate as symptomatic of a flourishing patriotism in the United States. But why should the reaction be so narrated? Taylor seems to concede the nominal character of his claim when he refers to the basic political commitments of citizens as "patriotism" (his scare quotes)—the implication being that he could just have easily called them something else. Citizens, that is, were needed to drive Nixon from office. But were patriots? Taylor does not make the case. "Cross-Purposes," 174–75.

128 See Hagan, *Northern Passage*.

129 Schaar, "The Case for Patriotism," 287.

130 Rorty, *Achieving Our Country*, 67.

131 Ibid., 57.

132 Ibid., 52.

3. THE MORTAL LOGIC OF ENMITY

1 Democracy alone can compromise its basic political principles and values. In the United States, a history of self-induced injury might start with the Alien and Sedition Acts of 1798, move to Lincoln's assaults on the Con-

stitution during the Civil War, the Supreme Court's sanction of suppression of free speech in the First World War I, the gratuitous imprisonment of Japanese-American citizens in 1942, and McCarthyism's staged spectacles, and conclude with the many constitutional depredations of George Bush's war on terror: an extralegal concentration camp in Cuba, secret CIA prisons in Europe and North Africa, the physical and psychological torture of America's captives, the detention of American citizens without charge or trial, the National Security Agency's program of warrantless searches of American citizens (with the knowledge of the *New York Times* and the *Washington Post*), and the prosecutorial targeting of journalists who report on governmental crime. See Stone, *Perilous Times*.

2 See Frankfurt, *The Reasons of Love*, 42–43.

3 For a superb account of this kind of ethical question (and much more) see Connolly, *Pluralism*.

4 James Colaiaco, on the other hand, noting that Socrates's defense "must be judged a failure according to the standards of forensic oratory later systematized by Aristotle in his *Rhetoric*," insists on a Socratic affirmation. "As George Grote observed: 'No one who reads the "Platonic *Apology*" of Sokrates will ever wish that he made any other defense.'" From this view I respectfully dissent. Colaiaco, *Socrates against Athens*, 179.

5 Villa, *Socratic Citizenship*, xi–xii.

6 Euben, *The Tragedy of Political Theory*, 202.

7 Euben, *Corrupting Youth*, 34.

8 Villa and Euben offer compelling, invaluable interpretations of Socrates. Nonetheless, I wish to contest their ownership claims.

9 Jonathan Lear writes: "Socrates . . . fashioned a method of cross-examination, designed to elicit conflicts which had hitherto remained unconscious inside the interlocutor. . . . The point of Socratic examination was to help people to be able to ask and answer the question for themselves." Thus Lear deems Socrates's defense unsuccessful "by any standard measure," and Socrates bears part of the responsibility for failing to recognize the likely reaction to his intervention. What I want to suggest is that Socrates himself did not lead the fully examined life that Lear presumes. Thus the problem is not that Socrates inadvertently provoked a "transference storm," but that he had not achieved sufficient self-transparency and thus provoked himself—not just the demos—"to act out [a] murderous impulse," as it were. Thus Lear and I part company on the question of whether Socrates sought acquittal. Lear, *Open Minded*, 56–57.

10 Alexander Nehamas poses quite well the problem that Socrates presents: "More than any other figure in our secular intellectual history he seems to have lived and died as he thought: holding that thought and action

are continuous, he actually drew no line between what he believed and what he did ... If Socrates was in reality radically different from his representations, then it is not clear that he deserves his status." Nehamas, *Virtues of Authenticity*, 85. What I am trying to explore here is whether his representations are what they purport (or are purported) to be.

11 Villa, *Socratic Citizenship*, 4.

12 Euben recognizes that Socrates's self-assigned task is not just difficult but ambiguous. Speaking of the Athenians, he writes: "Now corrupt, they are unable to adhere to what is best in their traditions or alter those traditions to realize better the highest aims of collective life as philosophy understands them. Like tragedy Socratic philosophy brings the city to think about the character of its collective goals and the implicit pattern of its actions." It is not necessary to convert citizens into philosophers, but Socrates "does want them to recognize what is problematic about the practices and decisions of their everyday lives, since the unexamined life is not worth living." How this can be fostered at trial Euben does not make clear. He suggests that Socrates can encourage collective self-examination by turning the tables on his accusers and judges and putting them on trial, which "creates a potentially uncorrupted public space around himself distinct from the public spaces already corrupted." Yet what would enable Athens to hear what Socrates has to say? Why would not Socrates end up talking to himself? And given that Socrates's defense, on Euben's own account, "turns into an offense in both senses," does not Socrates subvert his own case? Euben, *The Tragedy of Political Theory*, 211–12.

13 Ibid., 206, 208.

14 Hegel, *On Tragedy*, 361.

15 Ibid., 346.

16 See *Apology*, 29d–e, 30b, 30d–e, 36d.

17 Hegel, *On Tragedy*, 362, 346, 364, 365, 346, 358.

18 Ibid., 362.

19 Colaiaco, *Socrates against Athens*, 176–77; emphasis added.

20 Judith Shklar observes, "[Crito] is simply silenced with complex accounts of Socrates' familial and contractual obligations to Athens and to the ideal of a heroic philosopher indifferent to death." *Ordinary Vices*, 157–58.

21 Socrates's panegyric to the Laws cannot be squared with the actualities of his life—his protestations notwithstanding. Given Socrates's uniqueness, he defies the constitutive logic of identity that the Laws proclaim. Besides, no identity can be reduced to its context of creation. Identities exceed their place of origin. Socrates's identity is due not just to Athens's general nurturance and education; it is also forged independently of Athens. It is true that the life he lives in opposition to Athens presumes Athens, but this would be

true if Socrates lived in another city as well. Given Socrates's philosophical sensibility regarding convention, we can imagine him emerging in the interstices of a tyranny too. And it must not be forgotten that Socrates seeks Athens's utter transmogrification. Socrates's ethical success would be tantamount to parricide.

22 With consummate skill Euben recapitulates Socrates's engagement with the idealized Laws of Athens. If anything, he may suffer from success. Though he recognizes that the constitutive account of Socrates as an Athenian citizen is ultimately "one-sided," Euben still dismisses exile as "no solution." It would (allegedly) reduce Socrates to silence. Beyond Athens, the laws, and his fellow citizens, philosophy has no voice. The problem is that Euben does not rethink the possibilities of exile. He works within its conventional understanding, which means that his conclusion is prejudged, and his arguments designed to lead to the decision about exile he has already reached. In this Euben reflects Socrates's unthinking version of exile.

23 Colaiaco, *Socrates against Athens*, 199.

24 Ibid., 198–99.

25 See ibid., 176. Colaiaco seems to recognize Socrates's prearranged role, but claims that for Socrates to choose exile would be tantamount to collaboration with Athens in his victimization.

26 Ibid., 202, 203.

27 Ibid., 199.

28 Ibid., 209, 199, 210.

29 As Hegel noted, that Socrates formally proposed punishment cannot be squared with his later insistence that he not flee but remain in prison and "submit to the law." By this logic, moreover, he should not have participated in his trial.

30 Exile might appear an unpromising avenue of citizenship. Whether from force of economic circumstance or political tyranny, exile involves dislocation, dispossession, disempowerment, spiritual death. Yet it is exiles themselves who ultimately rethink it and concede not just the fundamental ambiguity of exile. They transform exile into something commonplace, perhaps universal, and productive. Moreover, as exiles reflect on the notion of home that governs their initial responses to exile, they come to realize that there is no place like home. The patriotism that would render exile unbearable itself becomes impossible after an encounter with exile and its successes. Exile becomes associated with possibility, patriotism with death. Exile thus poses a threat, if any, not to life, but to patriotism. See Hoffman, "The New Nomads"; and Said, *Reflections on Exile and Other Essays*.

31 Lendon, *Soldiers and Ghosts*, 81.

32 As Thucydides's account of Pericles's funeral oration reveals, Athens

was keenly aware of its comparative reputation in the Greek world. It distinguished itself vis-à-vis other city-states, Sparta for one. Athens would be sensitive to Socrates's discussion of it once he left.

33 White, *Acts of Hope*, 33–34. Much, if not most of the paragraph, is a paraphrase of White's argument. I am heavily indebted to him.

34 Ibid., 34.

35 Ibid., 34–35.

36 Nietzsche, *The Gay Science*, no. 340 [p. 272].

37 Socrates's patriotism disturbs many admirers, who deny but keep addressing it. Villa observes of Socrates: "He is, as the argument of the *Crito* shows, a kind of democrat. To call him a 'loyal' one, however, is misleading, if only because the vocabulary of loyalty and patriotism sets severe limits to the reach of philosophical questioning and moral criticism." Villa later insists that if anyone insists "on calling Socrates a 'patriot,' then it is necessary to qualify that description as a form of *constitutional* patriotism. But even then we risk losing sight of the true nature of his attachment." If so, Villa's concern should be addressed to Socrates—not his critics—for Socrates's philosophical questioning and moral criticism suffer limitations at key moments, as I have tried to demonstrate. Thus, when Villa writes that "we risk losing sight of the true nature of his attachment," the "we" designates those who view Socrates's citizenship as philosophical or dissident. I appreciate Villa's invitation but ultimately cannot accept it. Villa, *Socratic Citizenship*, 5, 49.

38 The instability of Euben's account manifests itself when he writes, "Socrates chooses to be a victim." For Euben, this is a matter of Socrates's patriotism. He practices philosophy for the city and its improvement. If Athens condemns him, it will harm itself more than it will harm him. At best Athens is "shortsighted, at worst self-destructive." Given Athens's incapacity, however, Socrates has created a new problem for himself, one that Euben does not address. Socrates has become complicit with Athenian perfidy. He makes no attempt to stop Athens, at trial, from doing its worst. If anything, when it comes to the jury (as opposed to the prosecutors), he in effect forces the city to take a course of action that it might otherwise have rejected. He is thus no victim; Athens is his victim. Yet Euben insists that Socrates "bravely defended his city against its foes and is doing no less here." In doing so, he maps Socratic thoughtlessness on the city's wars. I would suggest, however, that just as Athens created its own enemies on the battlefield through its imperial undertakings, Socrates converted the jury into his enemy through the conduct of his trial. Patriotism is what links these so-called defenses of Athens. In each case the seduction of death seems irresistible. Death's attractions peak as Socrates speculates that his death could lead to a kind of

thinly veiled civil war. Euben, *The Tragedy of Political Theory*, 216, 217, 218, 227, 228–29.

1 Schaar, "The Case for Patriotism," 285.

2 Ibid., 287–91.

3 Ibid., 288.

4 Ibid., 287.

5 Ibid., 289, 288, 287, 286, 290.

6 Ibid., 291.

7 Connolly, *Why I Am Not a Secularist*, 25–29. Connolly's invaluable work on the nexuses of brain, body, and culture illuminates the power and persistence of patriotism.

8 Ibid., 27.

9 Wills, *John Wayne's America*, 198, 273.

10 Wayne's reaction to film encompasses more than right-wing chauvinists. Rorty fixates on American intellectuals unduly influenced by postmodernism who might encounter Wayne's war films and wrongly adjudge America a "violent, inhuman, corrupt country." Rorty, *Achieving Our Country*, 7.

11 Maurizio Viroli describes the language of patriotism as "eminently rhetorical." It targets passions and seeks to take charge of the love that people feel for their country. Viroli too stresses the importance of patriotic stories with "morals to tell" that do not employ sustained arguments; hence the importance of film. Viroli, *For Love of Country*, 8–9.

12 Jane Tompkins writes of westerns: "Some of these films [such as *High Noon*] have become part of the permanent repertoire of American culture." Tompkins, *West of Everything*, 5.

13 Here I challenge more traditional readings of *High Noon*. Tompkins writes: "The price the Western exacts from its heroes is written in the expression on Gary Cooper's face throughout *High Noon* . . . The expression is one of fear, distaste, determination, and inward pain. It is impossible not to share that pain with Western heroes." For Tompkins the price exacted is "too high." Ibid., 19, 105, 219.

14 Wills, *John Wayne's America*, 274. Slotkin, *Gunfighter Nation*, 392–93, 394, writes: "There is also a social component among Kane's motives. His work was meaningful because it transformed Hadleyville into a 'progressive' little town where it is safe for women and children to walk the streets. He cannot permit society to revert to the savage regime of Miller, even if the

people who constitute that society are willing to permit it." Kane is no demo-crat. I would like to extend, perhaps radicalize, Slotkin's reading. He grounds his interpretation on a small but critical difference between Kane and Miller: "Kane's latent instinct for goodness." Though Slotkin attributes Kane's power and success to his affinity with Miller, he also insists that Kane can transcend evil given this instinct. This is the patriotic benefit of the doubt I would like to challenge, a challenge signaled by Slotkin's scare quotes around "progres-sive."

15 Ibid., 392.

16 In the film's optic, democracy is problematic. It equates speech with evasion and obfuscation. Given the self-evident character of right and wrong, talk becomes inherently suspicious. Kane thus refuses to engage the town in moral or political discourse. Slotkin considers the church scene in *High Noon* a "parody of democracy." He concludes: "In effect, the principle on which [Kane] acts is . . . that the defense of 'civilization' is more impor-tant than the procedures of 'democracy.'" Kane, of course, scorns not just democratic procedures but democracy's judgment. Slotkin, *Gunfighter Na-tion*, 392–93.

The church scene receives cinematic rebuke some fifty years later in Mel Gibson's *The Patriot*. America's revolutionary war faces recruitment short-ages in South Carolina. Appeal is made to Sunday churchgoers in a small village. It is met with little success until a young woman intervenes. She de-nounces the assembled for their timidity. For the patriot, word and deed must match. Once rebuked, the community answers the call for volunteers. Even the reverend, unlike the vacillating pastor in *High Noon*, joins the cause to tend his flock in battle.

Furthermore, *The Patriot* makes its own contribution to Socratic thinking about the irrelevance of consequences, namely of death. The British learn of the town's "traitorous" conduct and decide to make an example of it. Being no ordinary enemy, the British require demonization. And the colonists need an enemy that can justify the sacrifices self-imposed. The British order the church burned, which means that they effectively transform themselves into the Nazis who committed precisely such an atrocity in France. The choice of God's house in *The Patriot* is surely no accident. The heavenly future of those men and women who remained loyal cannot be left in doubt.

17 The audience cannot appreciate, let alone experience, the community's decision. It decided, reluctantly, not to deploy the overwhelming force at its disposal, a force that could easily have dispensed with Frank Miller and as-sociates.

18 Cf. Slotkin, *Gunfighter Nation*, 393, 394. When Kane finally returns to the office, his old friend Herb waits. Shocked that Kane has been unable to

enlist help, he starts to backpedal. He reminds Kane that he volunteered; no one had to ask. But he had not counted on being the only one to help. There is only so much that can be expected of one man. As he talks, he slowly holsters his gun. As he creeps backward toward the door his entire body recoils. Kane admits he had forgotten about Herb. So had we; hence the reminder. For us, not even too much anger suffices.

19 In the great seduction scene following serial rejection, where Kane's deputy tries to persuade and then force him to leave town, Kane, though tempted, ultimately resists. Fatigue fosters fear. Yet Kane does not rethink his position here, for when it comes to right and wrong there's nothing to think about. Kane's apparent bravery conceals his thoughtlessness.

20 Slotkin takes Miller's evil rule for granted and claims that he "terrorized" the town from his saloon. Drummond, *High Noon*, 59, also takes Miller's guilt for granted.

21 When Miller arrives he is as cool as can be. He belies his advance billing. And what of his three associates? They ride into town without incident, not wanted by the law.

22 Drummond, *High Noon*, 46, is silent on the matter.

23 Slotkin argues that Kane's authority derives from his character or manhood, not the badge. But if his authority lies elsewhere, perhaps it is from above. This may be why Kane does not attend church. It is ruled by infidels. Not even the pastor comes to Kane's defense. Slotkin, *Gunfighter Nation*, 393.

24 Ibid., 395.

25 Vincent Canby argues that the film "[restored] the nation's heroic image of itself." Beyond that he doubts its relevance. Canby, "Saving a Nation's Pride of Being: The Horror and Honor of a Good War," *New York Times*, August 10, 1998, § E, 1.

26 It is only later that you realize this man could not have seen what you are about to witness, namely the Normandy invasion. He was not there. But truth is the currency deployed here.

27 Upon its release *Saving Private Ryan* acquired a privileged place in American cinema. Stephen Hunter called it "the greatest war movie ever made, and one of the great American movies." Janet Maslin called it "the finest war movie of our time." David Edelstein wrote, "The opening battle might be the most visceral ever put on film" and the film's "battles . . . make most World War II pictures seem like Hollywood kid stuff." Stephen Hunter, "'Private Ryan': Steven Spielberg's Unflinching Tribute to the Men Who Conquered Hell," *Washington Post*, July 24, 1998; Janet Maslin, "Panoramic and Personal Visions of War's Anguish," *New York Times*, July 24, 1998; David Edelstein, "Apocalypse Then: The Viscera of War," *Slate*, July 24, 1998.

28 Despite the stunning visual properties of *Saving Private Ryan*, Spielberg concentrated on sound. See *New York Times*, June 24, 2001, 23–24.

29 Stephen Hunter has astutely observed: "In Spielberg's terrifying version [of Normandy], the bullets seem somehow angry." See note 27, above.

30 The United States is but one democracy with controversies over patriotism. Idith Zertal's genealogy of Israeli nationalism discloses the use of its people when it was not yet a state. Excavating the myth of Tel Hai, Zertal notes the fanciful origins of the heroic story and the ease with which its myth unfolded. It didn't matter whether Yosef Trumpeldor, leader of Jewish pioneers in Upper Galilee, actually said, "It's nothing. It's good to die for our country." It didn't matter that he and his comrades were settlers encroaching on Arab land and fought an unnecessary skirmish. Rather, Trumpeldor's death could be put to productive political use as a sign of newfound will and resistance. Thus adroit leaders like Ben-Gurion did not need to worry about evacuating isolated northern settlements, though reinforcement was impossible. Death would be salutary for incipient Israeli identity. Tel Hai thus became sacred symbolic ground flush, later, with the nation's first memorial. Necessity may have reduced Trumpeldor's life to political use value, but then how do you love a country that does not think twice about committing such sacrifice and then exploiting it? Zertal, *Israel's Holocaust and the Politics of Nationhood*, chapter 1.

31 Wendy Brown, "Political Idealization and Its Discontents," *Edgework: Critical Essays on Knowledge and Politics*.

32 Upham's protest triggers a veritable mutiny by one of Miller's men. Upham thus makes possible what ought to be, under the circumstances, unthinkable: American self-destruction.

33 Cf. Maslin's attribution of "immense dignity" to the film. See note 27, above.

5. THE ARCHITECTURE OF DEMOCRATIC MONUMENTS

1 Russell, "Crowding the Mall," 34.

2 This has been the success of the counter-monument movement in Germany. See Young, *The Texture of Memory* and *At Memory's Edge*.

3 Jeff Gerth, "Groundbreaking, of Sorts, for a Contested War Memorial," *New York Times*, November 12, 2000, 21. For data on the Second World War see Irvin Molotsky, "Panel Backs World War II Memorial on Mall in Washington," *New York Times*, July 21, 2000, § A, 13.

4 The inscriptions on the base of the flagpoles that frame the memorial's entrance read: "Americans came to liberate, not to conquer, to restore freedom and to end tyranny."

5 Rorty, *Achieving Our Country*, 3, 4, 13, 22.

6 Charles Krauthammer, "The WWI Memorial: Inadequate and Out of Place," *Washington Post*, July 28, 2000, § A, 25.

7 See Irvin Molotsky, "Design for World War II Memorial Awaits Review, with Detractors Vocal," *New York Times*, July 17, 2000, § E, 6.

8 Herbert Muschamp disagreed: "The design's best feature is its sensitivity to the site. Scale notwithstanding, the memorial is not the visual obstruction many have feared . . . The hemicircular arrangement enables the steles to be partly screened by trees." "An Appraisal: New War Memorial Is Shrine to Sentiment," *New York Times*, June 7, 2001, § A, 28.

9 "For the Record," at www.wwiimemorial.com/Response.htm.

10 Charles Krauthammer, "DON'T BUILD IT HERE!," *Time*, April 21, 1997.

11 Consider the announcement stone at the World War II Memorial. Invoking the nation's paternity and rebirth, it announces, "Here in the presence of Washington and Lincoln . . . we honor those twentieth century Americans who took up the struggle during the Second World War and made the sacrifices to perpetuate the gift our forefathers entrusted to us: a nation conceived in liberty and justice."

12 This is where I part company with Muschamp, who writes: "Friedrich St. Florian's design for the National World War II Memorial diminishes the substance of its architectural context. The design does not dare to know. It is, instead, a shrine to the idea of not knowing or, more precisely, of forgetting . . . It puts sentiment in the place where knowledge ought to be." Muschamp, "An Appraisal." Despite Muschamp's assessment that "Washington's core formal concept—its neo-Classical plan and architectural aesthetic—is symbolically sound," he writes one paragraph later that "Washington is relatively insubstantial architecturally . . . The city's Fine Arts Commission . . . is more or less in the business of preventing . . . challenges from materializing where they might distract visiting school children from the overwhelming impression of authority." I prefer the second Muschamp.

13 Muschamp notes—and then partially surrenders to—the nostalgia informing the World War II Memorial: "the cause of remembering the war has also served the objective of forgetting the unfolding of history before and since. Before Vietnam, before Watergate, before the cultural distortions of the cold war, there was an age of moral certainty, a time innocent of complexity, irony, or ambiguity. This time can be bracketed between the years 1939 and 1945. But this view of the war years is rooted in the moral uncertainties of our own day. So is the World War II Memorial's design. It represents our yearning for the timeless and eternal to distract us from the relative and the complex. After the failures of the so-called American Century, that yearning is understandable and even heroic, up to a point." My disagreement with

Muschamp's closing assessment regarding heroism should become clear below. Muschamp, "An Appraisal."

14 Rorty, *Achieving Our County*, 56–57, 32.

15 Nicolaus Mills presumes that location alone alters the balance of symbolic power on the Mall, that the Second World War should put the other wars in their historic places. What this presumption misses is that the political war on the Mall is fought over the Mall itself. Mills's problem isn't that the Vietnam War can't rival the Second World War in historical significance; Mills's problem is that no memorial can seize the status the Vietnam Memorial has secured for itself. Thus Mills wants to treat the respective memorials on historical grounds alone. Mills, *Their Last Battle*.

16 Russell, "Crowding the Mall," 33.

17 I would make a similar point with regard to his criticism of the Hart and Goodacre additions to the Vietnam grounds (that they "demean" Maya Lin's design). I know what Russell means aesthetically, but the rebuke overlooks their "contribution" to the Vietnam complex as a site of civic political space. See chapter 6.

18 Mills, *Their Last Battle*, 10, for example.

19 Roger Durbin, a Battle of the Bulge veteran who in Mills's book sets the memorial process in motion, dies before the memorial is built. The struggle took its toll on him. Nazis couldn't kill him; fellow citizens contributed to his death. Ibid., 46–53.

20 Ibid., 61, 75.

21 Ibid., 105.

22 Ibid., 43, 105. Constitution Gardens, one option, constitutes one of the most beautiful spaces on the Mall. It defines underuse. For the World War II Memorial, therefore, it also defined inadequacy: it fell outside (by a hundred yards) the central Washington-Lincoln axis. Apparently it never occurred to the American Battle Monuments Commission that the Memorial, properly designed, could transfigure the space it occupied. It's as if the memorial required a geographical head start to succeed.

23 Ibid., 109–13.

24 Consider Hugh Hardy's dogmatism: "Maya Lin's design for the Vietnam Veterans Memorial successfully challenges the use of historical references and heroic statuary. Traditional symbols of victory and valor do not apply to the Vietnam War ... However ... it offers no precedent for presenting the many facets of the Second World War." Hardy headed the board that selected the winning memorial. Brinkley, ed., *The World War II Memorial*, 33.

25 Mills, *Their Last Battle*, 120–29.

26 Ibid., 145, 148, 153.

27 Ibid., 147, 150.

28 Ibid., 148.

29 For example, Mills denounces comparisons of St. Florian's classicism with Albert Speer as "architectural McCarthyism." Ibid., 175.

30 Fifty-six equals the number of states, districts, and territories then constituting the nation.

31 Mills, *Their Last Battle*, 215–16; emphasis in original.

32 Ibid., 207.

33 Ibid., 216.

34 Ibid., 213–14, 217–18.

35 Ibid., xxiii–xxvi.

36 Ibid., 218.

37 "The Purpose," at www.wwiimemorial.com/aboutmemorial/purpose .htm; emphases added.

38 David Montgomery and Linda Wheeler, "Generations Gather in Gratitude," *Washington Post*, November 12, 2001, § A, 14; emphasis added.

39 Thus George Bush invokes (and misquotes) Marshall's words at his graduation speech at West Point in 2002, where he articulates his plans to remake the world in America's image of "[m]oral truth," which "is the same in every culture, in every time, and in every place." The speech is available at www.whitehouse.gov.

40 Even Charles Krauthammer inadvertently exposes the blindness of the memorial. Though he later described the Second World War as "the most monumental, most unequivocally righteous struggle in history," in 1997 he included the following as part of the memorial's work: "To mark the most shocking attack on (Pearl Harbor) and the most shocking attack by (Hiroshima) the U.S." Krauthammer, "DON'T BUILD IT HERE!"

41 According to George Mosse, nations deftly mask and transform mass death into legitimating myth. The World War II Memorial contributes to the architectural tradition of denial by effectively erasing war's horrors through sheer grandiosity. Turning from Asia to Europe, consider W. G. Sebald's *On the Natural History of Destruction*. The Allied bombing campaign on Germany in 1943 targeted Hamburg (among other cities). The Allies believed that the military and psychological reasons for the bombings were debatable. Once they learned that German war production and morale continued unabated, the campaign's rationales vanished. The bombing continued, however, and mass slaughter and apocalyptic destruction resulted. When patriots claim to love their country and take pride in its accomplishments, victory in war enjoys a place of privilege. If they celebrate the end of war, do they not also implicitly affirm the means deployed on its behalf? Can patriots knowingly love a country that would knowingly commit crimes for no legitimate

reason according to rules of war that they themselves establish? How do you love that which kills without hesitation on a mass scale? What does that mean? Sebald, *On the Natural History of Destruction*. See also Nossack, *The End*.

42 Consider the inscription at Lincoln temple's from his second inaugural. Slavery is identified without hesitation as the war's source. Yet the South cannot be singled out for blame. Slavery is an all-American institution, a national responsibility. Each side must come to understand the war's unprecedented carnage as just comeuppance for slavery's sins. While America prays that the war will conclude with all deliberate haste, there are no grounds for complaint if it continues. If anything, there would be justice should the war bankrupt America of the wealth it reaped from such an evil institution and if the horrors of the war ultimately matched the sufferings of slavery. Yet the words, towering over and above visitors, take on new meaning absent the original ceremonial context. They have been appropriated to serve America's self-image. The Civil War shifts from a gratuitous self-inflicted wound to an occasion to honor the quiet nobility of our suffering. In retrospect Lincoln's words, reinvented through inscription, give us permission. We have put them to maximum patriotic use. I recommend White, *Lincoln's Greatest Speech*.

43 Panel 52 bears an injunction from Senator Daniel K. Inouye: "The lessons learned must remain as a grave reminder of what we must not allow to happen again to any group." Yet the reminder has already failed. As the Bush administration's "war on terror" proves, the lesson learned by the state was to relocate detention centers outside the United States. *Patriotism, Perseverance, Posterity*, 131.

44 Ibid., 130. The accolades here include a salute from President Truman to Japanese American veterans of the Second World War at a White House ceremony honoring them in 1946. Truman, second in command in the administration that ordered detention, speaks of prejudice and overcoming it. America must be made to realize its ideals, and apparently responsibility falls to these veterans to "keep up that fight." If they do, "we will continue to win." These words are remarkable. Not just because of Truman's implication in the original injustice (unremarked here); not just because victims of injustice are made responsible for America's moral reformation; but also because the prejudice of which he speaks arguably informs the war's stunning Pacific conclusion. The silence here anticipates the silence at the World War II Memorial.

45 *Patriotism, Perseverance, Posterity*, 26. This obfuscation corresponds to what William Marutani, president of the nonprofit organization that brought the memorial into being, said at a hearing before the National Capital Memorial Commission (20): "It is ... not solely a military memorial. It is,

indeed, a significant chapter in American history. What other government apologizes to its citizens for having committed a wrong? That's beautiful. It makes me proud to be an American." Or as James Whitaker of the commission stated (21): "I think there is a much broader story [in the memorial] in terms of recognition of wrong, of repentance, of forgiveness. If it can be cast in historical significance and that kind of thing, and isn't this a wonderful country that we can turn ourselves around." Another memorial inscription refers to the nation's "admission of error committed in the hysteria of war." At the time of incarceration, however, Roosevelt knew from military and police sources that Japanese-American citizens posed no threat to their country. See Robinson's *By Order of the President*. To compound the injustice, some internees were drafted. When they refused, they were imprisoned (again, elsewhere). See Muller's *Free to Die for Their Country*.

46 Robert Musil insisted that more should be expected from monuments. Yet his seems a minority voice. Daniel Abramson, among others, though troubled by the narrowness of the memorial impulse, limits the possibilities of monumental space. As if responding to brute facts, he writes: "Admittedly monument making should not be expected to accomplish the same things as historical discourse. We cannot realistically expect, for instance, that a monument will spur debate about its subject within itself. Nor should we anticipate that monument makers will get out ahead of the public (which commissions monuments, after all)." Note the passivity with which he begins the argument. "Admittedly" here functions to create the concession that pretends to reasonableness and presupposes facts not in evidence. But even if it were agreed that monument making cannot effectively mimic historical discourse, cannot monuments be designed to spur debate? This premise defines the counter-monument movement, for example. Abramson, "Make History, Not Memory," 82.

47 Harry S. Truman, Message to Congress on the Atomic Bomb, October 3, 1945, available at www.atomicarchive.com/Docs/Deterrence/Truman.

48 Mills feels compelled to conclude, however: "In terms of scale there was nothing fascistic or even imperial about St. Florian's memorial." More specifically, "With a baldacchino inside each, the arches encourage contemplation, not exultation, on the part of anybody entering them." *Their Last Battle*, 176–77.

49 Harry S. Truman, White House Press Release, August 6, 1945, *American Experience* at www.pbs.org/wgbh/amex/presidents/33_Truman; J. Robert Oppenheimer at www.atomicmuseum.com/tour; the reference to Japanese housewife can be found in Schell, *The Fate of the Earth*, 39.

50 Dennis R. Montagu, locating the Grant in the political and cultural context of its creation in the early twentieth century, reads it in terms of

"military preparedness" and national "self-sacrifice." If, however, the Grant can be deemed pro-war and pro-empire, as Montagu contends, I would argue that effect belies intent. Montagu, "The Ulysses S. Grant Memorial in Washington, DC," 117.

51 Cf. Charles Griswold, who writes of the ambiguity of the Grant Memorial: "I would not go so far as to call it an antiwar monument; but it certainly neither glorifies war nor is heroic in any way." He concludes: "The Grant Memorial as a whole does not convey a moral lesson." I fear that Griswold's conclusion follows from his (somewhat) tepid description-cum-interpretation of the memorial itself. See Griswold, "The Vietnam Veterans Memorial and the Washington Mall," 84.

52 Levinson, *Written in Stone.*

53 The United States appropriated roughly 40 percent of Mexico and thereby increased its own territory by some 66 percent.

6. POLITICAL NOT PATRIOTIC

1 *New York Times*, July 4, 2000, § A, 8.

2 Washingtonpost.com/wp-dyn/articles/A39858–2000Jul13.html.

3 See the helpful introductory essay by David Chidester and Edward T. Linenthal in their edited volume *American Sacred Space.*

4 Mosse, *Fallen Soldiers*, 3, 6–7. Mosse analyzes what he calls the Myth of the War Experience from the French Revolution through the First and Second World Wars. Like Mosse, I seek patterns that transcend time and place to delineate and dissect the strategic repetitions apparently employed by all forms of patriotism to sustain themselves.

5 *New York Times*, July 17, 2000, § B, 6.

6 Charles Griswold describes how the Lincoln and Washington frame a visit to the Vietnam Memorial: "the architecture of the [Vietnam Veterans Memorial] encourages us to question America's involvement in the Vietnam War *on the basis of* a firm sense of both the value of human life and the still higher value of the American principles so eloquently articulated by Washington and Lincoln, among others." Griswold assumes this contextualization to be unproblematic, even desirable. Yet it insinuates preconditions into a consideration of the war and the issues it raises. Thus the interrogative character of the Wall is always already enclosed, and the range of possible answers to the questions it poses constricted. Griswold, "The Vietnam Veterans Memorial and the Washington Mall," 87, 93; emphasis in original. Griswold's reading of the memorial dovetails with Maya Lin's artistic and political intentions. Lin designed what she called an "apolitical" memorial, one

that allowed a "simple" inscription at the vertex. Lin can regard her creation as "apolitical" insofar as she presumes patriotism to be self-evidently void of politics. See Lin, *Boundaries*.

7 Berns, *Making Patriots*, 134.

8 As Robert Harbison points out: "Washington has memorials more chilling than Lincoln's; after all, the columns in that temple each have personal names, which are written over them. Each one is a state of the union, and there are thirty-six, the number of states when Lincoln was president . . . A more truthful monument would have found a way of representing architecturally the determined effort by eleven of these to leave the building. Like many others this monument represents an interesting conflict as stasis." Harbison, *The Built, the Unbuilt, and the Unbuildable*, 41.

9 See, for a very recent example, Richard Wightman Fox, "The President Who Died for Us," *New York Times*, April 14, 2006, § A, 21.

10 For an interesting account of Germany's efforts to deal with its violent national history see Till, *The New Berlin*.

11 Ibid., 82–83.

12 Young, *The Texture of Memory*, 27. I am deeply indebted here to Young's work.

13 Musil, "Monuments," 320–23.

14 The very city that Allied bombing destroyed without cause in the Second World War thus becomes the center of a movement for the rebirth of democratic public memorial architecture. In the United States, defeat in Vietnam engendered Maya Lin.

15 Young, *The Texture of Memory*, 28.

16 Rousseau warned that the theater, for example, unleashes emotions in patrons who congratulate themselves for their human response to tragedy. What more could be asked of them, they conclude? Certainly they need not do anything about the condition of the world. Rousseau, *Politics and the Arts*, 24.

17 Carhart, "Insulting Vietnam Vets."

18 Lin's design originally envisioned that the memorial would be approached head-on, from the south. The listing of the dead, arranged chronologically rather than alphabetically, begins and ends at the vertex.

19 Griswold, "The Vietnam Veterans Memorial," 87, 91.

20 Trees to a considerable degree block the Lincoln during certain seasons.

21 In November 2003 George Bush signed legislation sanctioning a Vietnam Veterans Memorial Center, the fifth memorial at the site. It will include exhibits to provide a history (a "patriotic" history) of the war as well as "in-

formational brochures" with patriotic accounts of the nearby monuments. The Vietnam Veterans Memorial Fund website (www.vvmf.org) furnished the information.

22 Griswold argues, "For all practical purposes, the visitor to the VVM must literally turn his back to these additions." He then concludes: "Yet the physical and aesthetic distance between these two additions and the VVM is so great that there exists no tension between them. All three finally seem to be separate memorials." Perhaps, but given the heavy flow of bodies moving from the Lincoln to the Wall, the Three Soldiers are often encountered first. As for the question of distance, the Three Soldiers stand at the western end of the Wall. There is no real distance between the two. And while the aesthetic difference between the Wall and its supplements may be great, the differences call attention to the whole.

23 Griswold has described the Wall as "fundamentally interrogative." "The Vietnam Veterans Memorial," 91.

24 This distinguishes it from the Korean Memorial, whose simulation of geographical severity, for example, grounds its effect.

25 This characterization may be misleading. While the Wall may have come first through the design competition, the Three Soldiers became, in effect, part of the original Vietnam Memorial complex. For the Wall would not have been built if the Three Soldiers had not been incorporated into the overall schema.

26 Scruggs, a Vietnam veteran, conceived the very idea of a Vietnam memorial and was the governing force of its realization.

27 Consider here Tom Carhart's assessment of the Wall as a "black gash of shame." Assume he's right. Is this a damning formulation that speaks for itself? Assume now that critics were right to condemn the war. Wouldn't it say more about a country and its normative commitments if it were capable of addressing its problematic—violent, deadly, tragic—past? Carhart's angry reaction troubles, because for dominant modes of patriotism a black gash of shame could not be imagined, let alone countenanced.

28 The Wall was designed so that new names could be added; the status of names already inscribed could be updated. It was also possible, encouraged even, for visitors to make paper tracings of the names.

29 Scruggs and Swerdlow, *To Heal a Nation*, 124. See also Hass, *Carried to the Wall*, 23, for an indispensable treatment of the offerings left at the Wall.

30 The reasons for this offering should become clear later in the chapter.

31 The criteria for the memorial included that it: "be reflective and contemplative in character . . . and . . . make no political statement about the war." Yet returning to Griswold's characterization, I would argue that the Wall is more than interrogative; it is also constitutively declarative. There

are two patriotic epigraphs at the vertex of the Wall that were not part of Lin's design (though she did subsequently revise the design to allow for and contain them). In addition, the POW/MIA campaign, symbolized by a menacing black flag that has become inextricable from the memorial, presents and performs a highly politicized understanding of the war, its conduct, and its aftermath. Here I depart from Marita Sturken, who writes about the Memorial: "It evokes contemplation rather than declaring its meaning." See Sturken, "The Wall, the Screen, and the Image," 123.

32 *New York Times*, July 5, 2000; emphases added. Scruggs takes the opportunity to refer to the controversy—and reiterate his position—surrounding the design of the Wall. He is also careful to restrict his ire to permanent new additions, since the offerings left daily at the wall are perpetual additions. It should be added that Scruggs and the Vietnam Veterans Memorial Fund (VVMF) later decided to support the plaque. Though the plaque was unveiled in 2004, it arrived invisible. A small inscription on existing flagstones reads: "In memory of the men and women who served in the Vietnam War and later died as a result of their service. We honor and remember their sacrifice." Unless you know in advance the precise location of the "plaque" at the edge of Hart's Three Soldiers, you are unlikely to notice it. If anything, its hyper-unobtrusiveness insults the memory of those whom it would salute. The inclusion of the word "later" also compromises the tribute. Again, here not all deaths are equal.

33 They certainly fit the inscription on the Wall that speaks of courage and sacrifice. Ironically, it denies recognition to war protestors while recognizing William Calley Jr. of the infamous My Lai massacre. Does the Memorial really wish to honor his courage and sacrifice?

34 Scruggs and Swerdlow, *To Heal a Nation*, 29; emphasis mine.

35 Given Scruggs's disapproval of additions, I wonder if he opposed the Korean War Veterans Memorial. I would suggest that the Korean War Veterans Memorial functions as a challenge to, even a check against, the Vietnam Wall. Opposite the Vietnam complex, the design of the Vietnam Wall informs and animates the Korean. The wall delimiting the southern edge of the memorial, which depicts the faces of the thousands of men and women of the four military branches, forms a backdrop that focuses attention on the memorial's core: a platoon of soldiers on the move across a harsh Korean landscape. It suggests that this war, unlike that in Vietnam, enjoyed widespread support. Men-at-war is the drama presented here. But which war exactly? And who's fighting it?

In contrast to the Vietnam Memorial, the Korean tapestry unfolds above ground. Designed to elicit sympathy, even pity, the larger than life-sized troops reek power. Masculinity and heroism are both on display—in abundance. While covered in rain gear to protect themselves from the nasty elements, they bulge beneath this outer layer. Armed to the teeth, ready for action, the men are in transit, on their way to the next engagement. They are tense, on alert.

Beyond the terrain that the soldiers patrol, a declaratory inscription can be found on a short wall. It reads: freedom is not free. As art, this memorial will not be allowed to speak for itself. The thinly veiled accusation points toward the Vietnam Wall rather than the soldiers who supposedly exemplify its truth. The words announce that there is a price to be paid to defend values in war. Freedom entails obligation and responsibility. For some this may mean fighting thousands of miles from home in a war where the outcome seems remote to American concerns and interests. But on occasion this is what nations call on their sons—and daughters—to do. And do it they must, if they are good Americans. They will not refuse to serve, they will not resist, and they will not flee the country. Freedom is not free. It's as if the Korean Memorial chastises pilgrims of the Vietnam Wall. Freedom is not free, you must remember. That's the way the world works. There's nothing to cry about here, in public, on the national Mall. The World War II Memorial's so-called Freedom Wall, 4,000 gold stars representing (roughly) 400,000 military deaths, reiterates the Korean's censure of the Vietnam wall: death made to moralize.

36 In addition, the introduction to the ceremony consisted of the presentation of the colors, the Pledge of Allegiance, the National Anthem, the colors retired, the invocation. Meanwhile, volunteers distributed official programs along with miniature American and POW/MIA flags.

37 I think Griswold may overestimate—at least I hope he does—the wholeness and reconciliation that in his view the monument has accomplished. See Griswold, "The Vietnam Veterans Memorial," 92–93, for example.

38 The looseness of the formulation could include antiwar protestors—many of whom would have been Vietnam veterans.

39 Rolling Thunder Inc. is a nonprofit organization whose "major function . . . is to publicize POW-MIA issues." See www.rollingthunder1.com.

40 Griswold, "The Vietnam Veterans Memorial," 73; emphasis added.

41 Ibid., 92.

42 Ibid.; emphasis added.

43 Scruggs, *To Heal a Nation*, 165; emphasis added.

44 Griswold, "The Vietnam Veterans Memorial," 92–93.

45 Ibid., 94.

46 Ibid.

47 As Marita Sturken observes, the Wall can be conceptualized as a screen.

"A screen can be a surface that is projected upon; it is also an object that hides something from view, that shelters or protects." "The Wall," 118.

48 Hubbard, "A Meaning for Monuments," 17–30.

49 Ibid., 21, 25, 26.

50 Ibid., 20.

51 Ibid., 20, 22, 25, 27.

52 Ibid., 27.

53 The quote is from Scruggs, *To Heal a Nation*, 98.

7. PATRIOTISM AND DEATH

1 Thucydides, *The Peloponnesian War*, 143.

2 Ibid., 144–45.

3 Ibid., 147.

4 Ibid., 150–51.

5 Ibid., 147.

6 Ibid., 147.

7 Rousseau, *Émile*, 40.

8 Thucydides, *The Peloponnesian War*, 146.

9 Ibid., 150.

10 For invaluable reflections on finitude, which have informed the reading of Pericles offered here, see Connolly, *Identity\Difference*, chapter 1, "Freedom and Resentment."

11 As Tim Luke pointed out to me, the U.S.S. Maine Memorial in Arlington (1913) and the U.S.S. Arizona Memorial at Pearl Harbor (1962) could be included here. For an insightful exploration of the construction of American innocence at Pearl Harbor see Turnbull, "Remembering Pearl Harbor."

12 George Bush, State of the Union, January 29, 2002. All Bush speeches in this chapter are available at www.whitehouse.gov/news/release/.

13 Bigler, *In Honored Glory*. This work is featured prominently in the cemetery's bookshop and seems to be the source for its web site.

14 Ibid., 91–94.

15 "During the first year, visitation at the Kennedy grave frequently reached 3,000 per hour and, on weekends, an estimated 50,000 people paid their respects daily. Incredibly, during the three years immediately following the President's death, 16 million people came to Arlington in what Superintendent Metzler called, 'the most tremendous demonstration [of respect in history].'" Ibid., 98–99.

16 Ibid., 107. The friend is Dave Powers.

17 George Lardner wrote a damning article in the *Washington Post* about

Stone's project. He accused Stone of "chasing a fiction," alleging mistakes, distortions, falsehoods, and manipulations. Though Lardner recognizes Vietnam's central role in *JFK*, his determination to argue the facts of the assassination obscures its significance. In a scathing reply, Stone signaled the film's patriotic ambition. *JFK* solicits "an emotional experience that speaks a higher truth than the Lardners of the world will ever know." George Lardner Jr., "On the Set: Dallas in Wonderland" and "Or Just a Sloppy Mess?," both reprinted in Stone and Sklar, eds., *JFK*, 191–98, 202–5. Stone, "Stone's *JFK*: A Higher Truth?," *JFK*, ed. Stone and Sklar, 202.

18 Stone's Vietnam thesis preempts proof or disproof: it must remain permanent possibility. Kennedy's murder means by definition that what he would have done cannot be known. Moreover, the limited withdrawal plan that he toyed with awaited developments on the ground in Vietnam. Kennedy was committed to winning the war against communism, and policy decisions were determined by whether they contributed to this end. Hence the lack of a formal withdrawal announcement. But Stone does not need truth, only possibility. Kennedy's death turns solid speculation on withdrawal into truth. Stone's insinuation: Why else would Kennedy have been killed?

19 This enables Stone to skirt critique of American society and the war that Vietnam provokes. On Stone's rendering, the Vietnam Veterans Memorial would vanish.

20 Simon, *Dangerous Knowledge*, 214, describes the foundational role of the opening sequence: "These images speak the 'truth' about JFK, helping to establish the film's thesis of conspiratorial motive even before Garrison's investigation is introduced. Of course the subsequent three hours elaborate a fictional scenario, but its crucial components have now been verified by the prologue's deployment of historical footage." Where I tend to differ with Simon is over my concern with *JFK* as a patriotic text.

21 Stone does not allow dissenters in the film—not for long, anyway. The lone voice of opposition, Bill Broussard, becomes a mole who compromises the investigation and the trial at the behest of the conspiracy. Here dissent becomes an act of treason. The film thus mimics the very logic it criticizes.

22 Stone's key witness, X, "testifies" in Washington, on the Mall, in the shadow of the Washington Monument. The symbolism is apt, for Stone's conspiracy tale presumes that some day America will be free of the corruption riddling it and the cabal running it. Alien forces rule America—temporarily. What was taken can be retrieved.

23 Rorty cites Neal Stephenson (*Snow Crash*) and Leslie Marmon Silko (*Almanac of the Dead*) for refusing hope to America's future. Rorty, *Achieving Our Country*, 4–8.

24 See DePietro, ed., *Conversations with Don DeLillo*.

25 For an English version of patriotism's self-destructive dynamic see John le Carré's *The Spy Who Came In from the Cold* (New York: Ballantine, 1992). Le Carré delineates how patriots become, in the name of freedom, the enemy they oppose by matching, even exceeding, the evil that the enemy commits in order to defeat it.

26 DeLillo, *Libra*.

27 Ibid., 54.

28 Machiavelli, *The Discourses*, 102–3, 385–87.

29 DeLillo, *Libra*, 147.

30 Ibid., 53.

31 Ibid.

32 Ibid., 22.

33 Ibid., 21–22.

34 Ibid., 51.

35 Ibid., 27–28.

36 Ibid., 362–63.

37 Ibid., 27–28.

38 Ibid., 302.

39 Ibid., 219.

40 Ibid., 298.

41 George Bush, Second Inaugural, January 20, 2005.

42 Garry Wills writes of the battle of Gettysburg: "Both sides, leaving fifty thousand dead or wounded or missing behind them, had reason to maintain a large pattern of pretense about this battle—Lee pretending that he was not taking back to the South a broken cause, Meade that he had not let the broken pieces fall through his fingers. It would have been hard to predict that Gettysburg, out of all this muddle, these missed chances, all the senseless deaths, would become a symbol of national purpose, pride, and ideals. Abraham Lincoln transformed the ugly reality into something rich and strange." Wills, *Lincoln at Gettysburg*, 20.

43 For a critique see Connolly, "Time to Break the Silence," and my complimentary response, "Staying the Course Will Add to Death Toll."

44 Hamilton, Madison, and Jay, *The Federalist Papers*, no. 1 [p. 33].

45 The Declaration of Independence likewise addresses "the opinions of mankind." Attuned to the protective bent of providence, this revolutionary document claims entitlement to that which God has granted the American people, namely, its rightful place "among the powers of the earth." The self-evident truths then invoked are truths that hold the world as well.

46 Ibid.

47 Hamilton's opening salvo in the ratification controversy situates him in the American missionary project. Not counting John Winthrop and the new Israel, the project can be traced to the manifest destiny of Jackson and Polk, the evangelical zeal of Lincoln, the imperial gambits of Alfred T. Mahan, Theodore Roosevelt, and Woodrow Wilson, and the Hegelian dramas of Richard Rorty and George Bush.

48 Hamilton invokes and enacts patriotism early in the first paper. For the term "true patriot" see Hamilton, Madison, and Jay, *The Federalist Papers*, no. 20 [p. 137].

49 Ibid., no. 24 [pp. 160–61], no. 25 [p. 163].

50 Ibid., no. 24 [p. 162].

51 Storing, ed., *The Anti-federalist*, 299, 306–7.

52 *The Federalist*, no. 4 [p. 47].

53 Ibid., no. 1 [p. 33].

54 Ibid., no. 11 [p. 91].

55 Ibid.

56 Ibid.

57 Ibid., no. 6 [pp. 56–58].

58 Ibid., no. 6 [p. 59].

59 Hamilton writes: "A cloud has been for some time hanging over the European world. If it should break forth into a storm, who can insure us that in its progress a part of its fury would not be spent upon us? No reasonable man would hastily pronounce that we are entirely out of its reach." Ibid., no. 34 [p. 208].

60 Hobbes, *Leviathan*, 363.

61 *The Federalist*, no. 14 [p. 104].

62 Ibid., no. 8 [p. 67].

63 Michael Igantieff, "It's War—But it Doesn't Have to Be Dirty."

64 George Bush, Address to the Nation, September 11, 2001.

65 Ibid. Note how Bush concludes by taking possession of the world.

66 Bush, Six-Month Anniversary Speech, March 11, 2002. See also Bush's speech from Ellis Island, New York, September 11, 2002, the source of the epigraph in this chapter.

67 Geoffrey Stone points out that Bush's Manichean optic was introduced in America in 1798 thanks to hysterical fear of revolutionary France. Stone, *Perilous Times.*

68 Bush, Address to a Joint Session of Congress, September 20, 2001.

69 Bush, State of the Union, January 28, 2003.

70 Bush, Second Inaugural, January 20, 2005.

71 George Bush, Graduation Speech at West Point, June 1, 2002.

72 George Bush Bush, State of the Union, January 29, 2002.

73 Hence the reading of the Gettysburg Address at New York City's first memorial service for the dead.

74 George Bush, A Proclamation, Patriot Day, 2002.

75 George Bush, Address to the United Nations, November 10, 2001.

76 George Bush, Address to the Nation, October 7, 2001.

77 Bruce Lincoln effectively delineates the religious parallels between George Bush and Osama bin Laden in *Holy Terrors*, 23. Lincoln analyzes the dueling speeches that they offered on October 7, 2003. He finds Bush's reference to the fourth-grader "cloying." At the same time, he notes: "This American girl was different, however. Although threatened by menacing forces herself, she responds as a subject in ways Bush offered as a model of how proper Americans do and ought to behave: courageous, self-sacrificing, and resolute (also utterly unquestioning of their leaders)." Lincoln's religious focus, I think, leads him to overlook the subtext of Bush's patriotic fourth-grader. It's not just that she functions as inspirational exemplar; she also defines as internal enemies those who question, let alone challenge, oppose, or refuse Bush's (America's) response to September 11. To have any disposition other than unwavering support means to take sides against America and lend aid and comfort to the enemy.

78 George Bush, Address to the Nation, World Congress Center, Atlanta, November 8, 2001.

8. BRUCE SPRINGSTEEN

1 ABC News, "Nightline," July 30, 2002. The quotes are from a tape of the interview.

2 Thanks to Foucault, *Discipline and Punish*, 3–7.

3 *Time*, September 24, 2001, 49.

4 Thirty percent of Americans, according to a poll by the *Washington Post*, do not know the year of the September 11 attacks. *Washington Post*, August 2, 2006, § A, 2.

5 Borradori, ed., *Philosophy in a Time of Terror*, 87.

6 Ibid. On the question of undecidability, Jürgen Habermas argues that only in retrospect can a judgment be made on the long-term significance of the September attacks. A determination that the event marks a break in history, that it is unique or unprecedented, awaits developments. Even so, as far as analogies go Habermas prefers the First World War to Pearl Harbor. He is no American patriot.

7 Borradori, ed., *Philosophy in a Time of Terror*, 27, 29.

8 Nietzsche, *The Birth of Tragedy and The Genealogy of Morals*, from *The Genealogy*, II, x, 205. See also *The Genealogy*, I, x, 173.

9 Cf. Peter Beinart, who sees the fight against "Islamic totalitarianism" as responsible for the future of American freedom. "The fight for national security *is* the fight for liberal values, not merely in the Muslim world . . . but also at home, where threats to American safety almost inevitably spawn threats to American freedom. Totalitarian Islam has already damaged both, and unless defeated, the damage could be exponentially worse." Peter Beinart, "TRB: The Good Fight," *New Republic*, December 20, 2004, 6.

10 Cf. Coles's *Bruce Springsteen's America*. Coles's book seems methodologically flawed. To focus on one or two songs and what they mean to this or that person ignores Springsteen's larger ambition, which takes a lifetime to unfold through a body of interrelated work that continually looks back, reflects on, and modifies itself.

11 While the claim that tragedy frames Springsteen's music runs counter to his self-conception as a romantic, I believe it radicalizes elements of his work that might otherwise remain inchoate. It may also correspond to tragic moments in his thinking. See the interviews by Paul Williams and Robert Hilburn in Sawyers, ed., *Racing in the Street*.

12 Interview by Hilburn in Sawyers, ed., *Racing in the Street*, 95, 96.

13 Ibid., 95.

14 Springsteen, "Chords for Change."

15 Eric Alterman understands *Darkness on the Edge of Town* as a call to resistance. It "is an album about responding to unseen and undefinable forms of domination and repression." Alterman is right, I think, that Springsteen's ethos disables a politics of blame and resentment, but the loci of responsibility are hardly unknown or unidentifiable. Silence does not equal ignorance. Alterman, *It Ain't No Sin to Be Glad You're Alive*, 96. Dave Marsh reads *Darkness* differently, embracing what he calls its macho refusal. The album thus becomes "an heroic parable . . . The ending is a glorious symbol of transcendence; the hero reaches the mountaintop." Yet Marsh overlooks the mountaintop's ambiguous character. To write, as he does, that "there is not a hint of defeat" obscures "the cost" that Springsteen insists must be paid for living any life. While Marsh writes of "the tragic vision captured on *Darkness*," he seems to be referring to the confrontation with life's everyday struggles. But why "taking life on its own terms, and never giving in" amounts to a tragic vision remains unclear. Marsh, *Bruce Springsteen*, 194, 228, 221, 193.

16 The American dream's cruelty finds perhaps consummate expression four years later in *Nebraska*. In "Mansion on the Hill," inspired by Guthrie, a man tells his life story. He has spied the mansion since he was a boy. Working men, like his father, built the very body of the mansion that dominates life and keeps them at bay. "Gates of hardened steel" were produced in the facto-

ries and mills below. Work, then, fosters the envy that renders them potential threats. Life is blessed for some, who enjoy their station at the expense of others, those disposable.

17 Cf. Colleen Sheehy, "Springsteen: Troubadour of the Highway," especially 353–55, and Simon Frith, "The Real Thing: Bruce Springsteen," 136, both in Sawyers, ed., *Racing in the Street*.

18 Alterman writes of the song: "To be born in the U.S.A. is a curse for its hero, a cross to bear, not cause for a rousing cheer." Though he invokes Springsteen to support it, Alterman's version seems to individualize what is a national experience. Alterman, *It Ain't No Sin to Be Glad You're Alive*, 157.

19 George F. Will, "Bruuuuuce," 108, 109.

20 Marsh, *Bruce Springsteen*, 433; emphasis in original.

21 Ibid.; emphasis added.

22 Ibid., 481, 482–83, 431.

23 Alterman, *It Ain't No Sin to Be Glad You're Alive*, 158–59.

24 Editors of Rolling Stone, *Bruce Springsteen*, 154.

25 Ibid., 158. Hence Springsteen's ambivalence about music videos.

26 Will, "Bruuuuuce," 108.

27 Editors of Rolling Stone, *Bruce Springsteen*, 153–54.

28 Ibid., 155.

29 Ibid.

30 Alterman, *It Ain't No Sin to Be Glad You're Alive*, 161.

31 Ibid., 374.

32 Ibid. 158.

33 Will, "Bruuuuuce," 108.

34 In "Blood Brothers," Springsteen fine-tunes his analysis of the American dream's frustration. The problem lies as much with the character of the world as with the structural injustices of American life. The world is not predisposed to meet our heart's desire: "Now *the hardness of this world* slowly grinds your dreams away / Makin' a fool's joke of the promises we make." Emphasis added.

35 "Youngstown" was included in the DVD production of *Live in New York City* (2001). When Springsteen cries out the city's name in the third chorus, he holds the last syllable like a curse. Youngstown becomes a four-letter word. The man who has spent his life burning it away by the blast furnace can look forward to nothing but his own death. Death as life's trajectory. Nils Lofgren's guitar solo, an angry blast against the fates and furies of life, concludes with a haze of feedback and gives amplified voice to Youngstown's agony. The guitar screams that the city refuses to go quietly into history's dustbin. But go it will.

36 See Julian E. Barnes, "Springsteen Song about Diallo Prompts Anger from Police," *New York Times*, June 13, 2000.

37 Springsteen portrays the police as consumed by the moment; they can do nothing but pray over the life of a dead man outside his apartment. Yet there is uncertainty—and thus empathy—here.

38 See Johnson, *Blowback*.

39 Alterman in Sawyers, ed., *Racing in the Street*, 373, 374.

40 Debate also engulfed the subject of *The Rising*. Most assumed it to be September 11. Others declared September 12 instead. Dave Marsh insisted that life and death were its concerns. Still others saw the album as mere eulogy void of politics. See Jon Pareles, "His Kind of Heroes, His Kind of Songs," *New York Times*, July 14, 2002; Josh Tyrangiel, "Bruce Rising: An Intimate Look at How Springsteen Turned 9/11 into a Message of Hope," *Time*, August 5, 2002; Kurt Loder, *Rolling Stone*, August 22, 2002; Dave Marsh, "Springsteen's *The Rising*: No Surrender," *CounterPunch*, August 31, 2002; Alan Maass, "The Boss on Bush: 'A War Well Handled': What's Missing from *The Rising*," *CounterPunch*, September 9, 2002.

41 See Pareles, "His Kind of Heroes."

42 Springsteen's ethos differs from the macho posturing of Toby Keith, author of "Courtesy of the Red, White, & Blue (The Angry American)" and Neil Young, author of "Let's Roll." Keith's authoritarian diktat takes evident pleasure in America's indiscriminate, murderous revenge. Young, in the name of living in a world free from fear, mimics George Bush's Manichaeism and fosters the very fear that he opposes. Yet he has no doubts about the crusade he would launch. Keith and Young both presume that the United States can restore the order of things with cleansing acts of violence.

43 Bruce Springsteen and the E Street Band, *Live in New York City* (Columbia Music Video, 2001).

Bibliography

Abramson, Daniel. "Make History, Not Memory." *Harvard Design Review*, fall 1999.

Alterman, Eric. *It Ain't No Sin to Be Glad You're Alive: The Promise of Bruce Springsteen*. Boston: Back Bay, 2001.

Anderson, Fred, and Andrew Cayton. *The Dominion of War: Empire and Liberty in North America, 1500–2000*. New York: Viking, 2005.

Baudrillard, Jean. *The Spirit of Terrorism*. New York: Verso, 2002.

Bazin, André. "The Evolution of the Western." *What Is Cinema?*, vol. 2, trans. Hugh Gray, 149–57. Berkeley: University of California Press, 2005.

Bennett, Jane. *The Enchantment of Modern Life: Attachments, Crossings, and Ethics*. Princeton: Princeton University Press, 2001.

Berns, Walter. *Making Patriots*. Chicago: University of Chicago Press, 2001.

Bigler, Philip. *In Honored Glory: Arlington National Cemetery: The Final Post*, 3rd edn. Arlington, Va.: Vandamere, 1999.

Boime, Albert. *The Unveiling of the National Icons: A Plea for Patriotic Iconoclasm in a Nationalist Era*. Cambridge: Cambridge University Press, 1998.

Borradori, Giovanna. *Philosophy in a Time of Terror: Dialogues with Jürgen Habermas and Jacques Derrida*. Chicago: University of Chicago Press, 2003.

Brickhouse, Thomas C., and Nicholas D. Smith. *Socrates on Trial*. Princeton: Princeton University Press, 1989.

Brinkley, Douglas, ed. *The World War II Memorial: A Grateful Nation Remembers*. Washington: Smithsonian, 2004.

Brooks, David. "The Osama Litmus Test." *New York Times*, October 30, 2004, § A, 19.

———. "The C.I.A. versus Bush." *New York Times*, November 13, 2004, § A, 15.

Brown, Wendy. *States of Injury: Power and Freedom in Late Modernity.* Princeton: Princeton University Press, 1995.

———. *Edgework: Critical Essays on Knowledge and Politics.* Princeton: Princeton University Press, 2005.

Callan, Eamonn. *Creating Citizens: Political Education and Liberal Democracy.* Oxford: Oxford University Press, 1997.

Carhart, Tom. "*Insulting Vietnam Vets.*" *New York Times*, October 24, 1981, § 1, 23.

Chidester, David, and Edward T. Linenthal, eds. *American Sacred Space.* Bloomington: Indiana University Press, 1995.

Colaiaco, James A. *Socrates against Athens: Philosophy on Trial.* New York: Routledge, 2001.

Coles, Robert. *Bruce Springsteen's America: The People Listening, a Poet Singing.* New York: Random House, 2003.

Connolly, William E. *Identity\Difference: Democratic Negotiations of Political Paradox.* Ithaca: Cornell University Press, 1991.

———. *The Ethos of Pluralization.* Minneapolis: University of Minnesota Press, 1995.

———. *Why I Am Not a Secularist.* Minneapolis: University of Minnesota Press, 2000.

———. *Neuropolitics: Thinking, Culture, Speed.* Minneapolis: University of Minnesota Press, 2002.

———. *Pluralism.* Durham: Duke University Press, 2005.

———. "Time to Break the Silence." *Baltimore Sun*, August 22, 2005.

DeLillo, Don. *Libra.* New York: Penguin, 1988.

DePietro, Thomas, ed. *Conversations with Don DeLillo.* Jackson: University Press of Mississippi, 2005.

Dietz, Mary G. "Patriotism." *Political Innovation and Conceptual Change*, ed. Terrence Ball, James Farr, and Russell L. Hanson. Cambridge: Cambridge University Press, 1989.

Douglass, Frederick. *Selected Speeches and Writings*, ed. Philip S. Foner. Chicago: Lawrence Hill, 1999.

Drummond, Phillip. *High Noon*, London: British Film Institute, 1997.

Editors of Rolling Stone. *Bruce Springsteen: The Rolling Stone Files.* New York: Hyperion, 1996.

Ellis, Joseph. *Founding Brothers: The Revolutionary Generation.* New York: Vintage, 2002.

Ellis, Richard J. *To the Flag: The Unlikely History of the Pledge of Allegiance.* Lawrence: University Press of Kansas, 2005.

Ellsberg, Daniel. *Secrets: A Memoir of Vietnam and the Pentagon Papers.* New York: Viking, 2002.

Euben, J. Peter. *The Tragedy of Political Theory: The Road Not Taken.* Princeton: Princeton University Press, 1990.

———. *Corrupting Youth: Political Education, Democratic Culture, and Political Theory.* Princeton: Princeton University Press, 1997.

Falk, Richard. *The Declining World Order: America's Imperial Geopolitics.* New York: Routledge, 2004.

Fletcher, George P. *Loyalty: An Essay on the Morality of Relationships.* Oxford: Oxford University Press, 1993.

Foucault, Michel. *Discipline and Punish: The Birth of the Prison,* trans. Alan Sheridan. New York: Vintage, 1977.

Frankfurt, Harry G. *The Reasons of Love.* Princeton: Princeton University Press, 2004.

Fredrickson, George M. *The Inner Civil War: Northern Intellectuals and the Crisis of the Union.* Urbana: University of Illinois Press, 1993.

Freud, Sigmund. *The Uncanny,* trans. David McLintock. New York: Penguin Classics, 2003.

Galston, William A. *Liberal Purposes: Goods, Virtues, and Diversity in the Liberal State.* Cambridge: Cambridge University Press, 1991.

Gillis, John R., ed. *Commemorations: The Politics of National Identity.* Princeton: Princeton University Press, 1994.

Gitlin, Todd. "Varieties of Patriotic Experience." *The Fight Is for Democracy,* ed. George Packer. New York: Perennial, 2003.

Griswold, Charles. "The Vietnam Veterans Memorial and the Washington Mall." *Critical Issues in Public Art,* ed. Harriet F. Senie and Sally Webster. Washington: Smithsonian Institution Press, 1998.

Hagan, John. *Northern Passage: American Vietnam War Resisters in Canada.* Cambridge: Harvard University Press, 2001.

Hamilton, Alexander, James Madison, and John Jay. *The Federalist Papers,* ed. Clinton Rossiter. New York: Mentor, 1961.

Hansen, Jonathan M. *The Lost Promise of Patriotism: Debating American Identity, 1890–1920.* Chicago: University of Chicago Press, 2003.

Harbison, Robert. *The Built, the Unbuilt, and the Unbuildable: In Pursuit of Architectural Meaning.* Cambridge: MIT Press, 1991.

———. *Thirteen Ways: Theoretical Investigations in Architecture.* Cambridge: MIT Press, 1997.

Harrison, Robert Pogue. *The Dominion of the Dead.* Chicago: University of Chicago Press, 2003.

Hass, Kristin Ann. *Carried to the Wall: American Memory and the Vietnam Veterans Memorial*. Berkeley: University of California Press, 1998.

Hayward, Susan. *Cinema Studies: The Key Concepts*, 2nd edn. New York: Routledge, 2000.

Hazlitt, William. *On the Pleasure of Hating*. New York: Penguin, 2000.

Hegel, G. W. F. *On Tragedy*, ed. Anne and Henry Paolucci. New York: Anchor, 1962.

Heidegger, Martin. *What Is Called Thinking?*, trans. J. Glenn Gray. New York: Harper, 1968.

———. *Introduction to Metaphysics*. New Haven: Yale University Press, 2000.

Higginson, Henry Lee. *Four Addresses*. Boston: D. B. Updike / Merrymount, 1902.

Hobbes, Thomas. *Leviathan*. New York: Penguin, 1982.

Hoffman, Eva. "The New Nomads." *Letters of Transit*, ed. Andre Aciman. New York: New Press, 1999.

Honig, Bonnie. *Democracy and the Foreigner*. Princeton: Princeton University Press, 2001.

Hubbard, William. "A Meaning for Monuments." *Public Interest* 74 (winter 1984), 17–30.

Ignatieff, Michael. "It's War—But It Doesn't Have to Be Dirty." *Guardian*, October 1, 2001.

James, William. "Address of the Annual Meeting of the New England Anti-Imperialist League" (1903), http://www.nps.gov/boaf/54th.htm.

———. "The Moral Equivalent of War" (1906), http://www.constitution.org/wj/meow.htm.

———. "Robert Gould Shaw." *Essays in Religion and Morality, The Works of William James*. Cambridge: Harvard University Press, 1982.

Jefferson, Thomas. *The Portable Thomas Jefferson*, ed. Merrill D. Peterson. New York: Penguin, 1975.

Johnson, Chalmers. *Blowback: The Costs and Consequences of American Empire*. New York: Henry Holt, 2000.

Johnston, Steven. *Encountering Tragedy: Rousseau and the Project of Democratic Order*. Ithaca: Cornell University Press, 1999.

———. "Political Not Patriotic: Democracy, Civic Space, and the American Memorial/Monument Complex." *Theory and Event* 5, no. 2 (2001).

———. "The Architecture of Democratic Monuments." *Strategies* 15, no. 2 (2002), 197–218.

———. "Staying the Course Will Add to Death Toll." Letter to the editor, *Baltimore Sun*, August 29, 2005.

Kateb, George. "Is Patriotism a Mistake?" *Social Research*, 67, no. 4 (2000).

Kennedy, Caroline, ed. *A Patriot's Handbook: Songs, Poems, Stories, and Speeches Celebrating the Land We Love.* New York: Hyperion, 2003.

Kingsolver, Barbara. "Flying." *Small Wonder*, 184–94. New York: Harper Collins, 2002.

Lear, Jonathan. *Open Minded: Working Out the Logic of the Soul.* Cambridge: Harvard University Press, 1998.

Lendon, J. E. *Soldiers and Ghosts: A History of Battle in Classical Antiquity.* New Haven: Yale University Press, 2005.

Levinson, Sanford. *Written in Stone: Public Monuments in Changing Societies.* Durham: Duke University Press, 1998.

Lin, Maya. *Boundaries.* New York: Simon and Schuster, 2000.

Lincoln, Bruce. *Holy Terrors: Thinking about Religion after September 11.* Chicago: University of Chicago Press, 2003.

Linenthal, Edward T. *The Unfinished Bombing: Oklahoma City in American Memory.* Oxford: Oxford University Press, 2001.

Machiavelli, Niccolò. *The Discourses*, trans. Leslie J. Walker, S.J. New York: Penguin, 1970.

MacIntyre, Alasdair. "Is Patriotism a Virtue?" *Political Thought*, ed. Michael Rosen and Jonathan Wolff, 269–84. Oxford: Oxford University Press, 1999.

Markell, Patchen. "Making Affect Safe for Democracy? On 'Constitutional Patriotism.'" *Political Theory* 28, no. 1 (2000), 38–63.

Marsh, Dave. *Bruce Springsteen: Two Hearts: The Definitive Biography, 1972–2003.* New York: Routledge, 2004.

Menand, Louis. *The Metaphysical Club.* New York: Farrar, Straus and Giroux, 2001.

Miller, David. *On Nationality.* Oxford: Oxford University Press, 1995.

Mills, Nicolaus. *Their Last Battle: The Fight for the National World War II Memorial.* New York: Basic, 2004.

Montagu, Dennis R. "The Ulysses S. Grant Memorial in Washington DC: A War Memorial for the New Century." *Critical Issues in Public Art*, ed. Harriet F. Senie and Sally Webster. Washington: Smithsonian Institution Press, 1998.

Morgan, Edmund S. *American Slavery/American Freedom: The Ordeal of Colonial Virginia.* New York: W. W. Norton, 1975.

Morone, James A. *Hellfire Nation: The Politics of Sin in American History.* New Haven: Yale University Press, 2003.

Mosse, George L. *Fallen Soldiers: Reshaping the Memory of the World Wars.* Oxford: Oxford University Press, 1990.

Muller, Eric L. *Free to Die for Their Country: The Story of the Japanese American Draft Resisters in World War II*. Chicago: University of Chicago Press, 2003.

Musil, Robert. "Monuments." *Selected Writings*. New York: Continuum, 1978.

Nash, Gary B. *The Forgotten Fifth: African Americans in the Age of Revolution*. Cambridge: Harvard University Press, 2006.

The National Security Strategy of the United States of America, 2nd edn. Falls Village, Conn.: Winterhouse, 2002.

Nehamas, Alexander. *Virtues of Authenticity*. Princeton: Princeton University Press, 1999.

Nietzsche, Friedrich. *The Birth of Tragedy and The Genealogy of Morals*, trans. Francis Golffing. New York: Anchor, 1956.

———. *Twilight of the Idols and The Anti-Christ*, trans. R. J. Hollingdale. New York: Penguin, 1968.

———. *The Gay Science*, trans. Walter Kaufmann. New York: Vintage, 1985.

Nossack, Hans Erich. *The End: Hamburg, 1943*, trans. Joel Agee. Chicago: University of Chicago Press, 2004.

Nussbaum, Martha. *For Love of Country: Debating the Limits of Patriotism*. Boston: Beacon, 1996.

Ober, Josiah. *Athenian Legacies: Essays on the Politics of Going On Together*. Princeton: Princeton University Press, 2005.

O'Leary, Cecilia Elizabeth. *To Die For: The Paradox of American Patriotism*. Princeton: Princeton University Press, 1999.

Patriotism, Perseverance, Posterity: The Story of the National Japanese American Memorial. Washington: National Japanese American Memorial Foundation, 2001.

Plato. *The Trial and Death of Socrates*, 2nd edn, trans. G. M. A. Grube. Indianapolis: Hackett, 1980.

Podhoretz, Norman. *My Love Affair with America: The Cautionary Tale of a Cheerful Conservative*. New York: Free Press, 2000.

———. "How to Win World War IV." *Commentary*, February 2002.

———. "World War IV: How It Started, What It Means, and Why We Have to Win." *Commentary*, September 2004.

Robinson, Greg. *By Order of the President: FDR and the Internment of Japanese-Americans*. Cambridge: Harvard University Press, 2001.

Rorty, Richard. *Contingency, Irony, and Solidarity*. Cambridge: Cambridge University Press, 1989.

———. *Achieving Our Country*. Cambridge: Harvard University Press, 1998.

———. *Philosophy and Social Hope*. New York: Penguin, 1999.

Rosenstone, Robert A. *Visions of the Past: The Challenge of Film to Our Idea of History*. Cambridge: Harvard University Press, 1995.

Rousseau, Jean-Jacques. *Politics and the Arts: Letter to M. d'Alembert on the Theater*, trans. Allan Bloom. Ithaca: Cornell University Press, 1968.

———. *On the Social Contract*, trans. Judith R. Masters. New York: St. Martin's, 1978.

———. *Émile*, trans. Allan Bloom. New York: Basic, 1979.

Russell, James S. "Crowding the Mall." *Harvard Design Review*, fall 1999.

Said, Edward W. *Representations of the Intellectual*. New York: Vintage, 1996.

———. *Reflections on Exile and Other Essays*. Cambridge: Harvard University Press, 2002.

Sandage, Scott A. *Born Losers: A History of Failure in America*. Cambridge: Harvard University Press, 2005.

Savage, Kirk. *Standing Soldiers, Kneeling Slaves: Race, War, and Monument in Nineteenth-Century America*. Princeton: Princeton University Press, 1997.

Sawyers, June Skinner. *Racing in the Street: The Bruce Springsteen Reader*. New York: Penguin, 2004.

Schaar, John. "The Case for Patriotism." *Legitimacy in the Modern State*, 285–311. New Brunswick: Transaction, 1981.

Schell, Jonathan. *The Fate of the Earth*. New York: Avon, 1982.

Scruggs, Jan C., and Joel L. Swerdlow. *To Heal a Nation: The Vietnam Veterans Memorial*. New York: Perennial, 1985.

Sebald, W. G. *On the Natural History of Destruction*, trans. Anthea Bell. New York: Modern Library, 2004.

Seery, John E. *Political Theory for Mortals: Shades of Justice, Images of Death*. Ithaca: Cornell University Press, 1996.

Shklar, Judith. *Ordinary Vices*. Cambridge: Harvard University Press, 1984.

Simon, Art. *Dangerous Knowledge: The JFK Assassination in Art and Film*. Philadelphia: Temple University Press, 1996.

Simon, Linda. *Genuine Reality: A Life of William James*. New York: Harcourt Brace, 1998.

Slotkin, Richard. *Gunfighter Nation: The Myth of the Frontier in Twentieth-Century America*. New York: Harper Perennial, 1992.

Springsteen, Bruce. *Born to Run*. Sony, 1975.

———. *Darkness on the Edge of Town*. Sony, 1978.

———. *The River*. Sony, 1980.

———. *Nebraska*. Sony, 1982.

———. *Born in the U.S.A.* Sony, 1984.

———. *Bruce Springsteen and the E Street Band Live, 1975–1985*. Sony, 1986.

———. *Greatest Hits*. Sony, 1995.

———. *The Ghost of Tom Joad*. Sony, 1995.

———. *Live in New York City*. Sony, 2001.

———. *The Rising*. Sony, 2002.

———. "Chords for Change." *New York Times*, August 5, 2004, § A, 23.

Steiner, George. "'Tragedy' Reconsidered.'" *New Literary History* 35, no. 1 (2004).

Stephanson, Anders. *Manifest Destiny: American Expansion and the Empire of Right*. New York: Hill and Wang, 1995.

Stone, Geoffrey R. *Perilous Times: Free Speech in Wartime*. New York: W. W. Norton, 2004.

Stone, Oliver, and Zachary Sklar, eds. *JFK: The Book of the Film*. New York: Applause, 1992.

Storing, Herbert J., ed. *The Anti-Federalist*. Chicago: University of Chicago Press, 1985.

Sturken, Marita. "The Wall, the Screen, and the Image: The Vietnam Veterans Memorial." *Representations* 35 (summer 1991), 118–42.

Taylor, Charles. "Cross-Purposes: The Liberal Communitarian Debate." *Liberalism and the Moral Life*, ed. Nancy L. Rosenblum, 159–82. Princeton: Princeton University Press, 1989.

Thucydides. *The Peloponnesian War*, trans. Rex Warner. New York: Penguin, 1954.

Till, Karen E. *The New Berlin: Memory, Politics, Place*. Minneapolis: University of Minnesota Press, 2005.

Tompkins, Jane. *West of Everything: The Inner Life of Westerns*. Oxford: Oxford University Press, 1992.

Toplin, Robert Brent, ed. *Oliver Stone's USA: Film, History, and Controversy*. Lawrence: University Press of Kansas, 2000.

Tumarkin, Nina. *The Living and the Dead: The Rise and Fall of the Cult of World War II in Russia*. New York: Basic, 1994.

Turnbull, Phyllis. "Remembering Pearl Harbor: The Semiotics of the *Arizona* Memorial." *Challenging Boundaries: Global Flows, Territorial Identities*, ed. Michael J. Shapiro and Hayward R. Alker. Minneapolis: University of Minnesota Press, 1996.

Twain, Mark. *The War Prayer*. New York: Perennial, 1970.

Villa, Dana. *Socratic Citizenship*. Princeton: Princeton University Press, 2001.

Virilio, Paul. *Ground Zero*, New York: Verso, 2002.

Viroli, Maurizio. *For Love of Country: An Essay on Patriotism and Nationalism*. Oxford: Oxford University Press, 1995.

Warshow, Robert. "Movie Chronicle: The Westerner." *The Immediate Experi-*

ence: *Movies, Comics, Theatre and other Aspects of Popular Culture.* New York: Doubleday, 1962.

White, James Boyd. *Acts of Hope: Creating Authenticity in Literature, Law, and Politics.* Chicago: University of Chicago Press, 1993.

White, Ronald C. *Lincoln's Greatest Speech: The Second Inaugural.* New York: Simon and Schuster, 2002.

Will, George F. "Bruuuuuce." *Racing in the Street: The Bruce Springsteen Reader,* ed. June Skinner Sawyers. New York: Penguin, 2004.

Wills, Garry. *Lincoln at Gettysburg: The Words That Remade America.* New York: Simon and Schuster, 1992.

———. *John Wayne's America: The Politics of Celebrity.* New York: Simon and Schuster, 1997.

Young, James E. *The Texture of Memory: Holocaust Memorials and Meaning.* New Haven: Yale University Press, 1993.

———. *At Memory's Edge: After-Images of the Holocaust in Contemporary Art and Architecture.* New Haven: Yale University Press, 2000.

Zertal, Idith. *Israel's Holocaust and the Politics of Nationhood,* trans. Chaya Galai. Cambridge: Cambridge University Press, 2005.

Zerubavel, Yael. *Recovered Roots: Collective Memory and the Making of Israeli National Tradition.* Chicago: University of Chicago Press, 1997.

Žižek, Slavoj. *Welcome to the Desert of the Real: Five Essays on September 11 and Related Dates.* New York: Verso, 2002.

Žižek, Slavoj. *Iraq: The Borrowed Kettle.* New York: Verso, 2004.

Index

Alterman, Eric, 216–17, 266 n. 15
American Dream: cruelty of, 212–14, 217–20, 266 n. 16; death and, 218; impossibility of, 209–27; necessity of, 210, 213, 214; paradoxes of, 221–23; September 11 and, 222–23; Springsteen and, 17–18, 209–10, 211–13, 217–23, 266 n. 16, 267 n. 34, 267 n. 35
Athens, 15, 67, 69, 71–75, 81–84, 85–87, 163–66, 228–29, 246 n. 32

Babbitt, Bruce, 138–39
Bennett, Jane, 242 n. 120
Berns, Walter, 142; America's founding and, 37–39; enemies and, 239 n. 45
Bigler, Philip, 168
Brooks, David, 12; murderous fantasies of, 4; politics of hate and, 3–4
Bush, George W., 12, 199–202; Hamilton and, 190, 194–95; patriotism's addiction to death and, 162–63, 183–84, 195–97; Pericles and, 166–68; religious fundamentalism of, 192; Rorty and, 34–35, 167, 196; September 11 exploited by, 162–63, 167–68, 183–84, 189–95; Springsteen and, 205, 208; in 2004 election, 2–4; war as memorial and, 190–91

Callan, Eamonn, 36–37
Citizenship, democratic, 18–20, 151–53, 234 n. 30; James and, 10–12
Colaiaco, James A., 76, 78, 80, 243 n. 4, 245 n. 25
Cold War, 34, 35, 50–51, 62, 103, 176–77, 178–80
Commemoration: dangers inherent to, 10, 115–17, 159; politics of, 121–26, 140–41, 154–56
Connolly, William E., 243 n. 3; Iraq War and, 262 n. 43; on visceral register of being, 90
Counter-monument movement, 141, 144–46
Crito, 68, 76–77, 79

Death, 2–4, 7–13, 15–18, 139–40, 161–65, 167–70, 175–76, 181–84, 195–97, 230–31, 246 n. 38, 253 n. 41

Rousseau, Jean-Jacques: love's ambiguity and, 57–58; Spartan patriotism and, 166, 197

Russell, James S., 120–21, 252 n. 17

Sacred space, 138–40

St. Florian, Friedrich, 106, 123, 140. *See also* World War II Memorial

Saving Private Ryan (Spielberg), 103–14, 230, 249 n. 27; audience as target of, 104–5; debt and, 113–14, 222; enemy within and, 104, 107–12; moralization of death and, 104–6, 111–14; political context of, 103; Rorty's storytelling ethos and, 109–10, 113; World War II Memorial and, 106

Schaar, John, 2, 6–7, 8–9, 26, 89–90, 113, 151, 211–12, 239 n. 61; enmity and, 40, 41–45, 58–62; exile and, 59, 61–62; self-subverting patriotism of, 41–45, 242 n. 127

Scruggs, Jan, 149, 151, 153, 157, 259 n. 32, 259 n. 35

September 11 attacks: American Dream and, 222–23; Bush's exploitation of, 162–63, 167–68, 183–84, 189–95; Derrida on, 206, 208; "forgetting" of, 227; Habermas on, 206, 265 n. 6; memorial to, 226–27; as patriotic mantra, 205–7; Springsteen and, 202–5, 207–8, 223–26

Shaw, Robert Gould, 9–12, 229–30

Slavery, 5–8, 15, 36–39, 43, 143, 234 n. 13, 253 n. 42, 255 n. 42

Slotkin, Richard, 94, 102, 248 n. 14, 248 n. 16, 249 n. 20, 249 n. 23

Socrates: exile and, 76–77, 81–83, 87–88; patriotic thoughtlessness of, 68, 73–74, 75–76, 80, 85–86, 88; rebirth of, 228–29; on trial, 69–76; will to death of, 69, 71, 74, 75–76, 86–88

Spielberg, Steven, 103, 104, 106,

107, 109–11, 128, 222, 223. *See also Saving Private Ryan*

Springsteen, Bruce: Alterman on, 216–17, 266 n. 15; American Dream and, 17–18, 209–10, 211–13, 217–23, 266 n. 16, 267 n. 34, 267 n. 35; Bush and, 205, 208; life and, 227–29; patriotism of, 210–11; patriotism's self-subversion and, 217–20; *The Rising*, 223–26, 268 n. 40; September 11 and, 202–5, 207–8, 223–26; tragedy and, 208–11, 217–22; Vietnam War and, 214–15; Will on, 215–17

Steiner, George, 18

Stone, Oliver, 169–76, 262 n. 17, 262 n. 18, 262 n. 19, 262 n. 21, 262 n. 22. *See also JFK*

Storytelling, 15, 23–24, 27–30, 36–39, 58, 64, 195–97, 247 n. 11

Stow, Simon, 241 n. 119

Taylor, Charles, 21, 25, 236 n. 2, 236 n. 6

Three Soldiers, 121, 147–48

Till, Karen E., 143–44

Tompkins, Jane, 247 n. 12, 247 n. 13

Tragedy, 21; democracy and, 19–20, 25–27; Springsteen and, 208–11, 217–22; Steiner and, 18

Truman, Harry S., 125, 254 n. 44

Trumpeldor, Yosef, 250 n. 30

Vietnam Veterans Memorial, 145, 146–47; ceremonial politics at, 154–56; dismantling of, 230–31; offerings left at, 149–51; patriotism of, 156–58. *See also* Lin, Maya

Vietnam Veterans Memorial complex, 146–53

Vietnam War: Gitlin and 45–46, 47; Podhoretz and 50–51, 54–55, 241 n. 113; Rorty and, 32–33, 62–63, 120; Schaar and 32–33, 62–63, 120; Springsteen and, 214–15

Vietnam Women's Memorial, 148–
49
Villa, Dana, 68, 246 n. 37
Viroli, Maurizio, 56–57, 239 n. 59, 242
n. 121, 247 n. 11

Washington Monument, 142–43
Wayne, John, 89–90
White, James Boyd, 76, 83–85
Will, George F., 215–17
Wills, Garry, 92, 262 n. 42
World War II Memorial, 117–29;
conquest of Mall and, 119–21;
death and, 123; debt and, 125, 127–
29; democratic reconstruction of,
131–34; Hiroshima and Nagasaki
and, 127–29; location controversy
and, 118–20, 122–23; Muschamp
on, 251 n. 8, 251 n. 12, 251 n. 13;
patriotic love and, 128–29; self-
subversion of, 123–24

Young, James E., 144

STEVEN JOHNSTON
teaches political theory at the
University of South Florida. He is the
author of *Encountering Tragedy: Rousseau
and the Project of Democratic Order.*

*Library of Congress
Cataloging-in-Publication Data*

Johnston, Steven.
The truth about patriotism / Steven Johnston.
p. cm.
Includes bibliographical references and index.
ISBN 978-0-8223-4089-8 (cloth : alk. paper)
ISBN 978-0-8223-4110-9 (pbk. : alk. paper)
1. Patriotism—United States. 2. United States—
Politics and government.
I. Title.
JK1759.J74 2007
323.6'50973—dc22   2007007936